Flavorful Seasons Cookbook

Flavorful Seasons Cookbook

**Great-Tasting Recipes
for Winter, Spring,
Summer, and Fall**

Robyn Webb

American Diabetes Association.

Publisher	Susan H. Lau
Editorial Director	Peter Banks
Book Acquisitions	Susan Reynolds
Book Editor	Laurie Guffey

Page design and typesetting services by Insight Graphics

Cover design by Wickham & Associates, Inc.

Cover photography by Aldo Tutino

Illustrations by Rebecca Grace Jones

Nutritional analyses by Nutritional Computing Concepts, Inc.

Printed in the United States of America

American Diabetes Association
1660 Duke Street
Alexandria, VA 22314

Library of Congress Cataloging-in-Publication Data

Webb, Robyn.
    Flavorful seasons cookbook : great-tasting recipes for winter, spring, fall, and summer / Robyn Webb.
      p.   cm.
  ISBN 0–945448–62–7 (pbk.)
  1. Cookery. 2. Low-fat diet--Recipes. I. Title.
TX714.W3196 1996
641.5--dc20
                                         96–36133
                                           CIP

To my husband, Allan,
who is my loving partner every season of the year.

Editorial Advisory Board

Connie C. Crawley, RD, BS, MS
The University of Georgia Cooperative Extension Service
Athens, Georgia

John T. Devlin, MD
Maine Medical Center
Portland, Maine

Alan M. Jacobson, MD
Joslin Diabetes Center
Boston, Massachusetts

Lois Jovanovic-Peterson, MD
Sansum Medical Research Foundation
Santa Barbara, California

Carolyn Leontos, RD, CDE, MS
The University of Nevada Cooperative Extension
Las Vegas, Nevada

Peter A. Lodewick, MD
Diabetes Care Center
Birmingham, Alabama

Carol E. Malcom, BSN, CDE
Highline Community Hospital
Seattle, Washington

Wylie McNabb, EdD
The University of Chicago Center for Medical Education and Health Care
Chicago, Illinois

Virginia Peragallo-Dittko, RN, MA, CDE
Winthrop University Hospital
Mineola, New York

Jacqueline Siegel, RN
St. Joseph Hospital
Seattle, Washington

Tim Wysocki, PhD
Nemours Children's Center
Jacksonville, Florida

Contents

Tips

Menus

Summer

Tips

Menus

Fall

Tips

Menus

Preface

To every thing there is a season, and a time to every purpose under heaven.

—Ecclesiastes 3:1–8

I love the changing seasons! From the first twinkling of snowflakes I see, to the delicious aroma of fresh spring flowers . . . while enjoying the hot sunshine, and admiring the gorgeous fall foliage . . . I have fun cooking creatively using the tastiest seasonal ingredients.

Cooking in season guarantees fresh flavors, beautiful colors, and friendly produce prices. Although new agricultural techniques are making many fruits and vegetables available year-round, you may find that you get the best results by using ingredients that are naturally in season.

This book is more than just a cookbook. I've included my most useful cooking tips to help you get the best results; shared great ideas for everything from holiday decorating to summer grilling; and suggested creative ways to include the best foods of each season in your meal planning.

The easy-to-make recipes are sophisticated enough to satisfy the most discriminating taste, but simple enough to make your time in the kitchen a breeze. Of course, the recipes all use healthy, low-fat ingredients and come with complete nutritional analyses, so you can enjoy great flavor without guilt! There are enough recipes here to enable you to take full advantage of each season's variety.

For those special occasions, I've added seasonally-appropriate, tempting menus to add an extra spark to your holiday entertaining. From Mother's Day to Thanksgiving, Memorial Day to Halloween, you'll find great ideas for complete dinners, brunches, picnics, and parties.

I hope you enjoy this collection of creative, delicious foods, and cherish each season as it comes your way!

Acknowledgments

Many thanks go to the people behind the scenes who made this monumental project possible: Susan Reynolds, Laurie Guffey, and Sherrye Landrum of the American Diabetes Association, for their support, encouragement, and undying commitment to this book; Lyn Wheeler, for her expertise in the nutritional calculations (it is no easy task to compute over 400 recipes, but Lyn does this with such ease); my wonderful staff, Austin Zackari and Kathy Chamberlain, for their excellent recipes and hard work (and many, many trips to the grocery store) to make sure this book was a reality; my mother, Ruth, who was there when I needed just one more recipe; and finally, my clients, whose commitment to lead healthy lives inspires me every day.

The American Diabetes Association would also like to thank the following organizations for contributing recipes to this book:

Association for Dressings and Sauces
Beef Board and Veal Committee/Beef Industry Council
Horseradish Information Council
National Broiler Council
National Fisheries Institute
National Honey Board
National Pork Producers
Olive Oil Association
Washington Apple Commission

Winter

Shepherd's Pie

Use both ground turkey and lean ground beef in this comforting winter classic.

Preparation Time:
30 minutes

6 Servings/Serving Size:
1 cup

Exchanges:
2	Starch
2	Very Lean Meat
1/2	Monounsaturated Fat

Calories	248
Calories from Fat	66
Total Fat	7 g
Saturated Fat	3 g

Cholesterol	43 mg
Sodium	160 mg
Carbohydrate	28 g
Dietary Fiber	4 g
Sugars	7 g

Protein	19 g

4 medium russet potatoes, peeled
1/2 cup skim milk, heated
1 Tbsp olive oil
1/2 lb ground turkey (have your butcher grind this for you)
1/4 lb lean ground beef
1 medium onion, chopped
2 carrots, sliced
1 cup low-fat, low-sodium beef broth
1 Tbsp cornstarch or arrowroot powder
2 Tbsp water
2 Tbsp tomato paste
Fresh ground pepper and salt to taste
1 cup frozen peas, thawed and drained
1/4 cup cheddar cheese

1. Place the peeled potatoes in a medium saucepan. Add water to cover. Bring to a boil and boil potatoes for about 20 minutes, until potatoes are tender. Drain. Mash potatoes with hot milk and olive oil until fluffy. Set aside. In a nonstick skillet, brown the turkey and ground beef. Add the onion and saute for 5 minutes. Add the carrot and saute for another 5 minutes. Drain off any accumulated fat. Add the beef broth and bring to a boil.

2. Mix together the cornstarch or arrowroot powder and water until smooth. Add the mixture to the beef. Add the tomato paste and cook until thickened. Add in the pepper and peas. Preheat the oven to 350 degrees. Spoon the mixture into a 2-quart casserole dish. Top the casserole with the potatoes. Sprinkle cheese over the top. Bake for 35 minutes until potatoes are browned.

Eggplant Parmesan

This eggplant parmesan is baked instead of fried, but it still has great classic flavor.

Preparation Time:
20 minutes

6 Servings/Serving Size:
1 cup

Exchanges:

2 1/2	Starch
1	Lean Meat
1/2	Fat

Calories	264
Calories from Fat	80
Total Fat	9 g
Saturated Fat	3 g

Cholesterol	82 mg
Sodium	381 mg
Carbohydrate	35 g
Dietary Fiber	5 g
Sugars	11 g

Protein	12 g

1 Tbsp olive oil
1/2 cup chopped onion
2 garlic cloves, minced
2 cups coarsely chopped plum tomatoes
3 Tbsp red wine
2 tsp sugar
1 Tbsp minced fresh oregano
2 tsp minced fresh basil
1 bay leaf
Fresh ground pepper and salt to taste
2 medium eggplants, unpeeled and sliced into
    1/2-inch rounds
2 eggs and 1 egg white, beaten together
1 1/2 cups plain bread crumbs
1 cup part-skim mozzarella cheese

1. Preheat the oven to 350 degrees. Heat the oil in a saucepan over medium-high heat. Add the onions and garlic and saute for 5 minutes. Add the remaining ingredients except the eggplant, egg, bread crumbs, and cheese and bring to a boil. Lower heat and simmer for 30 minutes.

2. Meanwhile, dip each eggplant round into the beaten egg and then the bread crumbs. Refrigerate the rounds for 15 minutes to help the coating adhere.

3. In a casserole dish, place a thin layer of tomato sauce, then a layer of eggplant, then more sauce, then some of the cheese. Keep layering, ending with cheese. Bake for 45 minutes until bubbly.

Indian Stuffed Peppers

This is a very colorful and appetizing vegetarian meal.

Preparation Time:
20 minutes

---

6 Servings/Serving Size:
1 pepper with 1/2 cup rice

Exchanges:

2	Starch
2	Fruit
1	Vegetable
1/2	Fat

Calories 321
 Calories from Fat 47
Total Fat ....5 g
 Saturated Fat.............1 g

Cholesterol ....0 mg
Sodium....................63 mg
Carbohydrate.............66 g
 Dietary Fiber ....5 g
 Sugars.....................21 g

Protein.........................7 g

6 medium peppers, any color, cored, seeded, and
  left whole
1 Tbsp canola oil
1/2 cup diced onion
1/4 cup diced tart apple
1 1/2 cups rinsed, uncooked brown rice
3 cups low-fat, low-sodium chicken broth
1 tsp turmeric
1 cup raisins
2 cups boiling water
1/2 cup minced scallions
1/2 tsp cayenne pepper

1. Slice off a little of the bottom of the peppers
    to help them stand upright. In a pot of boiling
    water, parboil each pepper for about 10
    minutes. Drain and set aside. Heat the oil in
    a skillet over medium-high heat. Add the
    onion and apple and saute for 5 minutes. Add
    the rinsed brown rice and saute for 5 more
    minutes. Add the chicken broth and turmeric
    and bring to a boil. Lower heat and simmer
    for 45 minutes until rice is tender.

2. Preheat the oven to 350 degrees. Rehydrate
    the raisins by placing them in a bowl and
    pouring boiling water over them. Let stand
    for 15 minutes. Drain. Add the raisins,
    scallions, and cayenne pepper to the rice.
    Stuff each pepper equally with the filling.
    Place the peppers in a casserole dish and fill
    the dish with 1 inch of water. Bake, covered,
    for 20 minutes. Uncover and bake an
    additional 15 minutes.

Moroccan Chicken Tajine

This is a tasty way to prepare moist chicken.

Preparation Time:	
10 minutes	

6 Servings/Serving Size:
3–4 oz

Exchanges:

1	Carbohydrate
4	Very Lean Meat

Calories	207
Calories from Fat	27
Total Fat	3 g
Saturated Fat	1 g

Cholesterol	69 mg
Sodium	64 mg
Carbohydrate	19 g
Dietary Fiber	2 g
Sugars	15 g

Protein	26 g

1 1/2 lb boneless, skinless chicken breasts
3 Tbsp honey
1 large onion, chopped
3 cloves garlic, minced
2 sticks cinnamon
3 Tbsp fresh lemon juice
2 tsp turmeric
1/2 cup dried apricot quarters

Preheat the oven to 350 degrees. Place the chicken in a casserole dish. Pour the honey over the chicken, and sprinkle with onion and garlic. Add the cinnamon sticks, lemon juice, and turmeric. Top with apricot quarters. Cover and bake for 35–40 minutes until the chicken is tender and juices run clear. Remove the cinnamon sticks prior to serving.

This adapted recipe is courtesy of the National Broiler Council.

Tabouli Chicken Casserole

Bulgur wheat adds fiber to this hearty casserole.

Preparation Time:
20 minutes

6 Servings/Serving Size:
3 oz chicken with 1/2 cup bulgur wheat and 1/3 cup beans

Exchanges:

2 1/2	Starch
1	Vegetable
4	Very Lean Meat

Calories	357
Calories from Fat	47
Total Fat	5 g
Saturated Fat	1 g

Cholesterol	69 mg
Sodium	374 mg
Carbohydrate	44 g
Dietary Fiber	9 g
Sugars	7 g

Protein	35 g

1 cup sliced artichoke hearts
2 cups garbanzo beans (chickpeas), drained and rinsed
1 15-oz can chopped tomatoes
2 medium carrots, coarsely grated
1/2 cup low-fat, low-sodium chicken broth
1/4 cup dry white wine
1 Tbsp minced fresh mint
2 garlic cloves, minced
1 cup dry bulgur wheat
1 Tbsp grated lemon peel
2 Tbsp cornstarch or arrowroot powder
4 Tbsp water
1 1/2 lb boneless, skinless chicken breasts, halved
1/2 cup chopped fresh parsley
1/4 cup chopped cucumber, peeled

Preheat the oven to 350 degrees. In a large casserole dish, combine all ingredients except the last five. Combine the cornstarch or arrowroot powder and water and add it to the vegetables. Place the chicken breasts on top. Bake, covered, for about 35 minutes. Remove cover and bake an additional 10 minutes. Garnish with parsley and cucumbers to serve.

This adapted recipe is courtesy of the National Broiler Council.

Turkey Tetrazzini In Crisp Stuffing Cups

You'll never find a more creative use for stuffing and turkey tetrazzini!

Preparation Time:
20 minutes

6 Servings/Serving Size:
1/2 cup

Exchanges:
2	Starch
1	Vegetable
1	Very Lean Meat

Calories.......................215
 Calories from Fat........33
Total Fat ....4 g
 Saturated Fat.............1 g

Cholesterol ....8 mg
Sodium..................331 mg
Carbohydrate............35 g
 Dietary Fiber ....4 g
 Sugars........................8 g

Protein ....13 g

3 cups leftover bread stuffing (see recipes, p. 32)
3 cups leftover Turkey Tetrazzini (see recipe, p. 331)

1. Preheat the oven to 350 degrees. In a standard nonstick 6-muffin tin, press about 1/2 cup stuffing into the bottom and sides of each cup. Bake for about 15–20 minutes until crisp. Remove from the oven and carefully remove from tin.

2. Meanwhile, heat the leftover turkey tetrazzini on the stove or in the microwave until hot. Fill each stuffing cup with 1/2 cup of the leftover turkey tetrazzini and serve.

Italian Turkey Saute

Be sure to use cooked turkey within the week for safety and best freshness. To freeze cooked turkey, wrap large pieces in plastic wrap, then in butcher paper or foil.

Preparation Time: 15 minutes	

6 Servings/Serving Size: 3–4 oz

Exchanges:

1	Vegetable
3	Very Lean Meat
1/2	Fat

Calories	159
Calories from Fat	35
Total Fat	4 g
Saturated Fat	1 g
Cholesterol	49 mg
Sodium	217 mg
Carbohydrate	7 g
Dietary Fiber	2 g
Sugars	4 g
Protein	23 g

2 tsp olive oil
1/2 cup diced onion
2 garlic cloves, minced
1 1/2 cups crushed tomatoes
2 Tbsp red wine
2 tsp minced fresh oregano
3 cups leftover, cubed cooked turkey (preferably white meat)
2 Tbsp minced fresh basil
2 Tbsp capers

Heat the oil in a large skillet over medium-high heat. Add the onion and saute for 5 minutes. Add the garlic and saute for 2 more minutes. Add the crushed tomatoes and wine. Bring to a boil. Lower the heat and simmer for 10 minutes. Add the remaining ingredients and simmer for 5 minutes.

If you're going out to eat and you're afraid you'll eat too much, ask for a doggie bag and put the extra servings away before you start eating. This works at home, too, with those dishes that are so tasty you just keep going back for more.

Oriental Turkey Meatloaf

Put a low-fat spin on traditional meatloaf with turkey and Asian spices. (If you use egg substitute instead of egg, the cholesterol value is 75 mg.)

Preparation Time:
15 minutes

6 Servings/Serving Size:
3–4 oz

Exchanges:

1/2	Starch
3	Very Lean Meat

Calories......................157
 Calories from Fat.......14
Total Fat.......................2 g
 Saturated Fat.............0 g

Cholesterol...........111 mg
Sodium..................163 mg
Carbohydrate..............5 g
 Dietary Fiber.............0 g
 Sugars.......................1 g

Protein.......................29 g

1 1/2 lb ground turkey (have your butcher grind this for you)
1/2 cup cooked white rice
1 egg or egg substitute
1 tsp ginger
1 Tbsp oyster sauce
1 Tbsp dry sherry
2 garlic cloves, minced

Preheat the oven to 350 degrees. Combine all ingredients. Place into a nonstick loaf pan. Bake for 40 minutes until top is browned. Serve with lite soy sauce on the side (not included in nutritional analysis).

Pork and Veal Loaf Français

This meatloaf is great to serve at a casual dinner party. (If you use egg substitute instead of egg, the cholesterol value is 78 mg.)

Preparation Time:
15 minutes

---

6 Servings/Serving Size:
3–4 oz

Exchanges:

1/2	Starch
4	Very Lean Meat
1/2	Fat

Calories	198
Calories from Fat	57
Total Fat	6 g
Saturated Fat	2 g

Cholesterol	114 mg
Sodium	149 mg
Carbohydrate	7 g
Dietary Fiber	0 g
Sugars	0 g

Protein	27 g

1 lb lean ground pork (have your butcher grind this for you)
1/2 lb ground veal
2 Tbsp white wine
1/2 cup dry bread crumbs
2 tsp minced fresh thyme
1 tsp minced fresh rosemary
1 egg or egg substitute

Preheat the oven to 350 degrees. Combine all ingredients and place into a nonstick loaf pan. Bake for 45–50 minutes until top is browned.

Some fats are friendlier than others. If you can pour it, like olive or canola oil, it's healthier for you than solid sticks like butter or margarine.

Savory Rice and Bean Loaf

This hearty vegetarian loaf is great sliced and served on a crusty roll. (If you use egg substitute instead of egg, the cholesterol value is 0 mg.)

Preparation Time:
15 minutes

---

6 Servings/Serving Size:
about 1 cup

Exchanges:

1	Starch
1	Vegetable
1/2	Monounsaturated Fat

Calories	133
Calories from Fat	37
Total Fat	4 g
Saturated Fat	1 g

Cholesterol	0 mg
Sodium	126 mg
Carbohydrate	20 g
Dietary Fiber	3 g
Sugars	4 g

Protein	5 g

1 Tbsp olive oil
1 medium onion, chopped
1 cup canned garbanzo beans (chickpeas),
  drained, rinsed, and mashed slightly
1 cup cooked brown rice
1 egg or egg substitute
1 Tbsp sesame seeds
1 Tbsp minced fresh parsley
1 cup canned tomatoes, coarsely chopped

Preheat the oven to 350 degrees. Heat the oil in a skillet over medium heat. Saute the onions for 5 minutes. In a bowl, combine the remaining ingredients except the canned tomatoes. Shape into a loaf pan. Bake for 40 minutes. Add chopped tomatoes on top of loaf. Bake an additional 10 minutes.

Quick Hoppin' John

Hoppin' John is a nutritious blend of black-eyed peas, rice, and vegetables. (If you need to substitute regular turkey for the smoked turkey in this recipe, use the nutrient analysis in parentheses.)

Preparation Time:
20 minutes

6 Servings/Serving Size:
1 cup

Exchanges:

3	Starch
1	Vegetable
1	Very Lean Meat

Calories 292 (299)
  Calories from Fat........38
Total Fat ....4 g
  Saturated Fat.............1 g

Cholesterol..7 mg (12 mg)
Sodium ..392 mg (229 mg)
Carbohydrate.............51 g
  Dietary Fiber ....8 g
  Sugars.......................6 g

Protein ....15 g (16 g)

1 Tbsp canola oil
1 medium onion, chopped
1/2 cup diced carrots
1/2 cup diced celery
2 garlic cloves, minced
2 15-oz cans black-eyed peas, drained
1 tsp minced fresh thyme
1/2 lb fresh collard greens, stems removed, washed, and torn (or 2 packages frozen collard greens, thawed slightly)
1 cup white rice
2 1/2 cups low-fat, low-sodium chicken broth
1/2 cup diced smoked turkey breast (or regular diced turkey)
Fresh ground pepper to taste

1. Heat the oil in a stockpot over medium-high heat. Add the onion and carrots and saute for 5 minutes. Add the celery and garlic and saute for 3 more minutes.

2. Add the black-eyed peas, collard greens, and rice. Saute for 2 minutes. Add the chicken broth and bring to a boil. Cover and lower the heat for 20 minutes, until water is absorbed and rice is tender. Add the turkey and cook 5 more minutes.

Winter Beef Stew

Pears and apples, winter's finest fruits, complement lean beef in this hearty stew.

Preparation Time:
25 minutes

6 Servings/Serving Size:
1 cup with 3–4 oz beef

Exchanges:

1	Starch
3	Very Lean Meat
1	Monounsaturated Fat

Calories	223
Calories from Fat	69
Total Fat	8 g
Saturated Fat	2 g

Cholesterol	59
Sodium	156
Carbohydrate	14 g
Dietary Fiber	3 g
Sugars	9 g

Protein	27 g

1 Tbsp canola oil
1 cup chopped onion
3 garlic cloves, minced
2 carrots, cut into 1-inch slices
1 1/2 lb lean stew beef, cut into 1-inch cubes
3 cups low-fat, low-sodium beef broth
1 tsp paprika
Fresh ground pepper and salt to taste
1 1/2 cups mixed pears and apples, unpeeled and
   chopped into 1-inch pieces

1. Heat the oil in a large stockpot over medium-high heat. Add the onion and garlic and saute for 5 minutes. Add the carrots and saute another 5 minutes. Add the meat and brown. Drain off any accumulated fat. Add the broth, paprika, pepper, and salt (if desired).

2. Bring to a boil over high heat. Reduce the heat and simmer, uncovered, for 1 1/4 hours. Add the apples and pears and cover. Cook over low heat for 15–20 minutes until the apples and pears are soft, but not mushy.

Tender Pork and Bean Stew

A bit of almonds inspire this Basque-like stew.

Preparation Time:
25 minutes

6 Servings/Serving Size:
3–4 oz pork with 1/4 cup beans

Exchanges:
1	Starch
4	Very Lean Meat
1	Monounsaturated Fat

Calories	274
Calories from Fat	79
Total Fat	9 g
Saturated Fat	2 g

Cholesterol	71 mg
Sodium	417 mg
Carbohydrate	18 g
Dietary Fiber	5 g
Sugars	3 g

Protein	31 g

1 1/2 lb pork tenderloin, cut into 1-inch cubes
2 Tbsp unbleached white flour
1/2 tsp salt
1/2 tsp pepper
1 Tbsp olive oil
1/2 cup chopped onion
1 cup low-fat, low-sodium chicken broth
1 cup diced canned tomatoes
2 Tbsp slivered almonds
1 tsp chili powder
1/4 tsp cayenne pepper
1/2 tsp cinnamon
1 15-oz can black beans, drained and rinsed

In a plastic bag, combine the flour, salt, and pepper with the pork cubes. Shake the bag well. Heat the oil in a large stockpot over medium-high heat. Add the pork and brown on all sides for about 10 minutes. Add the broth, tomatoes, almonds, and spices. Bring to a boil, lower the heat, and simmer for 30 minutes. Add the beans and simmer for 10 more minutes.

Chicken and Zucchini Stew

Use yellow squash in this recipe if zucchini is unavailable.

Preparation Time:
20 minutes

6 Servings/Serving Size:
3–4 oz chicken

Exchanges:
1	Vegetable
4	Very Lean Meat

Calories 169
 Calories from Fat 32
Total Fat .... 4 g
 Saturated Fat .... 1 g

Cholesterol .... 69 mg
Sodium .... 241 mg
Carbohydrate .... 7 g
 Dietary Fiber .... 2 g
 Sugars .... 4 g

Protein .... 27 g

1 18-oz can tomatoes
1 cup low-fat, low-sodium chicken broth
1 small green pepper, coarsely chopped
2 garlic cloves, minced
2 medium zucchini, coarsely chopped
Fresh ground pepper and salt to taste
2 tsp minced fresh basil
1 1/2 lb boneless, skinless chicken breasts,
 cooked and cubed into 2-inch pieces

1. Drain the liquid from the tomatoes into a saucepan. Chop the tomatoes and set aside. Add the broth, green pepper, and garlic to the tomato liquid. Bring to a boil, reduce heat to medium, and cook for 10 minutes.

2. Add reserved tomatoes, zucchini, pepper, salt, and basil. Simmer until zucchini is tender, about 10 minutes. Reduce heat to low and add the chicken. Cook for 5 minutes.

Oven Turkey Stew

Using sweet potatoes instead of white potatoes adds a delightfully different taste to this warm stew.

Preparation Time:
20 minutes

6 Servings/Serving Size:
1 cup with 3–4 oz turkey

Exchanges:

1 1/2	Starch
4	Very Lean Meat
1/2	Monounsaturated Fat

Calories	281
Calories from Fat	54
Total Fat	6 g
Saturated Fat	1 g

Cholesterol	76 mg
Sodium	86 mg
Carbohydrate	25 g
Dietary Fiber	4 g
Sugars	9 g

Protein	31 g

1 1/2 lb turkey breast filets
2 Tbsp olive oil
1/4 cup chopped onions
2 medium sweet potatoes (about 1 lb), peeled
  and cut into 8ths
6 large shallots, peeled and left whole
3 garlic cloves, finely chopped
2 Tbsp unbleached white flour
1 1/4 cups low-fat, low-sodium chicken broth
1 cup dry white wine
1 Tbsp minced fresh thyme
1/2 lb small white mushrooms, cut in half
1 cup chopped fresh parsley

1. Preheat the oven to 350 degrees. Cut the turkey into 1-inch pieces. Heat the oil in an ovenproof pot on the stove over medium heat. Add the turkey to the pot. Cook, stirring occasionally, until the turkey is no longer pink, about 5–6 minutes.

2. Add the onion, sweet potatoes, shallots, and garlic, and cook for 2–3 minutes. Sprinkle the flour over the mixture. Cook for 1 minute. Stir in the chicken broth, wine, and thyme. Bring to a boil. Add the mushrooms. Transfer to the oven and bake uncovered for 35 minutes. Stir in the parsley and serve.

Chicken and Apple Stew

This is a sweet and nutritious chicken stew.

Preparation Time:	
25 minutes	
6 Servings/Serving Size:	
3–4 oz	
Exchanges:	
2	Fruit
4	Very Lean Meat
1/2	Fat
Calories	286
Calories from Fat	60
Total Fat	7 g
Saturated Fat	1 g
Cholesterol	69 mg
Sodium	180 mg
Carbohydrate	32 g
Dietary Fiber	5 g
Sugars	25 g
Protein	27 g

1 Tbsp canola oil
1 1/2 lb boneless, skinless chicken breasts, halved
1/2 tsp nutmeg
Fresh ground pepper and salt to taste
1 Tbsp Dijon mustard
2 cups low-fat, low-sodium chicken broth
1/4 cup apple cider vinegar
6 whole cloves
3 medium carrots, peeled and sliced
6 medium apples, peeled and sliced
1 cup shredded cabbage
1 cup unsweetened applesauce

1. Heat the oil in a Dutch oven over medium-high heat. Add the chicken breasts and saute on both sides for a total of 10 minutes. Sprinkle with nutmeg, pepper, and salt. Spread the mustard on the chicken. Add the broth, vinegar, cloves, and carrots and bring to a boil. Cover and simmer for 15 minutes.

2. Add the apples and cook for 5 minutes. Add the cabbage and cook, covered, for 10 more minutes. With a slotted spoon, remove the chicken and vegetables from the broth. Keep warm. Add the applesauce to the liquid and boil for 5 minutes. Pour over the chicken and serve.

This adapted recipe is courtesy of the National Broiler Council.

Corn Biscuit Chili Pie

Preparation Time:
25 minutes

6 Servings/Serving Size:
1 cup with 1 2-inch
biscuit

Exchanges:

4	Starch
3	Very Lean Meat
1/2	Fat

Calories	459
Calories from Fat	81
Total Fat	9 g
Saturated Fat	3 g

Cholesterol	94 mg
Sodium	626 mg
Carbohydrate	59 g
Dietary Fiber	9 g
Sugars	13 g

Protein	36 g

1 Tbsp canola oil
1 medium onion, chopped
2 garlic cloves, minced
1/2 cups chopped red pepper
1 1/2 lb lean stew meat, cut into 2-inch cubes
1 Tbsp minced jalapeno pepper
3 cups canned tomatoes, coarsely chopped,
    undrained
1 cup canned black beans, drained and rinsed
3 Tbsp chili powder
1 tsp coriander
1/2 tsp cinnamon
1 cup unbleached white flour
1 cup yellow cornmeal
1/2 tsp baking soda
1 tsp baking powder
1 egg, beaten
1 cup low-fat buttermilk
1 Tbsp sugar
1/2 cup corn kernels

1. Heat the oil in a large pot over medium-high
    heat. Add the onion and saute for 5 minutes.
    Add the garlic and red pepper and saute for 5
    more minutes. Add the stew beef and saute
    until meat is browned on all sides. Drain off
    any accumulated fat. Add the next 6
    ingredients and bring to a boil. Lower the
    heat and let simmer for 1 hour, until meat is
    tender. Add a little more water if necessary.

2. Preheat the oven to 400 degrees. Combine all
    remaining ingredients and mix until smooth.
    Do not over-mix! When the chili has
    simmered, transfer it to a casserole dish. By
    large tablespoonsful, drop the corn biscuits
    onto the chili. Bake for about 25 minutes,
    until biscuits are cooked.

Lentil Chili

Bulgur wheat gives texture to this meatless chili.

Preparation Time:
15 minutes

6 Servings/Serving Size:
1 cup

Exchanges:
3   Starch
1/2 Monounsaturated Fat

Calories	271
Calories from Fat	63
Total Fat	7 g
Saturated Fat	1 g

Cholesterol	0 mg
Sodium	218 mg
Carbohydrate	43 g
Dietary Fiber	16 g
Sugars	7 g

Protein	15 g

2 Tbsp canola oil
1 medium onion, chopped
4 garlic cloves, minced
1 cup dried lentils
1 cup dry bulgur wheat
3 cups low-fat, low-sodium chicken or vegetable broth
2 cups canned tomatoes, drained and coarsely chopped
2 Tbsp chili powder
1 Tbsp cumin

Heat the oil in a large stockpot over medium-high heat. Add the onions and garlic and saute for 5 minutes. Add the dry lentils and bulgur wheat and stir. Add all the remaining ingredients and bring to a boil. Simmer for 30 minutes until the lentils are tender.

Turkey Pinto Bean Chili

Try Drop Biscuits (see recipe, p. 420) dipped into this tasty turkey chili.

Preparation Time:
15 minutes

6 Servings/Serving Size:
1 cup

Exchanges:

2	Starch
4	Very Lean Meat

Calories	287
Calories from Fat	41
Total Fat	5 g
Saturated Fat	1 g

Cholesterol	77 mg
Sodium	335 mg
Carbohydrate	29 g
Dietary Fiber	8 g
Sugars	9 g

Protein	36 g

2 tsp canola oil
2 cups diced onion
3 garlic cloves, minced
1 1/2 lb ground turkey breast (have your butcher grind this for you)
2 tsp paprika
2 tsp cumin
2 Tbsp chili powder
1 tsp cinnamon
1 24-oz can tomatoes, coarsely chopped with their juice
1 cup diced red pepper
3 cups low-fat, low-sodium chicken broth
2 cups canned pinto beans, drained and rinsed
Fresh ground pepper and salt to taste

Heat the oil in a large saucepan over medium heat. Add the onion and garlic and saute for 5 minutes. Add the turkey and saute until browned. Sprinkle the mixture with the spices and saute for 5 more minutes. Add the tomatoes, red pepper, and beans. Bring to a boil, then cover and simmer for 2 hours. Season with pepper and salt to serve.

Black Bean, Corn, and Rice Chili

Cornbread sticks (see recipe, p. 75) taste great with this spicy chili.

(see recipe, p. 75)

Preparation Time:	
20 minutes	

6 Servings/Serving Size:
1 cup

Exchanges:

2 1/2	Starch

Calories	208
Calories from Fat	32
Total Fat	4 g
Saturated Fat	0 g

Cholesterol	0 mg
Sodium	219 mg
Carbohydrate	38 g
Dietary Fiber	4 g
Sugars	14 g

Protein	31 g

1 Tbsp canola oil
1 small onion, chopped
2 garlic cloves, minced
1/4 cup chopped green pepper
1 cup raw brown rice
1 cup water
1 cup crushed tomatoes
1 15-oz can black beans, drained and rinsed
1 cup corn kernels, frozen or fresh
1 Tbsp chili powder
2 tsp cumin
1 tsp cinnamon
Dash hot pepper sauce

Heat the oil in a large saucepan over medium heat. Add the onion and garlic and saute for 3 minutes. Add the green pepper and saute for 3 more minutes. Add the rice, water, and crushed tomatoes. Bring to a boil, lower the heat, cover, and simmer for 40 minutes. Add the beans, corn, and seasonings and cook for 20 more minutes until the rice is tender.

Vegetarian Chili

You won't miss the meat in this hearty chili!

Preparation Time:	
20 minutes	

6 Servings/Serving Size:
1 cup

Exchanges:

1	Starch
1	Vegetable
1/2	Monounsaturated Fat

Calories	123
Calories from Fat	33
Total Fat	4 g
Saturated Fat	1 g

Cholesterol	0 mg
Sodium	488 mg
Carbohydrate	21 g
Dietary Fiber	6 g
Sugars	8 g

Protein	6 g

1 Tbsp olive oil
1 cup diced onion
3 garlic cloves, minced
2 cups chopped green cabbage
1 28-oz can tomatoes, coarsely chopped, drained
1 cup low-fat, low-sodium chicken broth
1 8-oz can tomato sauce
1 cup canned black beans, drained and rinsed
2 Tbsp chili powder
1 bay leaf
1 tsp cumin
1/4 tsp cayenne pepper
Fresh ground pepper to taste

Heat the oil in a large stockpot over medium-high heat. Add the onion and garlic and saute for 5 minutes. Add the remaining ingredients and bring to a boil. Lower heat and simmer for 1–2 hours until thick. Add a little water if necessary.

A Hill of Beans

Long thought of as part of a "poor man's diet," beans, like grains, have made a culinary comeback. Now recognized for their superior nutrition, beans are showing up on the most sophisticated of dinner plates. Beans are very low in fat, rich in soluble fiber, and are brimming with potassium, iron, magnesium, B vitamins, and calcium. Canned beans are quick and easy to use, but when you have more time, consider preparing them yourself from dried beans.

All beans except for lentils and split peas require presoaking before cooking, which helps to reduce their gas-producing qualities. (If you add baking soda while cooking beans to achieve this, the B vitamin content will be greatly reduced!) Be sure your pot for soaking and cooking is big enough, because beans swell when they cook. Cook slowly over low heat, or the beans will separate from their skins. Adding salt while cooking may make beans tougher.

Soak all of the following beans in two to three times their volume of water for 6–24 hours before cooking. To cook, change to fresh water (still using two to three times the volume of water). Bring the water to a boil, lower the heat, cover, and simmer until the beans are tender.

Cooking times for some favorite bean varieties

Black Beans	1 1/2–2 hours
Black-Eyed Peas	1 1/2–2 hours
Fava Beans	2–3 hours
Garbanzo Beans (Chickpeas)	1/2–2 hours
Kidney Beans	1/2–2 hours
Lentils	45 minutes
Lima Beans	45 minutes
Navy and Pea Beans	1/2–2 hours
Pinto Beans	1/2–2 hours
Small Pink Beans	1/2–2 hours
Soybeans	3 hours
Split Peas	45 minutes
White Beans	1/2–2 hours

Pasta Vegetable Soup

This hearty soup will warm you up on a rainy winter night.

Preparation Time:
15 minutes

6 Servings/Serving Size:
1 cup

Exchanges:
1	Starch
1/2	Monounsaturated Fat

Calories	87
Calories from Fat	36
Total Fat	4 g
Saturated Fat	1 g

Cholesterol	0 mg
Sodium	136 mg
Carbohydrate	12 g
Dietary Fiber	3 g
Sugars	4 g

Protein	4 g

1 Tbsp olive oil
2 cloves garlic, minced
1/2 cup minced scallions
4 cups low-fat, low-sodium chicken broth
1 cup frozen peas, thawed
1/2 cup diced tomato
1 cup diced carrot
1/2 tsp minced fresh rosemary
1/2 cup cooked wagon wheel pasta (or any other shaped pasta)
Fresh ground pepper and salt to taste

Heat the oil in a stockpot over medium-high heat. Add the garlic and scallions and saute for 2 minutes. Add the remaining ingredients except the pasta, cover, and simmer for 25 minutes. Add the cooked pasta, pepper, and salt to serve.

Turkey and Wild Rice Soup

This slightly spicy soup will warm you up on a cold winter day!

Preparation Time:
15 minutes

6 Servings/Serving Size:
1 cup

Exchanges:

1	Starch
3	Very Lean Meat
1/2	Fat

Calories	202
Calories from Fat	51
Total Fat	6 g
Saturated Fat	2 g

Cholesterol	49 mg
Sodium	146 mg
Carbohydrate	14 g
Dietary Fiber	2 g
Sugars	3 g

Protein	26 g

4 1/2 cups low-fat, low-sodium chicken broth
2 tsp olive oil
1/2 cup sliced red onion
2 medium carrots, diced
1 tsp turmeric
1/2 tsp ground red pepper
3 cups diced cooked turkey (preferably white meat)
1 1/2 cups cooked wild rice
Fresh ground pepper to taste

In a large stockpot, bring the chicken broth to a simmer. Heat the oil in a small skillet over medium-high heat. Add the onions and carrots and saute for 10 minutes. Add the turmeric and ground red pepper and saute for 2 more minutes. Add the sauteed mixture to the broth. Simmer for 10 minutes. Add the remaining ingredients and simmer for 10 more minutes.

Chicken Vegetable Soup

Potatoes, peppers, and corn make this a heartier chicken soup than the traditional broth version.

Preparation Time:
15 minutes

6 Servings/Serving Size:
1 cup

Exchanges:
1 1/2	Starch
2	Very Lean Meat
1/2	Monounsaturated Fat

Calories	200
Calories from Fat	48
Total Fat	5 g
Saturated Fat	1 g

Cholesterol	36 mg
Sodium	146 mg
Carbohydrate	22 g
Dietary Fiber	2 g
Sugars	8 g

Protein	19 g

2 tsp olive oil
1/2 cup chopped onion
2 Tbsp minced fresh parsley
1 cup cubed, peeled russet potatoes
1 cup chopped red pepper
1/2 lb cooked chicken, cut into 2-inch cubes
1 cup fresh or frozen corn
2 cups low-fat, low-sodium chicken broth
1 1/2 cups evaporated skim milk
2 tsp cornstarch or arrowroot powder
4 tsp water

1. Heat the oil in a stockpot over medium-high heat. Add the onion and parsley and saute for 5 minutes. Add the potatoes and saute for 5 more minutes. Add the red pepper and saute for 5 more minutes.

2. Add the remaining ingredients except for the cornstarch or arrowroot powder and water. Bring to a simmer and cook an additional 5–8 minutes. Mix together the cornstarch or arrowroot powder and water until smooth. Add to the soup and cook until thickened.

Cream of Chicken Soup

There is nothing like homemade cream of chicken soup to warm you up on a cold day.

Preparation Time:
20 minutes

6 Servings/Serving Size:
1 cup with 2–3 oz chicken

Exchanges:

1	Starch
3	Very Lean Meat
1/2	Fat

Calories	213
Calories from Fat	62
Total Fat	7 g
Saturated Fat	2 g
Cholesterol	41 mg
Sodium	209 mg
Carbohydrate	17 g
Dietary Fiber	1 g
Sugars	10 g
Protein	21 g

1 Tbsp canola oil
1/2 cup minced onion
1/2 cup diced carrots
3 cups low-fat, low-sodium chicken broth
2 cups evaporated skim milk
2 Tbsp dry sherry
1 1/2 cups diced cooked white chicken meat
2 Tbsp cornstarch or arrowroot powder
4 Tbsp cold water
3 Tbsp minced fresh parsley
Fresh ground pepper to taste

1. Heat the oil in a large stockpot over medium-high heat. Add the onion and saute for 5 minutes. Add the carrots and saute another 5 minutes. Add in the chicken broth and sherry and bring to a boil. Lower the heat and add the milk. Add the chicken and simmer for 5 minutes.

2. Combine the cornstarch or arrowroot powder with the water. Mix until smooth and add to the pot. Cook the soup until thickened. Sprinkle with parsley and ground pepper and serve.

White Bean and Turkey Soup

Pureed and whole white beans give this soup a wonderful texture.

Preparation Time:
15 minutes

6 Servings/Serving Size:
1 cup with 2 oz turkey

Exchanges:
2 1/2	Starch
2	Very Lean Meat

Calories	281
Calories from Fat	53
Total Fat	6 g
Saturated Fat	1 g

Cholesterol	27 mg
Sodium	499 mg
Carbohydrate	38 g
Dietary Fiber	8 g
Sugars	7 g

Protein	22 g

1 Tbsp canola oil
1 medium onion, minced
3 carrots, diced
3 stalks celery, sliced
3 cups low-fat, low-sodium chicken broth
2 15-oz cans white beans (navy or cannellini), drain and rinse one can
1 1/4 cups diced cooked turkey
2 tsp paprika
1 tsp minced fresh thyme
Fresh ground pepper to taste

1. Heat the oil in a large stockpot over medium-high heat. Add the onion and saute for 5 minutes. Add the carrots and saute for another 5 minutes. Add the celery and saute for 2 minutes. Add the broth and bring to a boil. Simmer over low heat for 5 minutes.

2. Puree one can of the beans with its liquid. Add to the soup. Simmer for 10 minutes. Add the other can of whole beans (drained), turkey, paprika, thyme, and pepper. Continue to simmer for 20 minutes.

Five Onion Soup

Five different onions add a twist to this classic favorite.

Preparation Time:
20 minutes

6 Servings/Serving Size:
1 cup

Exchanges:
1/2   Starch

Calories..........................47
  Calories from Fat........24
Total Fat ....3 g
  Saturated Fat.............1 g

Cholesterol ....4 mg
Sodium..................108 mg
Carbohydrate...............6 g
  Dietary Fiber ....1 g
  Sugars......................3 g

Protein ....4 g

1/2 cup thinly sliced yellow onion
1/2 cup thinly sliced red onion
1/4 cup thinly sliced leeks (white part only)
1/4 cup chopped shallots
1/4 cup sliced scallions
2 cups dry white wine
6 cups low-fat, low-sodium beef broth
Fresh ground pepper to taste

Preheat the oven to 400 degrees. Place the onions in a casserole dish with the wine and bake for 1 hour. Add a little water if necessary. There should be little liquid left after baking and onions should be brown. Heat the beef broth to boiling. Add the cooked onions and grind in black pepper. Serve immediately.

Chickpea and Pasta Soup

Fresh rosemary turns this soup into a Tuscan feast!

Preparation Time: 15 minutes	
6 Servings/Serving Size: 1 cup	
Exchanges:	
1 1/2	Starch
1/2	Monounsaturated Fat
Calories	144
Calories from Fat	36
Total Fat	4 g
Saturated Fat	1 g
Cholesterol	0 mg
Sodium	303 mg
Carbohydrate	23 g
Dietary Fiber	4 g
Sugars	7 g
Protein	6 g

1 Tbsp olive oil
7 garlic cloves, minced
2 Tbsp minced fresh rosemary
2 cups crushed tomatoes
2 cups low-fat, low-sodium chicken broth
1 cup canned chickpeas (garbanzo beans),
    drained and rinsed
1 cup cooked elbow macaroni
Fresh ground pepper to taste

1. Heat the oil in a large stockpot over medium-high heat. Add the garlic and saute for 3 minutes. Add the rosemary and saute for 2 more minutes.

2. Add the crushed tomatoes and simmer for 15 minutes. Add the broth and beans and simmer for 10 minutes. Add the elbow macaroni and pepper. Simmer for 5 minutes. Serve.

Basic Bread Stuffing with Variations

Preparation Time:
20 minutes

---

12 Servings/Serving Size:
1/2 cup

Exchanges:
1   Starch

Calories 59
  Calories from Fat 11
Total Fat ....1 g
  Saturated Fat ....0 g

Cholesterol ....0 mg
Sodium ....119 mg
Carbohydrate ....11 g
  Dietary Fiber ....2 g
  Sugars ....3 g

Protein ....3 g

2 1/2 cups low-fat, low-sodium chicken broth
3 medium onions, diced
6 cups diced whole-grain bread
1 Tbsp paprika
1 egg substitute
Fresh ground pepper and salt to taste

Heat 1/2 cup of the chicken broth in a skillet over medium-high heat. Add the onions and saute for 10 minutes until the onions have softened. In a bowl, combine the cooked onions, remaining broth, bread, paprika, egg, pepper, and salt. Mix well. Place inside the cavity of a 12-lb turkey or place in a casserole dish. If baking stuffing separately from the turkey, place stuffing in a preheated 350-degree oven and bake for 45 minutes.

Variations (Exceptions to nutrient analysis are in parentheses.)
Herb Stuffing: Add 1 Tbsp chopped fresh sage, rosemary, and parsley.
Fruit Stuffing: Add 1/2 cup diced tart apples, cranberries, or diced pears.
Sweet Stuffing: Add 1 tsp allspice, cinnamon, nutmeg, or ginger.
Mushroom Stuffing: Add 1 cup sliced mushrooms (white or wild). Saute with the onions. Cook until mushrooms are soft.
Cornbread Stuffing: Replace 3 cups of the whole-grain bread with 3 cups cornbread (see recipe, p. 75). (Starch Exchange = 1 1/2, Calories = 113, Calories from Fat = 13, Cholesterol = 18 g, Sodium = 155 mg, Carbohydrate = 21 g, Sugars = 5 g, and Protein = 5 g.)
Chestnut Stuffing: Add 1 cup roasted chestnuts, peeled. Buy chestnuts in jars packed in water; this saves you roasting time. Chestnuts are low in fat! (Calories = 90, Calories from Fat = 12, Carbohydrate = 18 g, Sugars = 4 g, and Protein = 4 g.)
Dried Fruit Stuffing: Add 1 cup diced dried apricots, apples, figs, cranberries, or cherries. (Starch Exchange = 1 1/2, Sodium = 167 mg, Carbohydrate = 20 g, Dietary Fiber = 3 g, and Sugars = 4 g.)

Wild Rice and Vegetable Stuffing

This is a great stuffing for Cornish game hens or chicken, too.

Preparation Time:
20 minutes

12 Servings/Serving Size:
1/2 cup

Exchanges:
1 1/2   Starch

Calories	128
Calories from Fat	27
Total Fat	3 g
Saturated Fat	1 g
Cholesterol	0 mg
Sodium	84 mg
Carbohydrate	22 g
Dietary Fiber	2 g
Sugars	2 g
Protein	6 g

2 cups raw wild rice, rinsed
8 cups low-fat, low-sodium chicken broth
1 Tbsp canola oil
1/2 cup diced yellow pepper
1/2 cup diced red pepper
1/4 cup sliced scallions
1 cup sliced celery
1/4 cup minced fresh parsley
2 Tbsp red wine
1 tsp minced fresh thyme

1. In a saucepan, combine the rice and broth. Bring to a boil, lower the heat, and cover. Simmer for 50 minutes until all the broth has been absorbed. Meanwhile, heat the oil in a skillet over medium-high heat. Add the peppers and saute for 5 minutes.

2. Add the scallions and celery and saute for 3 more minutes. Add the parsley, red wine, and thyme. Cook for 3 more minutes. Combine the rice with the vegetable mixture. Stuff a 12-lb turkey, 2 6-lb chickens, or 12 Cornish game hens with this mixture, or serve stuffing separately.

Italian Wild Rice Stuffing

A few crunchy pine nuts and plump sun-dried tomatoes dress up this stuffing.

Preparation Time:
20 minutes

12 Servings/Serving Size:
1/2 cup

Exchanges:
1 1/2   Starch
1/2 Monounsaturated Fat

Calories.....................148
  Calories from Fat........36
Total Fat ....4 g
  Saturated Fat.............1 g

Cholesterol ....0 mg
Sodium..................188 mg
Carbohydrate.............25 g
  Dietary Fiber ....3 g
  Sugars.......................2 g

Protein ....7 g

2 cups wild rice, rinsed
8 cups low-fat, low-sodium chicken broth
1 Tbsp olive oil
1 medium onion, chopped
3 garlic cloves, minced
20 sun-dried tomatoes, rehydrated (to rehydrate, pour boiling water over the tomatoes until they are covered; let stand for 10–15 minutes and drain)
2 Tbsp toasted pine nuts (to toast, place the pine nuts in a nonstick, dry skillet and shake over medium heat until they are light brown)
1/4 cup minced fresh parsley
Fresh ground pepper and salt to taste

1. In a saucepan, combine the rice with the broth. Bring to a boil, lower the heat, and cover. Cook for 50 minutes until water is absorbed. Meanwhile, heat the oil in a skillet over medium-high heat. Add the onion and garlic and saute for 5 minutes.

2. Add the tomatoes, pine nuts, and parsley and cook for 3 more minutes. Grind in pepper and add salt. Combine the rice with the tomato mixture. Stuff a bird with this mixture, or serve stuffing separately.

Mushroom and Barley Stuffing

This hearty stuffing is a great vegetarian side dish.

Preparation Time:
20 minutes

13 Servings/Serving Size:
1/2 cup

Exchanges:
2	Starch
1	Vegetable

Calories......................185
  Calories from Fat........24
Total Fat.......................3 g
  Saturated Fat.............0 g

Cholesterol...............0 mg
Sodium....................30 mg
Carbohydrate.............37 g
  Dietary Fiber.............8 g
  Sugars.......................4 g

Protein.........................5 g

2 Tbsp olive oil
1 medium onion, chopped
4 large carrots, peeled and diced
2 cups rehydrated shiitake mushrooms, stems removed and sliced, or 2 cups sliced fresh shiitake mushrooms (you may substitute regular button mushrooms, but try to use the more flavorful, exotic shiitakes)
2 1/2 cups pearl barley
7 cups water
Fresh ground pepper to taste

Heat the oil in a large stockpot over medium heat. Add the onion and saute for 7 minutes. Add the carrots and saute for 10 minutes. Add the mushrooms and saute for 5 minutes. Add the water and the barley. Bring to a boil, cover, lower the heat, and simmer for 60 minutes until barley is tender. Cook longer if necessary until all water is absorbed. Grind in pepper. Stuff a bird with this mixture, or serve stuffing separately.

❊❊❊❊❊❊❊❊❊❊❊❊❊❊❊❊❊❊❊❊❊❊❊

At dinner parties, eat slowly.
Decline offers of seconds.
A great side benefit: you won't feel overstuffed.

❊❊❊❊❊❊❊❊❊❊❊❊❊❊❊❊❊❊❊❊❊❊❊

Quinoa Stuffing

Quinoa is a high-protein, high-fiber grain—and it only takes 15 minutes to prepare! Look for quinoa in natural food stores. It is very important to rinse quinoa well. This removes some of the bitterness naturally present in the outside ring of the grain. Quinoa stuffing is best served separately in a casserole dish instead of baked in a bird.

Preparation Time:
17 minutes

6 Servings/Serving Size:
1/2 cup

Exchanges:

2	Starch
1	Vegetable
1/2	Monounsaturated Fat

Calories	205
Calories from Fat	47
Total Fat	5 g
Saturated Fat	1 g
Cholesterol	0 mg
Sodium	82 mg
Carbohydrate	35 g
Dietary Fiber	4 g
Sugars	3 g
Protein	8 g

1 1/2 cups dry quinoa, rinsed well
3 cups low-fat, low-sodium chicken broth
2 tsp olive oil
1 medium onion, diced
2 garlic cloves, minced
1/2 cup diced celery
1/2 cup diced carrots
1/2 cup minced scallions
Fresh ground pepper to taste

1. In a medium saucepan, bring the broth to a boil. Add the rinsed quinoa and return to a boil. Lower the heat, cover, and cook for about 15 minutes until all the water is absorbed.

2. Meanwhile, heat the oil in a skillet over medium-high heat. Add the onion and garlic and saute for 5 minutes. Add the celery and carrots and saute for 5 minutes. Add the scallions and saute for 2 minutes. Combine the vegetables with the quinoa and grind in pepper to serve.

Forty Clove-of-Garlic Holiday Chicken

Use some of the roasted garlic from this recipe to spread on crusty bread—it's better than butter! Just squeeze out the garlic flesh from its skin and spread it on.

Preparation Time:
15 minutes

6 Servings/Serving Size:
3–4 oz (no skin)

Exchanges:
4	Very Lean Meat
1/2	Fat

Calories	173
Calories from Fat	68
Total Fat	8 g
Saturated Fat	2 g

Cholesterol	76 mg
Sodium	94 mg
Carbohydrate	0 g
Dietary Fiber	0 g
Sugars	0 g

Protein	25 g

1 roasting chicken (about 3 lb)
1 Tbsp olive oil
2 Tbsp minced fresh rosemary
Fresh ground pepper and salt
1 Tbsp paprika
40 cloves garlic, skins left on
1 cup low-fat, low-sodium chicken broth

1. Wash the chicken inside and out. Remove and discard the giblets. Combine the next four ingredients. Rub this mixture all over the chicken and place in the refrigerator overnight.

2. The next day, preheat the oven to 350 degrees. Place the chicken in a roasting pan. Surround the chicken with garlic and then pour the broth over the chicken. Roast the chicken, covered, for 1 hour. Uncover and roast an additional 1/2 hour or until juices run clear.

Spiced Turkey Roast

Using a boneless breast of turkey means nothing is wasted!

Preparation Time:	
15 minutes	

6 Servings/Serving Size:
3–4 oz

Exchanges:

4	Very Lean Meat

Calories	155
Calories from Fat	23
Total Fat	3 g
Saturated Fat	1 g

Cholesterol	75 mg
Sodium	65 mg
Carbohydrate	4 g
Dietary Fiber	1 g
Sugars	2 g

Protein	28 g

1 1/2 lb boneless turkey roast
2 tsp olive oil
2 tsp cinnamon
2 tsp cloves
1 tsp allspice
1 Tbsp coarsely cracked peppercorns
1 cup low-fat, low-sodium chicken broth
1 cup fresh cranberries
2 cups water
2 Tbsp orange juice
1 Tbsp cornstarch or arrowroot powder
2 Tbsp water

1. Preheat the oven to 350 degrees. Place the turkey roast in a roasting pan. Rub with olive oil. Combine the four spices. Rub over the turkey roast. Pour the chicken broth into the bottom of the pan. Place the turkey in the oven and roast for about 1 hour until the juices run clear, basting occasionally with the broth.

2. Combine the cranberries and water in a saucepan. Bring to a boil. Lower the heat and cook until the cranberries begin to pop. Add the orange juice. Combine the cornstarch or arrowroot powder with water and add to the sauce. Cook until thickened. Slice the turkey roast and serve the sauce with the sliced turkey.

Triple Apple Cornish Game Hens

This is an elegant holiday main dish.

Preparation Time:
15 minutes

6 Servings/Serving Size:
1/2 hen (3 oz, no skin)
with 1 Tbsp sauce

Exchanges:
2   Very Lean Meat

Calories 77
  Calories from Fat 16
Total Fat ....2 g
  Saturated Fat ....0 g

Cholesterol ....47 mg
Sodium ....29 mg
Carbohydrate ....4 g
  Dietary Fiber ....0 g
  Sugars ....3 g

Protein ....11 g

3 Cornish game hens (about 3/4 lb each)
1 cup unsweetened apple juice
2 Tbsp unsweetened apple butter
1/2 cup diced Granny Smith apple, unpeeled
1/4 cup minced onion
1 Tbsp cornstarch or arrowroot powder
2 Tbsp water

1. Preheat the oven to 350 degrees. Wash the hens inside and out. Remove giblets and discard. In a small saucepan, mix together all sauce ingredients except for the cornstarch or arrowroot powder and water. Bring to a boil and lower the heat. Cook for 5 minutes.

2. Combine the cornstarch or arrowroot powder and water. Mix until smooth. Add to the sauce and cook until thickened. Pour sauce over the game hens, reserving 1/4 cup. Keep reserved sauce warm. Bake hens for 45–60 minutes until juices run clear. Cut in halves and serve with reserved sauce.

Vanilla-Raisin Cornish Game Hens

Brush the raisin sauce on the hens during the last 20 minutes of baking for a splendid glaze.

Preparation Time:
15 minutes

6 Servings/Serving Size:
1/2 hen (3 oz, no skin)

Exchanges:
1/2	Fruit
2	Very Lean Meat

Calories	84
Calories from Fat	16
Total Fat	2 g
Saturated Fat	0 g

Cholesterol	47 mg
Sodium	29 mg
Carbohydrate	6 g
Dietary Fiber	0 g
Sugars	4 g

Protein	11 g

3 Cornish game hens (about 3/4 lb each)
1/2 cup raisins
1 1/4 cups boiling water
2 Tbsp apple cider
2 tsp cinnamon
2 Tbsp cornstarch or arrowroot powder
4 Tbsp water
2 tsp vanilla

1. Preheat the oven to 350 degrees. Wash the hens inside and out. Remove giblets and discard. Pat hens dry. Place the hens in a roasting pan, cover, and bake for 40 minutes. Place the raisins in a small measuring cup. Add the boiling water and let raisins soak for 10 minutes. Drain, reserving the raisin water. Add the raisin water to a small saucepan. Add the apple cider and bring to a boil. Add the cinnamon and lower the heat.

2. Mix together the cornstarch or arrowroot powder and water. Add to the pan. Cook over low heat until thickened. Remove from the heat and add in the raisins and vanilla. Brush the vanilla raisin sauce over the hens. Continue to bake for 20 more minutes, uncovered. Split the hens and serve.

Three French Hens

Herbs and garlic spice up this classic dish.

Preparation Time:
15 minutes

6 Servings/Serving Size:
1/2 hen (3 oz, no skin)

Exchanges:
2   Very Lean Meat

Calories	70
Calories from Fat	26
Total Fat	3 g
Saturated Fat	1 g
Cholesterol	47 mg
Sodium	28 mg
Carbohydrate	0 g
Dietary Fiber	0 g
Sugars	0 g
Protein	10 g

3 Cornish game hens (about 3/4 lb each)
2 Tbsp minced fresh rosemary
2 tsp minced fresh tarragon
1 Tbsp minced fresh sage
1 Tbsp minced fresh thyme
1 Tbsp olive oil
12 unpeeled garlic cloves
Fresh ground pepper to taste

Wash hens inside and out. Remove giblets and discard. Combine all the herbs and the olive oil. Rub over the surface of the hens and place in the refrigerator overnight. The next day, preheat the oven to 350 degrees. Place the hens on a roasting rack. Surround the hens with the garlic and grind pepper over each hen. Roast the hens, covered, for about 40 minutes. Uncover and continue to bake for 20 more minutes until juices run clear. Split the hens and serve.

Red Wine Beef Roast

Marinating this roast in an aromatic mixture of red wine and herbs makes it tender.

Preparation Time:
10 minutes

6 Servings/Serving Size:
3–4 oz

Exchanges:
4   Very Lean Meat
1/2   Monounsaturated Fat

Calories	165
Calories from Fat	54
Total Fat	6 g
Saturated Fat	2 g
Cholesterol	57
Sodium	75
Carbohydrate	0 g
Dietary Fiber	0 g
Sugars	0 g
Protein	24 g

1 1/2 lb boneless beef roast
2 cups dry red wine
2 Tbsp olive oil
4 sprigs fresh thyme
2 sprigs fresh rosemary
4 garlic cloves, minced
Fresh ground pepper and salt to taste

1. Combine the marinade ingredients. Place the roast in a non-metallic bowl and pour the marinade over the roast. Place in the refrigerator to marinate overnight.

2. The next day, preheat the oven to 350 degrees. Drain the marinade and place the roast on a roasting rack. Roast the beef according to the following guidelines: 1 1/4 hours for rare, 1 1/2 hours for medium, or 1 3/4 hours for well done.

Onion and Herb Pork Roast

Boneless pork tenderloin can be a nice low-fat alternative to beef.

Preparation Time:
10 minutes

6 Servings/Serving Size:
3–4 oz

Exchanges:
3	Lean Meat
1	Monounsaturated Fat

Calories 213
 Calories from Fat 107
Total Fat ....12 g
 Saturated Fat............3 g

Cholesterol ....63 mg
Sodium ....70 mg
Carbohydrate..............2 g
 Dietary Fiber ....0 g
 Sugars.......................1 g

Protein ....23 g

1 1/2 lb boneless pork loin roast
1 medium onion, minced
1 Tbsp minced fresh rosemary
2 tsp minced fresh thyme
2 tsp minced fresh parsley
2 Tbsp olive oil
Fresh ground pepper and salt to taste

1. Preheat the oven to 350 degrees. Place the pork roast in a roasting pan. Combine the remaining ingredients and mix well, until the mixture resembles a paste. Rub the paste over the pork roast.

2. Place the pork roast in the oven and roast for about 1 1/2 hours, until there is no trace of pink. Slice and serve.

*Eat a snack before a party.
Then you won't be eating too many high-fat foods
just to fill your empty stomach.*

Orange Pork Roast

This glazed pork roast will look like a jewel on your pretty holiday table.

Preparation Time:
10 minutes

6 Servings/Serving Size:
3–4 oz

Exchanges:

1	Carbohydrate
3	Very Lean Meat
1	Fat

Calories	227
Calories from Fat	70
Total Fat	8 g
Saturated Fat	2 g
Cholesterol	71 mg
Sodium	129 mg
Carbohydrate	12 g
Dietary Fiber	0 g
Sugars	8 g
Protein	26 g

1 1/2 lb boneless pork loin roast
1/4 cup low-calorie margarine
2 tsp sugar
2 cups low-fat, low-sodium chicken broth
1/4 cup cornstarch or arrowroot powder
1/4 cup Grand Marnier
1/4 cup low-sugar orange marmalade
2 Tbsp grated orange peel
1/8 tsp cloves
Orange slices
Parsley

1. Preheat the oven to 375 degrees. Place the pork roast on a roasting rack. Melt the margarine in a large saucepan and add the sugar. Combine the chicken broth and the cornstarch or arrowroot powder. Add to the saucepan and stir until thickened. Add the remaining ingredients except the orange slices and parsley. Cook for 2 minutes on low heat.

2. Brush one-half of the sauce over the pork. Roast the pork for about 60 minutes until there are no traces of pink. Heat the remaining glaze to serve on the side. Slice the pork and garnish with orange slices and parsley to serve.

Tuscan-Peppered Pork Loin

The combination of wine and herbs will fill your kitchen with a delicious aroma as this roast cooks!

Preparation Time:
20 minutes

6 Servings/Serving Size:
3–4 oz

Exchanges:
4   Lean Meat

Calories 237
  Calories from Fat 94
Total Fat ....10 g
  Saturated Fat.............3 g

Cholesterol ....69 mg
Sodium.....................52 mg
Carbohydrate...............3 g
  Dietary Fiber ....0 g
  Sugars.......................2 g

Protein ....25 g

1 1/2 lb boneless pork loin roast
1 Tbsp olive oil
2 Tbsp coarsely ground pepper
3 garlic cloves, crushed
1 sprig fresh thyme
1 sprig fresh rosemary
1 medium onion, quartered
1 cup dry white wine
1/3 cup Irish whiskey
2 Tbsp coarsely cracked black pepper
3 Tbsp minced fresh parsley

1. Preheat the oven to 350 degrees. Rub the surface of the pork roast with the olive oil and pepper. Place the pork in a roasting pan with the garlic, herbs, and onion and roast for 30 minutes. Add the wine and continue to roast for 30–40 minutes until there are no traces of pink.

2. Remove the roast from the pan and set aside. Save the pan drippings. In a saucepan, combine the drippings with the whiskey and peppercorns. Bring to a boil. Reduce the heat and cook until sauce is reduced by half. Stir in the parsley and serve the sauce with the sliced pork.

This adapted recipe is courtesy of the National Pork Producers.

Herbed Pork Roast

Fresh herbs make all the difference in this dish.

Preparation Time:
5 minutes

6 Servings/Serving Size:
3–4 oz

Exchanges:

4	Very Lean Meat
1	Fat

Calories	188
Calories from Fat	76
Total Fat	8 g
Saturated Fat	3 g
Cholesterol	71 mg
Sodium	52 mg
Carbohydrate	1 g
Dietary Fiber	0 g
Sugars	0 g
Protein	25 g

1 Tbsp paprika
3 Tbsp minced fresh parsley
1/2 tsp minced fresh oregano
1/4 tsp minced fresh tarragon
1/4 tsp minced fresh thyme
1/4 tsp minced fresh dill
1 2-lb boneless pork rib end roast

Preheat the oven to 350 degrees. Mix together the paprika and the herbs. Coat the roast with the herb mixture. Place the roast on a rack in an open roasting pan. Roast, uncovered, for 1 1/2 hours, until meat thermometer registers 150–160 degrees. Remove from the oven and let stand 10 minutes before serving.

This adapted recipe is courtesy of the National Pork Producers.

Spinach-Stuffed Pork Roast

Try serving this flavorful stuffed pork with roasted potatoes and baby peas.

Preparation Time:
15 minutes

6 Servings/Serving Size:
3 oz

Exchanges:

1/2	Starch
4	Very Lean Meat
1 1/2	Fat

Calories	250
Calories from Fat	100
Total Fat	11 g
Saturated Fat	3 g

Cholesterol	71 mg
Sodium	165 mg
Carbohydrate	9 g
Dietary Fiber	1 g
Sugars	1 g

Protein	27 g

1 2-lb boneless pork roast, rolled and tied
1 Tbsp olive oil
1/4 cup chopped fresh mushrooms
1/4 cup chopped onion
1/4 cup chopped red pepper
1/2 10-oz package frozen chopped spinach,
    thawed
1/2 cup bread crumbs
Fresh ground pepper and salt to taste

1. Untie roast and set aside. Preheat the oven to 325 degrees. Heat the oil in a skillet over medium-high heat. Add the mushrooms, onion, and red pepper and saute for 3 minutes. Stir in spinach, bread crumbs, pepper, and salt.

2. Spread stuffing over the roast and roll up. Tie securely with string. Place the roast on a rack in an open roasting pan. Roast, uncovered, for 1 1/2 hours, until meat thermometer registers 150–160 degrees. Remove from the oven and let stand 10 minutes before serving.

This adapted recipe is courtesy of the National Pork Producers.

Grilled Pepper Pork

To make this dish more spicy, try using white Szechwan peppercorns, available in Asian grocery stores.

Preparation Time:	
15 minutes	

6 Servings/Serving Size:
3 oz

Exchanges:
3 Lean Meat

Calories	140
Calories from Fat	55
Total Fat	6 g
Saturated Fat	2 g
Cholesterol	52 mg
Sodium	189 mg
Carbohydrate	1 g
Dietary Fiber	0 g
Sugars	1 g
Protein	19 g

2 garlic cloves, crushed
1 Tbsp crushed coriander seeds
8 crushed black or white peppercorns
1 tsp brown sugar
3 Tbsp lite soy sauce
6 4–5-oz pork loin chops, about 1 inch thick

Combine all ingredients except the pork chops, then add the chops and marinate for 30 minutes. Grill or broil the chops, brushing with marinade and turning once, for about 12–14 minutes.

This adapted recipe is courtesy of the National Pork Producers.

Tex-Mex Pork Chops

This is a quick, one-skillet dish with an olé touch!

Preparation Time:
15 minutes

6 Servings/Serving Size:
3 oz

Exchanges:	
3	Lean Meat

Calories	168
Calories from Fat	70
Total Fat	8 g
Saturated Fat	2 g

Cholesterol	52 mg
Sodium	279 mg
Carbohydrate	4 g
Dietary Fiber	1 g
Sugars	2 g

Protein	19 g

2 tsp olive oil
6 4–5-oz boneless pork loin chops
1 1/2 cups salsa
1 4-oz can diced green chilies
1/2 tsp ground cumin

Heat the oil in a skillet over medium-high heat. Add the pork chops and saute for about 3 minutes on each side. Add the remaining ingredients. Lower the heat, cover, and simmer for 10 minutes.

This adapted recipe is courtesy of the National Pork Producers.

Teriyaki Pork Chops

This easy marinade tenderizes the pork beautifully.

Preparation Time: 5 minutes	

6 Servings/Serving Size:
3 oz

Exchanges:

3	Lean Meat

Calories	160
Calories from Fat	65
Total Fat	7 g
Saturated Fat	2 g

Cholesterol	52 mg
Sodium	239 mg
Carbohydrate	3 g
Dietary Fiber	0 g
Sugars	3 g

Protein	19 g

1/4 cup lite soy sauce
1/4 cup dry sherry
2 Tbsp sugar
3 garlic cloves, minced
1 Tbsp peanut oil
6 4–5-oz pork loin chops

Combine all marinade ingredients. Add the pork chops and marinate in the refrigerator for 4–24 hours. Grill or broil the pork chops, turning once, for 12–13 minutes until juices run clear.

This adapted recipe is courtesy of the National Pork Producers.

Grilled Ham Steak with Apricot Glaze

Just a few ingredients turn ham into something special! (This recipe is high in sodium.)

Preparation Time:
10 minutes

6 Servings/Serving Size:
3 oz

Exchanges:

1/2	Fruit
3	Very Lean Meat
1/2	Fat

Calories......................160	
Calories from Fat........46	
Total Fat......................5 g	
Saturated Fat............2 g	

Cholesterol............50 mg	
Sodium...............1224 mg	
Carbohydrate.............4 g	
Dietary Fiber.............0 g	
Sugars.......................4 g	

Protein........................23 g	

1/4 cup low-sugar apricot jam
2 tsp Dijon mustard
2 tsp cider vinegar
1 1/2 lb boneless, lean ham, cut into 6 1/2-inch-thick slices

In a small bowl, mix together the jam, mustard, and vinegar. Broil or grill the ham slices, brushing with the basting sauce and turning once, for 8–10 minutes.

This adapted recipe is courtesy of the National Pork Producers.

Ham with Peach Chutney

Ham and peaches make a great combination. (This recipe is high in sodium.)

Preparation Time:
15 minutes

6 Servings/Serving Size:
3 oz

Exchanges:

1 1/2	Fruit
4	Very Lean Meat
1/2	Fat

Calories	247
Calories from Fat	57
Total Fat	6 g
Saturated Fat	2 g

Cholesterol	60 mg
Sodium	1452 mg
Carbohydrate	19 g
Dietary Fiber	2 g
Sugars	16 g

Protein	28 g

1 2-lb fully cooked, boneless ham
3 cups unsweetened peach slices (canned or fresh)
1/4 cup cider vinegar
2 Tbsp brown sugar
1/2 cup minced onion
1 tart apple, peeled and coarsely chopped

Preheat the oven to 325 degrees. Place the ham in a shallow pan and roast until the meat thermometer reads 140 degrees (about 1 to 1 1/2 hours). Meanwhile, coarsely chop the peaches. Combine the peaches with the remaining ingredients in a large saucepan and simmer 20 minutes until thickened slightly. Allow to cool and cover until serving. Slice the ham and serve with the sauce.

This adapted recipe is courtesy of the National Pork Producers.

Ham with Blueberry Sauce

Juicy, plump blueberries form the basis of this delicious sauce. (This recipe is high in sodium.)

Preparation Time:
15 minutes

6 Servings/Serving Size:
3 oz

Exchanges:

1	Fruit
4	Very Lean Meat
1/2	Fat

Calories	224
Calories from Fat	56
Total Fat	6 g
Saturated Fat	2 g

Cholesterol	60 mg
Sodium	1463 mg
Carbohydrate	12 g
Dietary Fiber	1 g
Sugars	9 g

Protein	27 g

1 2-lb, fully cooked, center slice of ham, cut
   1 inch thick
1/3 cup water
1 Tbsp cornstarch or arrowroot powder
1/3 cup low-sugar apricot jam
1 Tbsp brown sugar
2 Tbsp dry red wine
4 tsp lemon juice
1 cup blueberries

1. Preheat the oven to 350 degrees. Trim the fat from the edge of the ham slice, if necessary. Place the ham slice on a rack in a shallow baking pan and bake for 30 minutes.

2. In a small saucepan, combine the cornstarch or arrowroot powder and water. Stir in the apricot jam, brown sugar, wine, and lemon juice. Cook over medium-low heat for 5–6 minutes until the sauce is thickened and bubbly. Stir in the blueberries and cook 2–3 minutes. Spoon the sauce over the ham and serve.

This adapted recipe is courtesy of the National Pork Producers.

Holiday Decorating Magic

The special meals and desserts you prepare for the holidays will look even better against a festive backdrop. Try these ideas to add those special touches around the house:

❄ Mood candles look elegant; purchase all sizes and colors and set them everywhere! Be careful to place them away from curtains and flammable areas. Arrange a cluster of red candles in assorted shapes and sizes on the mantle. Use tall white candles as a contrast. Set candles inside a collection of antique coffee cups. Purchase glass, engraved votive candles and place on silver trays on coffee tables.

❄ Pine cone baskets look great on coffee tables or in bathrooms. Simply spray gold paint on baskets in all shapes and sizes, tie ribbon around them, and fill with natural and gold-sprayed pine cones.

❄ Potpourri will make your whole house smell wonderful. Fill different containers with your favorite and set in every room of the house. Place some packets in lingerie drawers, too.

❄ Think green with pine boughs and holly placed on staircases, mantles, and over door frames. White is a great complementary color—include white poinsettias and narcissus as a contrast. Be careful to keep all greenery away from small children. Try more unusual colors, such as deep blues and purples, to lend a Mardi Gras feel to the holidays.

❄ Play old-fashioned holiday music all day long!

Some creative ways to decorate your holiday table

✳ Centerpieces can include gourds, pears, apples, or pine cones stacked high or in baskets. Look for arrangements of dried flowers and whole spices using holiday colors. For a very elegant look, splurge on red and white roses.

✳ Use beautiful platters for serving golden turkey, chicken, or roasts. On the bottom of a silver platter, set white kale leaves. Place the turkey, chicken, or roast on top. Surround the sides with seckel pears (little pears); clusters of green and red grapes; orange cups filled with cranberries (halve oranges, hollow out, and fill with cranberries); and rosemary sprigs coming out from the base of the turkey, chicken, or roast.

✳ Serve soups from a hollowed-out pumpkin or large turban squash. Or serve each person soup in half an acorn squash.

✳ Place settings are made more special if you use a small framed photograph of each person taken from a previous holiday season as a placecard. Each person can keep the photo and the memory!

✳ For New Year's Eve, do place settings in gold by sprinkling base plates with gold stars. Make placecards with large gold stars and write each person's name in gold glitter. Give each person gold wands. Set the table with tall gold candles.

Apple-Glazed Baby Carrots

No need for sticky brown sugar and high-fat butter—let the natural, sweet taste of the carrots shine through.

Preparation Time:
15 minutes

6 Servings/Serving Size:
1/2 cup

Exchanges:
2   Vegetable

Calories 61
  Calories from Fat 12
Total Fat ....1 g
  Saturated Fat.............0 g

Cholesterol ....0 mg
Sodium...................77 mg
Carbohydrate.............12 g
  Dietary Fiber ....2 g
  Sugars.......................7 g

Protein ....1 g

3 cups baby carrots (about 1 1/2 bags)
1 Tbsp lemon juice
1 Tbsp low-calorie margarine
3 Tbsp apple juice concentrate
2/3 cup low-fat, low-sodium chicken broth
1 tsp cinnamon
2 tsp cornstarch or arrowroot powder
1 tsp water

In a steamer over 2 inches of boiling water, steam the carrots, covered, for 3 minutes. Sprinkle with lemon juice. Melt the margarine in a medium skillet over medium heat. Add the apple juice concentrate and cook until it melts. Add the broth and cinnamon and bring to a boil. Mix together the cornstarch or arrowroot powder with the water. Add to the skillet, lower the heat, and cook until thickened. Add the carrots and toss well to coat.

Brussels Sprouts and Chestnuts

Although Brussels sprouts usually make their way to holiday tables, this fiber-rich vegetable should be served all winter long.

Preparation Time:
20 minutes

6 Servings/Serving Size:
1/2 cup

Exchanges:

1	Starch
1	Vegetable
1/2	Monounsaturated Fat

Calories	126
Calories from Fat	29
Total Fat	3 g
Saturated Fat	0 g

Cholesterol	0 mg
Sodium	50 mg
Carbohydrate	23 g
Dietary Fiber	4 g
Sugars	8 g

Protein	4 g

3 cups Brussels sprouts
1 cup whole roasted chestnuts (see directions below to prepare yourself, or buy chestnuts in jars packed in water at the grocery store)
1 orange, peeled, separated into sections, and seeded
1/2 cup low-fat, low-sodium chicken broth
1 Tbsp canola oil
Fresh ground pepper and salt to taste

1. Trim each sprout by cutting a little piece off the bottom. With a small paring knife, make an "X" in the top of the sprout. Repeat with all sprouts. In a steamer over 2 inches of boiling water, steam the sprouts, covered, for about 10 minutes.

2. Remove the steamed sprouts from the pot. Let cool. Cut each sprout in half and place in a casserole dish. Layer the chestnuts on top of the sprouts. Place the orange sections on top of the chestnuts. Add the broth and pour over all ingredients. Drizzle the casserole with oil. Grind in pepper and add salt. Bake in a preheated 350-degree oven for 15 minutes, until oranges are soft.

To prepare your own chestnuts, mark an "X" on the rounded side of the chestnut with a small paring knife. Place all the chestnuts on a baking sheet and roast in a 350-degree oven for about 30 minutes, until soft. Let cool. Then peel, trying to keep the chestnuts as whole as possible.

Cauliflower with Low-Fat Cheese Sauce

Tender cauliflower gets a little flavor boost from this creamy cheese sauce.

Preparation Time:
15 minutes

6 Servings/Serving Size:
1/2 cup with 2–3 Tbsp sauce

Exchanges:

1	Starch
1	Monounsaturated Fat

Calories 126
 Calories from Fat 44
Total Fat ....5 g
 Saturated Fat.............1 g

Cholesterol ....1 mg
Sodium ....58 mg
Carbohydrate ....18 g
 Dietary Fiber ....1 g
 Sugars........................5 g

Protein ....3 g

1 medium cauliflower, broken into florets (about 3 cups)
2 Tbsp low-calorie margarine
1 Tbsp unbleached flour
1 cup evaporated skim milk
1/4 cup low-fat cheddar cheese
2 Tbsp low-fat cottage cheese
2 tsp Parmesan cheese
1 tsp paprika
Fresh ground pepper and salt to taste

1. Steam the cauliflower in a steamer over boiling water, covered, for 5–6 minutes until the florets just turn tender. Set aside. Melt the margarine in a medium skillet over medium heat. Add the flour and stir until smooth.

2. Add the milk and cook over medium-low heat until slightly thickened. Add the cheeses. Cook until cheeses melt, about 3 minutes. (Add a little liquid if the sauce is too thick.) Add the paprika, pepper, and salt. Pour the sauce over steamed cauliflower and serve.

Baked Vegetable Casserole

This one-pot side dish will stick to your ribs on cold winter days.

Preparation Time:
15 minutes

---

6 Servings/Serving Size:
1/2 cup

Exchanges:
1 1/2   Starch

Calories......................123
 Calories from Fat........19
Total Fat......................2 g
 Saturated Fat.............0 g

Cholesterol ....3 mg
Sodium.................555 mg
Carbohydrate...........22 g
 Dietary Fiber ....3 g
 Sugars......................6 g

Protein.........................5 g

1/2 cup evaporated skim milk
3 cups frozen mixed vegetables, thawed slightly
1 11-oz can reduced fat cream of mushroom
    soup
1 Tbsp Dijon mustard
1 tsp minced garlic
1 tsp dill
1/2 cup dry bread crumbs

Preheat the oven to 350 degrees. Mix all
ingredients together except the bread crumbs
and place in a 9-inch glass casserole dish.
Sprinkle the bread crumbs over the top and
bake for 30 minutes.

Broccoli with Sun-Dried Tomatoes and Pine Nuts

Preparation Time:
15 minutes

---

6 Servings/Serving Size:
1/2 cup

Exchanges:

2	Vegetable
1	Fat

Calories	95
Calories from Fat	50
Total Fat	6 g
Saturated Fat	1 g

Cholesterol	0 mg
Sodium	140 mg
Carbohydrate	10 g
Dietary Fiber	4 g
Sugars	3 g

Protein	5 g

1 1/2 lb fresh broccoli (stems sliced and
   separated into florets)
2 tsp olive oil
1/2 cup diced red onion
10 sun-dried tomatoes, rehydrated
1/2 cup low-fat, low-sodium chicken broth
1 Tbsp fresh lemon juice
1/4 cup toasted pine nuts

1. Fill a large stockpot with water and bring to a
    boil. Add the broccoli and boil gently for 1
    minute. Drain. Plunge the broccoli into a
    bowl of ice water. Drain again and set aside.
    Heat the oil in a saucepan over medium-high
    heat. Add the red onion and saute for 5
    minutes.

2. Dice the sun-dried tomatoes and add to the
    onion. Add the broth and bring to a boil.
    Lower the heat, cover, and let steam for 2
    minutes. Add the lemon juice to the tomato
    mixture. Add the broccoli and stir well to coat
    it with the tomatoes and onion. Place broccoli
    in a serving bowl, top with toasted pine nuts,
    and serve.

Roasted Potato Medley

Try this medley of roasted potatoes as a change or addition to mashed potatoes on your holiday table.

Preparation Time:	
15 minutes	

6 Servings/Serving Size:
1/2 cup

Exchanges:
| 1 | Starch |
| 1/2 | Monounsaturated Fat |

Calories	108
Calories from Fat	42
Total Fat	5 g
Saturated Fat	1 g
Cholesterol	0 mg
Sodium	11 mg
Carbohydrate	16 g
Dietary Fiber	2 g
Sugars	5 g
Protein	2 g

1 medium russet potato, cut into 2-inch cubes
1 medium red potato, cut into 2-inch cubes
1 medium sweet potato, cut into 2-inch cubes
2 Tbsp olive oil
2 Tbsp balsamic vinegar
2 tsp minced fresh thyme
3 garlic cloves, minced
1/4 cup low-fat, low-sodium chicken broth

Preheat the oven to 375 degrees. In a bowl, combine all ingredients. Toss well to coat. Place potatoes in a casserole dish. Roast uncovered for about 40 minutes, until potatoes are tender.

❋❋❋❋❋❋❋❋❋❋❋❋❋❋❋❋❋❋❋❋❋❋❋❋

Potatoes are a potent package.
A serving of French fries from a medium-size potato has 480 calories. If that medium-size potato was boiled or baked instead, it would have 90 calories. If you eat the skin, too, you get carbohydrate and fiber, half the recommended daily allowance of vitamin C, the protein of half an egg, and very little fat.

❋❋❋❋❋❋❋❋❋❋❋❋❋❋❋❋❋❋❋❋❋❋❋❋

*H*erbed Garlic Mashed Potatoes

Roasting garlic is easy, and adds a great flavor to these mashed potatoes!

Preparation Time:
15 minutes

6 Servings/Serving Size:
1/2 cup

Exchanges:
1	Starch
1	Monounsaturated Fat

Calories	126
Calories from Fat	44
Total Fat	5 g
Saturated Fat	1 g

Cholesterol	1 mg
Sodium	58 mg
Carbohydrate	18 g
Dietary Fiber	1 g
Sugars	5 g

Protein	3 g

1 head of garlic (slice off a little of the top to expose the cloves)
1/2 cup low-fat, low-sodium chicken broth
3–4 medium russet potatoes, peeled and cubed
1 cup warm skim milk
2 Tbsp olive oil
1 Tbsp minced fresh thyme
1/2 tsp minced fresh rosemary
Fresh ground pepper and salt to taste

1. Preheat the oven to 350 degrees. In a small casserole dish, place the whole head of garlic and the broth. Cover the casserole dish and roast in the oven for 1 hour. Remove from the oven and set aside. Meanwhile, boil the cubed potatoes in water for about 20 minutes, until soft. Drain.

2. Add the warm milk and olive oil. With electric beaters, whip until potatoes are fluffy. Add the herbs. Gently squeeze the garlic out from each of the cloves, leaving behind the skins. Add all the garlic pulp to the potatoes. Whip again. Season with pepper and salt and serve.

Herb-Roasted Potatoes

Serve these for a great change from plain old baked potatoes.

Preparation Time:
10 minutes

---

6 Servings/Serving Size:
1 small potato

Exchanges:
1   Starch
1   Monounsaturated Fat

Calories......................114
  Calories from Fat.......41
Total Fat ....5 g
  Saturated Fat............1 g

Cholesterol ....0 mg
Sodium....................28 mg
Carbohydrate............17 g
  Dietary Fiber ....2 g
  Sugars......................1 g

Protein.........................2 g

6 small russet potatoes
2 Tbsp olive oil
1/4 cup dry white wine
10 sprigs fresh rosemary
10 sprigs fresh thyme
Fresh ground pepper and salt to taste

Preheat the oven to 350 degrees. Cut each potato in half and place in a baking dish. Cover the potatoes with oil, wine, herbs, pepper, and salt. Cover and bake for 1 hour. Uncover and bake for 10 more minutes.

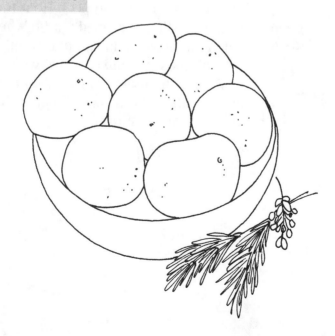

Savory Sweet Potatoes

Packed with fiber and Vitamin A, the sweet potato adorns every holiday table. Most people have a memory of mashed sweet potatoes (often canned) with burnt mini-marshmallows on top! For a healthier spud, just sprinkle a baked sweet potato with lots of cinnamon and nutmeg. Or scoop out the flesh, mash it with 1/2 cup crushed pineapple (canned in its own juice), spoon the mixture back into the shell, and bake at 375 degrees for an additional 5 minutes until the pineapple is bubbly. In the recipe below, savory garlic and onion add a twist to the sweet flavor of orange.

Preparation Time:
15 minutes

---

6 Servings/Serving Size:
1/2 cup

Exchanges:
1 1/2   Starch

Calories	124
Calories from Fat	16
Total Fat	2 g
Saturated Fat	0 g

Cholesterol	1 mg
Sodium	33 mg
Carbohydrate	24 g
Dietary Fiber	2 g
Sugars	14 g

Protein	3 g

3 medium sweet potatoes (about 1 1/4 lb total)
2 tsp canola oil
1/2 cup diced onion
2 garlic cloves, minced
1/2 cup fresh orange juice
1/2 cup evaporated skim milk
1 tsp cinnamon
Fresh ground pepper to taste

Cook the sweet potatoes by pricking their skins and baking them directly on the oven rack at 375 degrees for 45–60 minutes. Remove from the oven, let cool, and peel. Heat the oil in a medium skillet over medium-high heat. Add the onion and garlic and saute for 5 minutes. Mash the potatoes in a mixing bowl with electric beaters or a potato masher. Add the remaining ingredients. Add the onion and garlic mixture and beat again until fluffy.

Sweet Potatoes and Pears

Choose from the variety of pears available in the winter. Red d'Anjou or Bosc pears are particularly good.

Preparation Time:
20 minutes

6 Servings/Serving Size:
1/2 cup

Exchanges:

1	Starch
1 1/2	Fruit

Calories......................148
  Calories from Fat..........5
Total Fat......................1 g
  Saturated Fat............0 g

Cholesterol ....0 mg
Sodium.....................8 mg
Carbohydrate............36 g
  Dietary Fiber ....5 g
  Sugars....................24 g

Protein ....2 g

3 pears, washed, unpeeled, and thinly sliced
1 Tbsp lemon juice
3 medium sweet potatoes (about 1 1/4 lb total), peeled and sliced thin
1/4 cup apple cider
1 tsp nutmeg
1 tsp cinnamon
1/2 cup dried cranberries, rehydrated (pour boiling water over 1/2 cup dried cranberries, let sit for 10 minutes, and drain)

Preheat the oven to 350 degrees. Toss the pears with the lemon juice. In a casserole dish, layer the pears and sweet potatoes. Pour apple cider over the top and sprinkle with nutmeg, cinnamon, and rehydrated cranberries. Cover and bake for 40 minutes. Uncover and bake an additional 15 minutes.

Vanilla Brandy Sweet Potatoes

Immerse a whole vanilla bean in creamy sweet potatoes and add a splash of brandy for holiday cheer!

Preparation Time:
15 minutes

6 Servings/Serving Size:
1/2 cup

Exchanges:

2	Starch

Calories	135
Calories from Fat	1
Total Fat	0 g
Saturated Fat	0 g

Cholesterol	0 mg
Sodium	9 mg
Carbohydrate	31 g
Dietary Fiber	2 g
Sugars	20 g

Protein	2 g

3 medium sweet potatoes (about 1 1/4 lb total), peeled and sliced thin
2 cups orange juice
2 tsp honey
1 vanilla bean, split
1/4 cup brandy
2 tsp grenadine
1 Tbsp cornstarch or arrowroot powder
2 Tbsp water

1. Preheat the oven to 350 degrees. Place the sweet potatoes in a casserole dish. In a small saucepan over medium heat, add the orange juice, honey, vanilla bean, and brandy. Bring to a boil. Add the grenadine.

2. Mix together the cornstarch or arrowroot powder with the water. Add to the sauce. Cook over low heat until thickened. Pour the sauce over the potatoes and bake, covered, for 45–60 minutes.

Sweet Potato Timbales

Pumpkin and sweet potatoes combine in this side dish rich in beta-carotene.

Preparation Time:	
20 minutes	
6 Servings/Serving Size:	
1/2 cup	
Exchanges:	
1 1/2	Starch
Calories	131
Calories from Fat	17
Total Fat	2 g
Saturated Fat	1 g
Cholesterol	72 mg
Sodium	54 mg
Carbohydrate	24 g
Dietary Fiber	3 g
Sugars	12 g
Protein	5 g

2 cups peeled, shredded sweet potatoes (about 2 medium)
1 cup water
1 cup canned pumpkin puree (not pumpkin pie filling)
2 eggs, beaten
1/2 cup evaporated skimmed milk
1 Tbsp unbleached white flour
2 tsp honey
1 tsp cinnamon
Nonstick cooking spray

1. Preheat the oven to 350 degrees. In a small saucepan, cook the sweet potatoes in the water for 8 minutes until tender. Drain any water from the sweet potatoes. In a bowl, combine all the remaining ingredients and mix well.

2. Spray 6 glass custard cups with nonstick cooking spray. Pour the sweet potato mixture into the cups. Fill a baking pan with 2 inches of water and place the cups in the pan. Place the pan in the oven and bake for 30–35 minutes until custards are set. Serve.

Sweet Potato and Turnip Swirl

This combination of sweet potatoes and spicy turnips could make turnip lovers out of us all!

Preparation Time:
15 minutes

6 Servings/Serving Size:
1/2 cup

Exchanges:
1   Starch

Calories.......................73
  Calories from Fat..........9
Total Fat ....1 g
  Saturated Fat.............0 g

Cholesterol ....0 mg
Sodium...................34 mg
Carbohydrate............16 g
  Dietary Fiber ....2 g
  Sugars......................8 g

Protein ....1 g

1/2 lb turnips, peeled and cubed
2 medium sweet potatoes (about 13 oz), peeled and cubed
1 tsp minced ginger
1 Tbsp low-calorie margarine
1 Tbsp sugar
2 tsp grated orange peel

In a medium saucepan, cook the turnips and sweet potatoes in boiling water to cover for about 15–20 minutes until soft. Drain. Transfer to a food processor and puree. In a saucepan, combine the ginger, margarine, sugar, and orange peel. Add the puree and toss to coat with the margarine mixture. Serve warm.

Pumpkin Parfait

This is a light way to serve a pumpkin dessert.

Preparation Time:
15 minutes

6 Servings/Serving Size:
1/2 cup

Exchanges:
1/2	Starch
1/2	Skim Milk

Calories	75
Calories from Fat	3
Total Fat	0 g
Saturated Fat	0 g
Cholesterol	2 mg
Sodium	149 mg
Carbohydrate	13 g
Dietary Fiber	1 g
Sugars	7 g
Protein	5 g

1 cup pumpkin puree
1 package artificially sweetened, low-fat, instant vanilla pudding
1 tsp pumpkin pie spice
1 cup evaporated skim milk
1 cup skim milk

Mix all ingredients together in a mixer bowl. Place in parfait glasses and chill.

The holidays should be a happy, festive time. But worrying about what you eat can make them less happy. Don't deprive yourself of the foods you love. Instead, just have a taste of your favorites. The first bite is usually the best, anyway.

Pumpkin Cider Bread

This spicy bread is packed with flavor, fiber, and vitamin A.

Preparation Time:
15 minutes

9 Servings/Serving Size:
One 1-inch slice

Exchanges:	
2	Starch

Calories	167
Calories from Fat	16
Total Fat	2 g
Saturated Fat	0 g
Cholesterol	47 mg
Sodium	98 mg
Carbohydrate	34 g
Dietary Fiber	4 g
Sugars	9 g
Protein	6 g

2 1/2 cups whole-wheat flour
2 tsp baking powder
1 tsp cinnamon
1/2 tsp nutmeg
2 eggs, beaten
1/2 cup unsweetened applesauce
1/4 cup sugar
1/2 cup apple cider
1/3 cup canned pumpkin (not pumpkin pie filling)

Preheat the oven to 350 degrees. In a medium bowl, combine the whole-wheat flour, baking powder, cinnamon, and nutmeg. In a large bowl, combine the remaining ingredients. Add the dry ingredients slowly to the large bowl and mix until blended. Do not overbeat. Pour the batter into a 9-inch loaf pan and bake for 40 minutes until the tester comes out clean.

Sweet Squash Pie

This is a great way to sneak vegetables into your meal plan!

Preparation Time:
15 minutes

9 Servings/Serving Size:
1/9th of pie

Exchanges:
2   Carbohydrate
1/2 Monounsaturated Fat

Calories......................185
  Calories from Fat.......41
Total Fat ....5 g
  Saturated Fat.............1 g

Cholesterol ....25 mg
Sodium..................200 mg
Carbohydrate............32 g
  Dietary Fiber ....2 g
  Sugars.....................18 g

Protein........................5 g

1 egg
1 egg white
1/2 tsp nutmeg
1/2 tsp allspice
3 Tbsp honey
1 1/2 tsp vanilla
2 cups cooked, pureed squash (use acorn, butternut, or hubbard)
1 cup evaporated skim milk
1 9-inch graham cracker crust, baked (see recipe, p. 437)

Preheat the oven to 425 degrees. Beat egg and egg white well in a large bowl and then add the spices, honey, and vanilla. Add the squash and milk. Pour the squash mixture into the prepared shell and bake for 10 minutes. Then reduce heat to 350 degrees and continue to bake for 45 minutes until set. Remove and cool on a rack.

Sweet Smell of Spices

Cinnamon wafting through the house, clove-studded pomander balls turning in the air, the spicy essence of cardamom, hot cider warming on the stove—these aromas make the holidays special. Using sweet spices in holiday cooking will help reduce the amount of other sweeteners that need to be used. Here are a few tips to help you get the most flavorful baking results.

✳ Try to keep your ground spices for only one year. The essential oils in ground spices that give them their flavor will dry out after that.

✳ For the best flavor, consider grinding your own spices. For example, purchase whole nutmeg and grate it yourself. Cinnamon chunks you can grate yourself are also available from some mail-order companies.

Use the following seed and bark derivatives in your holiday cooking:

✳ Anise tastes sweet and spicy, and has long been used in cakes, breads, sweets, and even cough medicine. Anise is cultivated in North Africa and Europe.

✳ Cardamom is a member of the ginger family and is native to southern India and Sri Lanka. It's often used in Swedish baking, or used whole in marinades.

❋ Cinnamon comes from the bark of trees, generally young shoots cut close to the ground once every two years in the rainy season. After the bark is planed off, the strips are dried and curl into quills. Cinnamon tastes great in baked goods, lamb, and even chili.

❋ Coriander has a sweet, aromatic taste, a bit like orange peel. It grows in all of the Northern hemisphere, especially India. It is good with fish, lamb, sweet dishes, breads, and cakes.

Try some of these sweet roots and fruits:

❋ Allspice is a berry that, when ground, tastes like a mixture of cloves, cinnamon, and mace. It is used primarily in cakes, but try whole berries in marinades.

❋ Cloves are an important ingredient of curry powders and of sweet spice mixtures used in baking. Use whole cloves for marinades, mulled drinks, soups, and sweet potatoes, and ground cloves for cakes, cookies, and quick breads.

❋ Ginger is cultivated in tropical Asia. Fresh grated ginger gives the best flavor. Ground ginger is fine to use, but is not nearly as pungent.

❋ Mace is just the outer covering of nutmeg, and has a gentler flavor. Try mace in fruit desserts made with plums and peaches, or sprinkled into carrots, Brussels sprouts, fish, and potatoes.

❋ Nutmeg tastes very good with spinach, in cheese dishes, and in classic baked goods like pumpkin pie.

Sweet Potato and Zucchini Muffins

Golden sweet potato and zucchini add fiber to this moist muffin.

Preparation Time:	
20 minutes	

12 Servings/Serving Size:
1 muffin

Exchanges:	
1 1/2	Starch

Calories	111
Calories from Fat	11
Total Fat	1 g
Saturated Fat	0 g
Cholesterol	35 mg
Sodium	73 mg
Carbohydrate	22 g
Dietary Fiber	3 g
Sugars	7 g
Protein	4 g

2 cups whole-wheat pastry flour
2 tsp baking soda
2 tsp allspice
2 eggs
1/2 cup applesauce
1/4 cup sugar
2 tsp vanilla
1/2 cup peeled and shredded sweet potato
1/2 cup shredded zucchini

1. Preheat the oven to 350 degrees. Combine the flour, baking powder, and allspice in a medium bowl. Set aside. In a large bowl, combine the eggs, applesauce, sugar, and vanilla and mix well. Slowly add the dry ingredients to the large bowl and mix until blended. Do not overbeat.

2. Fold in the shredded sweet potato and zucchini. Pour the batter into 12 nonstick muffin cups and bake for 25–30 minutes. Remove muffins from oven and let cool slightly. Remove muffins from pan and let cool completely.

Golden Cornbread, Muffins, or Sticks

Adding corn kernels to this crispy cornbread makes it unique. Try the loaf recipe for stuffing, too. (The nutrient analysis for muffins or sticks is in parentheses, below.)

Preparation Time:
10 minutes

**Bread: 9 Servings/
 Serving Size:**
One 1-inch slice

**Muffins or Sticks: 12
 Servings/Serving Size:**
1 muffin or stick

Exchanges:
2 1/2 (2)   Starch

Calories 190 (143)
 Calories from Fat...13 (10)
Total Fat..............1 g (1 g)
 Saturated Fat....0 g (0 g)

Cholesterol..47 mg (35 mg)
Sodium ...197 mg (147 mg)
Carbohydrate...35 g (26 g)
 Dietary Fiber.....2 g (1 g)
 Sugars...............5 g (4 g)

Protein ....6 g (5 g)

1 cup unbleached white flour
1 cup yellow cornmeal
1 tsp baking powder
1/2 tsp baking soda
2 cups nonfat sour cream
2 eggs, beaten
2 tsp honey
1/2 cup corn kernels

1. Preheat the oven to 400 degrees. Combine the flour, cornmeal, baking powder, and soda. Mix together the sour cream, eggs, and honey. Add this mixture to the flour mixture. Add in the corn and mix. Do not overbeat. Pour the batter into a 9-inch loaf pan, a 12-muffin tin, or corn stick molds. Bake the loaf for 35 minutes, muffins and sticks for 25 minutes, until a toothpick comes out clean.

Early-Morning Muffins

Oats, raisins, and high-fiber bran make these muffins nutritious and delicious!

Preparation Time:
15 minutes

12 Servings/Serving Size:
1 muffin

Exchanges:
1 1/2	Starch

Calories......................117
  Calories from Fat........20
Total Fat ....2 g
  Saturated Fat.............0 g

Cholesterol ....18 mg
Sodium..................109 mg
Carbohydrate............21 g
  Dietary Fiber ....2 g
  Sugars.......................9 g

Protein..........................4 g

3/4 cup low-sugar bran cereal (flakes or nuggets)
3/4 cup skim milk
1 egg
1 egg white
1 Tbsp canola oil
1/4 cup unsweetened applesauce
1 Tbsp honey
1 Tbsp brown sugar
1 cup quick-cooking oats
1/3 cup whole-wheat flour
1/3 cup white flour
1/2 cup currants or raisins
1 tsp vanilla
1 tsp cinnamon
2 tsp baking powder

Preheat the oven to 375 degrees. Combine all ingredients and mix until blended. Do not overbeat. Pour the batter into 12 nonstick muffin cups and bake for 20–25 minutes. Remove muffins from oven and let cool slightly. Remove muffins from pan and let cool completely.

Light Lemon-Glazed Muffins

Add a zip to your morning with these tangy muffins.

Preparation Time:
20 minutes

12 Servings/Serving Size:
1 muffin

Exchanges:
1 1/2	Starch
1/2	Saturated Fat

Calories	141
Calories from Fat	21
Total Fat	2 g
Saturated Fat	1 g
Cholesterol	24 mg
Sodium	186 mg
Carbohydrate	26 g
Dietary Fiber	2 g
Sugars	6 g
Protein	4 g

1 1/2 cups unbleached white flour
1 cup whole-wheat flour
2 tsp baking powder
1 tsp baking soda
1 egg
1 egg white
3 Tbsp fresh lemon juice
1 cup low-fat sour cream
1/4 cup unsweetened applesauce
2 tsp vanilla
2 Tbsp sugar
1/2 cup fresh orange juice
1/2 tsp orange rind
2 Tbsp powdered sugar
1 Tbsp water
1 tsp butter extract
1 tsp cornstarch or arrowroot powder
2 tsp water

1. Preheat the oven to 350 degrees. Combine the flours, baking powder, and baking soda in a medium bowl. Set aside. In a large bowl, combine the egg, egg white, lemon juice, sour cream, applesauce, vanilla, and sugar. Beat well. Slowly add the dry ingredients to the large bowl and mix until blended. Do not overbeat. Pour the batter into 12 nonstick muffin cups and bake for 25–30 minutes.

2. Meanwhile, combine all remaining ingredients except the cornstarch or arrowroot powder and water in a saucepan. Bring to a boil. Mix together the cornstarch or arrowroot powder and water, add it to the orange juice mixture and cook over medium heat until thickened. Remove muffins from the oven and pour glaze over them. Cool completely before eating.

Poppy Seed Orange Muffins

Poppy seeds give this muffin its texture.

Preparation Time: 15 minutes	
12 Servings/Serving Size: 1 muffin	
Exchanges:	
1 1/2	Starch
1/2	Fat
Calories	142
Calories from Fat	34
Total Fat	4 g
Saturated Fat	0 g
Cholesterol	18 mg
Sodium	94 mg
Carbohydrate	24 g
Dietary Fiber	2 g
Sugars	4 g
Protein	4 g

1 1/2 cups unbleached white flour
1 cup whole-wheat flour
1 tsp baking powder
1/2 tsp baking soda
1 egg
1 egg white
3 Tbsp orange juice
2 Tbsp poppy seeds
1 tsp almond extract
1/2 cup unsweetened applesauce
2 Tbsp canola oil
2 Tbsp sugar

1. Preheat the oven to 375 degrees. Combine the flours, baking powder, and baking soda in a medium bowl. Set aside. In a large bowl, combine the remaining ingredients. Mix well. Slowly add the dry ingredients to the large bowl and mix until blended. Do not overbeat.

2. Pour the batter into 12 nonstick muffin cups and bake for 20–25 minutes. Remove muffins from oven and let cool slightly. Remove muffins from pan and let cool completely.

Sweet Spiced Muffins

Cinnamon, cloves, cardamom, and nutmeg spice up this muffin.

Preparation Time:
15 minutes

12 Servings/Serving Size:
1 muffin

Exchanges:
1 1/2	Starch
1/2	Monounsaturated Fat

Calories	138
Calories from Fat	29
Total Fat	3 g
Saturated Fat	0 g
Cholesterol	18 mg
Sodium	105 mg
Carbohydrate	24 g
Dietary Fiber	2 g
Sugars	4 g
Protein	4 g

1 1/2 cups white flour
1 cup whole-wheat flour
1 tsp baking powder
1/2 tsp baking soda
1 tsp cinnamon
1 tsp cardamom
1/2 tsp nutmeg
1/4 tsp cloves
1/2 cup unsweetened applesauce
1 egg
1 egg white
1/2 cup low-fat buttermilk
2 Tbsp brown sugar
2 Tbsp canola oil

1. Preheat the oven to 350 degrees. Combine the flours, baking powder, baking soda, and spices in a medium bowl. Set aside. In a large bowl, combine the remaining ingredients. Slowly add the dry ingredients to the large bowl and mix until blended. Do not overbeat.

2. Pour the batter into 12 nonstick muffin cups and bake for 25–30 minutes. Remove muffins from oven and let cool slightly. Remove muffins from pan and let cool completely.

Banana Ginger Muffins

Grating real ginger into these muffins is the secret to their flavor.

Preparation Time:	
20 minutes	

12 Servings/Serving Size:
1 muffin

Exchanges:

2	Starch

Calories	156
Calories from Fat	29
Total Fat	3 g
Saturated Fat	0 g

Cholesterol	18 mg
Sodium	83 mg
Carbohydrate	28 g
Dietary Fiber	2 g
Sugars	7 g

Protein	5 g

1 1/2 cups white flour
1 cup whole-wheat flour
2 tsp baking powder
1 tsp cinnamon
1 egg
1 egg white
1 cup skim milk
1/4 cup unsweetened applesauce
2 Tbsp canola oil
2 Tbsp brown sugar
2 bananas, mashed
2 tsp grated fresh ginger

1. Preheat the oven to 350 degrees. Combine the flours, baking powder, and cinnamon in a medium bowl. In a large bowl, combine the remaining ingredients and mix well. Slowly add the dry ingredients to the large bowl and mix until blended. Do not overbeat.

2. Pour the batter into 12 nonstick muffin cups and bake for 20–25 minutes. Remove muffins from oven and let cool slightly. Remove muffins from pan and let cool completely.

Pumpkin Spice Muffins

These spicy muffins are moist and delicious.

Preparation Time:	
20 minutes	

18 Servings/Serving Size:	
1 muffin	

Exchanges:	
1	Starch

Calories	86
Calories from Fat	22
Total Fat	2 g
Saturated Fat	0 g
Cholesterol	24 mg
Sodium	119 mg
Carbohydrate	15 g
Dietary Fiber	2 g
Sugars	4 g
Protein	3 g

2 cups whole-wheat flour
2 tsp baking powder
2 tsp cinnamon
1/2 tsp nutmeg
1 tsp baking soda
2 eggs, beaten
1 cup pumpkin puree
1/4 cup sugar
1/2 cup unsweetened applesauce
2 Tbsp canola oil
1 tsp almond extract

1. Preheat the oven to 350 degrees. Mix together the flour, baking powder, cinnamon, nutmeg, and baking soda in a medium bowl. Combine the remaining ingredients in a large bowl. Slowly add the dry ingredients to the large bowl and mix until blended. Do not overbeat.

2. Pour the batter into 18 nonstick muffin cups and bake for 25–30 minutes. Remove muffins from oven and let cool slightly. Remove muffins from pan and let cool completely.

Frozen Yogurt Muffins

These muffins, topped with fresh fruit and frozen yogurt, are great to serve for dessert.

Preparation Time:
15 minutes

12 Servings/Serving Size:
1 muffin

Exchanges:
2 1/2   Carbohydrate

Calories 204
  Calories from Fat 23
Total Fat .... 3 g
  Saturated Fat .... 1 g

Cholesterol .... 36 mg
Sodium .... 113 mg
Carbohydrate .... 40 g
  Dietary Fiber .... 3 g
  Sugars .... 14 g

Protein .... 7 g

1 1/2 cups whole-wheat flour
1 cup white flour
1/4 cup sugar
2 tsp baking powder
2 eggs, beaten
1 cup evaporated skim milk
1 Tbsp canola oil
1/4 cup unsweetened applesauce
2 Tbsp cinnamon
1/4 cup warm water
3 cups sliced bananas
1 1/2 cups sugar-free, low-fat, frozen yogurt (any flavor)

1. Preheat the oven to 350 degrees. Combine the flours, sugar, and baking powder in a medium bowl. In a large bowl, combine the eggs, skim milk, oil, and applesauce. Slowly add the dry ingredients to the large bowl and mix until blended. Do not overbeat.

2. Mix together the cinnamon and water. Swirl this mixture through the batter. Pour the batter into 12 nonstick muffin cups and bake for 25–30 minutes. Remove muffins from oven and let cool slightly. Remove muffins from pans, split them, and place on dessert plates. Fill muffin centers with bananas and yogurt to serve.

Winter Menus

New Year's Day Brunch

Grand Marnier Overnight French Toast

Herbed Chicken Sausage

Sweet Potato Biscuits

Winter Fruit Bowl

85–88

Super Bowl Sunday

Marinated Chicken Livers

Caesar Salad Sandwiches

Tri-Colored Rotini Salad

Carob Brownies

89–92

Après Ski Party

Savory Veal Stew

Dijon Vegetable Salad

Herbed Garlic Rolls

Bourbon-Raisin Baked Apples

93–96

Caribbean Vacation

Caribbean Pork Kabobs

Black Beans and Rice

Cucumber Salad

Tropical Mango Mousse

98–101

Valentine Dinner

Chicken Jubilee

Orzo with Spinach and Feta Cheese

Sauted Cherry Tomatoes and Multicolored Peppers

Gingerbread Pudding with Ginger Vanilla Sauce

102–105

Kids' Time

Pita Pizza Pizzazz

Chicken Nuggets

Fun Veggies and Dips

Pineapple Sundaes

106–109

Grand Marnier Overnight French Toast

You can prepare this French toast before the party begins on New Year's Eve and leave it in the refrigerator overnight.

Preparation Time:
15 minutes

6 Servings/Serving Size:
1 2-inch slice

Exchanges:
1 1/2	Starch
1	Lean Meat

Calories	166
Calories from Fat	26
Total Fat	3 g
Saturated Fat	1 g
Cholesterol	73 mg
Sodium	279 mg
Carbohydrate	24 g
Dietary Fiber	1 g
Sugars	8 g
Protein	10 g

6 2-inch slices of French bread (2 inches thick with a 2-inch diameter, approximately 1 oz each)
2 eggs
4 egg whites
2 Tbsp Grand Marnier (or any other orange liqueur)
1 cup evaporated skim milk
2 tsp almond extract

Place the slices of bread in a nonstick casserole dish. Combine the remaining ingredients in a bowl and beat well. Pour the mixture over the bread and cover. Place in the refrigerator overnight. The next day, preheat the oven to 350 degrees. Bake the French toast for about 35–40 minutes, until it is golden brown and puffy.

Herbed Chicken Sausage

This version of spicy sausage is much lower in fat than store-bought varieties.

Preparation Time:
10 minutes

6 Servings/Serving Size:
3 oz

Exchanges:
4   Very Lean Meat

Calories 154
  Calories from Fat 40
Total Fat .... 4 g
  Saturated Fat .... 1 g

Cholesterol .... 69 mg
Sodium .... 61 mg
Carbohydrate .... 1 g
  Dietary Fiber .... 0 g
  Sugars .... 1 g

Protein .... 25 g

1 1/2 lb ground chicken (have your butcher grind white meat for you)
4 garlic cloves, minced
1 tsp minced fresh oregano
2 tsp minced fresh thyme
2 Tbsp finely minced red onion
2 Tbsp dry white wine
2 tsp paprika
2 tsp olive oil

Combine all ingredients together and place in the refrigerator. Let the flavors blend together for 4–24 hours. Then shape into patties. Heat the oil in a skillet over medium-high heat. Cook sausage patties for 5 minutes on each side.

Sweet Potato Biscuits

These light biscuits are also great served with roast chicken or beef.

Preparation Time:
15 minutes

24 Servings/Serving Size:
1 biscuit

Exchanges:
1/2   Starch

Calories.........................57
  Calories from Fat..........9
Total Fat.......................1 g
  Saturated Fat.............0 g

Cholesterol ....0 mg
Sodium....................73 mg
Carbohydrate............10 g
  Dietary Fiber ....0 g
  Sugars.......................2 g

Protein.........................1 g

1 small sweet potato, peeled, cooked, and
  mashed
2 Tbsp low-calorie margarine, melted
1 Tbsp brown sugar
2 cups unbleached white flour
2 tsp baking powder
1/2 tsp baking soda
3/4 cup low-fat buttermilk
2 Tbsp finely minced toasted pecans

1. Preheat the oven to 400 degrees. Combine
    the sweet potato, margarine, and brown
    sugar in a bowl and beat well. In a separate
    bowl, combine the flour, baking powder, and
    baking soda. Add the buttermilk. Combine the
    sweet potato and flour mixtures. Fold in the
    pecans.

2. Turn the dough out on a lightly floured
    surface. Knead only for 8 strokes. Roll the
    dough out to 1/2-inch thickness. Cut with the
    floured rim of a glass or use a floured biscuit
    cutter. Place on an ungreased cookie sheet
    and bake for 16–18 minutes until tops are
    browned and biscuits are flaky.

Winter Fruit Bowl

You can still savor the taste of sweet fruit in the wintertime.

Preparation Time:	
10 minutes	

6 Servings/Serving Size:
1/2 cup

Exchanges:

1	Fruit

Calories	59
Calories from Fat	3
Total Fat	0 g
Saturated Fat	0 g

Cholesterol	0 mg
Sodium	2 mg
Carbohydrate	15 g
Dietary Fiber	2 g
Sugars	11 g

Protein	1 g

1 tart apple, unpeeled and diced
1 medium banana, peeled and sliced
2 Tbsp lemon juice
1/2 cup green or red grapes
1 small orange, sectioned and seeded
1 Tbsp minced crystallized ginger
2 tsp minced fresh mint, if available (or use dried mint)

Combine the apple and bananas and sprinkle with lemon juice. Add the remaining ingredients, toss well, and chill for several hours before serving.

❊ ❊

Even though it is a time of celebration,
stress levels can build at holidays. Stress can make your
blood sugar level go up. Make your lists, do the essential
things, and then take time to sit and breathe deeply.
Stretch and relax. A calm house is a welcoming house.
Hand joy to your guests in your smile.

❊ ❊

Marinated Chicken Livers

These easy-to-eat appetizers are lower in fat than the traditional version.

Preparation Time:
15 minutes

6 Servings/Serving Size:
2 chicken liver halves

Exchanges:
1   Medium-Fat Meat

Calories 76
  Calories from Fat 34
Total Fat ....4 g
  Saturated Fat.............1 g

Cholesterol ....189 mg
Sodium ....245 mg
Carbohydrate...............1 g
  Dietary Fiber ....0 g
  Sugars.......................1 g

Protein.........................9 g

1/2 cup dry sherry
3 Tbsp unsweetened pineapple juice
1 Tbsp minced fresh ginger
2 Tbsp lite soy sauce
6 chicken livers, cut in half
6 slices turkey bacon, cut in half

1. Combine the sherry, juice, ginger, and soy sauce. Add the chicken livers and marinate in the refrigerator for 2 hours. Preheat the oven to 350 degrees. Wrap each chicken liver with a piece of bacon and insert a toothpick through the center to secure it.

2. Place the chicken livers on a nonstick cookie sheet and bake for 10–12 minutes until the bacon is cooked through. Cool slightly before serving.

Caesar Salad Sandwiches

This is a healthy alternative to sandwiches made with processed meats.

Preparation Time:
15 minutes

6 Servings/Serving Size:
1 3-oz roll with 3 oz chicken and 1/2 cup salad greens

Exchanges:

3	Starch
4	Very Lean Meat
1/2	Fat

Calories......................401
 Calories from Fat........84
Total Fat ....9 g
 Saturated Fat.............3 g

Cholesterol ....72 mg
Sodium..................793 mg
Carbohydrate............44 g
 Dietary Fiber ....7 g
 Sugars........................5 g

Protein ....36 g

6 medium hard rolls (preferably whole grain)
3 cups torn romaine lettuce
1/2 cup fat-free Caesar salad dressing
1/3 cup grated fresh Parmesan cheese
1 1/2 lb chicken breasts, cut into strips about 3
    inches long
2 tsp olive oil

1. Set the oven on broil. Cut each roll in half and scoop out the dough to form a pocket in one side of the bread. Combine the lettuce, dressing, and cheese in a bowl.

2. Place the chicken strips on a broiler pan and brush with the olive oil. Broil the strips of chicken for a total of about 7 minutes, turning once. Add the chicken to the salad and pile the mixture into the bread pocket. Top with the other half of bread and serve.

Tri-Colored Rotini Salad

Using colorful pasta makes this dish a little more festive.

Preparation Time:
15 minutes

6 Servings/Serving Size:
1/2 cup

Exchanges:
1   Starch

Calories........................92
 Calories from Fat........21
Total Fat.....................2 g
 Saturated Fat............0 g

Cholesterol...............0 mg
Sodium..................162 mg
Carbohydrate............16 g
 Dietary Fiber.............2 g
 Sugars........................3 g

Protein.........................3 g

Salad
2 cups cooked tri-colored rotini pasta
1/2 cup halved cherry tomatoes
1/4 cup diced red pepper
1 Tbsp sliced black olives
1 15-oz can artichoke hearts, drained and halved

Dressing
1/4 cup balsamic vinegar
2 tsp olive oil
1 Tbsp Dijon mustard
2 tsp minced fresh basil
Fresh ground pepper to taste

Combine all salad ingredients in a large bowl. Whisk together the dressing ingredients. Pour the dressing over the salad and toss to coat well. Serve at room temperature.

Carob Brownies

Try this delicious version of a classic favorite!

Preparation Time:
10 minutes

12 Servings/Serving Size:
1 2-inch brownie

Exchanges:
1/2	Carbohydrate
1/2	Fat

Calories 61
  Calories from Fat 11
Total Fat .... 1 g
  Saturated Fat .... 0 g

Cholesterol .... 35 mg
Sodium .... 72 mg
Carbohydrate .... 12 g
  Dietary Fiber .... 2 g
  Sugars .... 5 g

Protein .... 2 g

1/2 cup unsweetened applesauce
1/4 cup sugar
2 eggs
1 tsp vanilla
1/3 cup carob powder or cocoa
2/3 cup whole-wheat pastry flour
2 tsp baking powder

Preheat the oven to 325 degrees. Beat together the applesauce, sugar, eggs, and vanilla. Combine the carob, flour, and baking powder. Add to the applesauce egg mixture and mix well. Pour into an 8 x 8-inch baking dish and bake for 20–25 minutes. Cool and cut into squares.

Some seasons are more filled with light than others. If this is a dark season for you, fill your meals with light, warmth, and sustenance.

Savory Veal Stew

This stew will warm you up after a cold day on the slopes!

Preparation Time:
20 minutes

6 Servings/Serving Size:
3–4 oz veal with 1/2 cup vegetables

Exchanges:
1 1/2	Starch
3	Very Lean Meat
1/2	Monounsaturated Fat

Calories	243
Calories from Fat	63
Total Fat	7 g
Saturated Fat	2 g

Cholesterol	96 mg
Sodium	322 mg
Carbohydrate	19 g
Dietary Fiber	3 g
Sugars	5 g

Protein	27 g

1 1/2 lb veal for stew, cut into 1-inch cubes
1/4 cup unbleached flour
1/2 tsp salt
1/2 tsp pepper
1 1/2 Tbsp olive oil
1 medium onion, chopped
2 garlic cloves, minced
1 14-oz can low-fat, low-sodium chicken broth
1/2 lb baby carrots
1/2 lb small red new potatoes, cut in half
1/2 cup frozen peas

1. In a medium bowl, combine the flour, salt, and pepper. Add the veal and toss to coat. Heat the oil in a large stockpot over medium-high heat. Add the veal and saute on all sides until browned. Remove the veal from the pot.

2. In the same pot, saute the onions and garlic for 2 minutes. Add the broth. Return the veal to the pot and bring to a boil. Lower the heat, cover, and simmer for 30 minutes. Stir in the carrots and potatoes. Cover and continue cooking for 15–20 minutes, until potatoes are tender. Stir in the peas and cook until they are heated through.

This recipe is courtesy of the Beef Board and Veal Committee/Beef Industry Council.

Dijon Vegetable Salad

This fresh mustard vinaigrette perks up winter vegetables.

Preparation Time:
20 minutes

6 Servings/Serving Size:
1/2 cup

Exchanges:
1	Vegetable
2	Monounsaturated Fat

Calories	116
Calories from Fat	86
Total Fat	10 g
Saturated Fat	1 g

Cholesterol	0 mg
Sodium	93 mg
Carbohydrate	7 g
Dietary Fiber	3 g
Sugars	3 g

Protein	2 g

1/2 head medium cauliflower, separated into
   florets
1/2 lb broccoli, separated into florets
1 cup sliced carrots
1/2 red pepper, sliced into strips
1/4 cup red wine vinegar
2 Tbsp lemon juice
1/4 cup olive oil
2 Tbsp Dijon mustard
1 Tbsp capers
Fresh ground pepper to taste

In a large stockpot, bring about 10 cups of water to a boil. Add the vegetables and let cook for 2 minutes. Drain. Immediately plunge the vegetables into a bowl of ice water. Drain again. Place the vegetables in a large bowl. In a small bowl, whisk together the dressing ingredients. Pour over the salad and mix well. Chill for 1 hour before serving.

Herbed Garlic Rolls

These crusty, garlic-flavored rolls are delicious dipped into the veal stew.

Preparation Time:
6 minutes

6 Servings/Serving Size:
1 small roll

Exchanges:
1   Vegetable
1   Monounsaturated Fat

Calories.......................135
  Calories from Fat........53
Total Fat ....6 g
  Saturated Fat.............1 g

Cholesterol ....0 mg
Sodium..................178 mg
Carbohydrate.............18 g
  Dietary Fiber ....1 g
  Sugars.......................3 g

Protein ....3 g

6 small, crusty, hard rolls
2 Tbsp olive oil
1/2 tsp dried basil
1/2 tsp dried oregano
1/4 tsp dried chives
1/2 tsp dried thyme
4 garlic cloves, finely minced
1 Tbsp paprika

Split each roll in half. Combine all remaining ingredients. Drizzle over each half of the roll. Place the two halves together and wrap each roll in foil. Bake at 400 degrees for 5 minutes.

Bourbon-Raisin Baked Apples

A spike of bourbon livens up an old favorite.

Preparation Time:
15 minutes

6 Servings/Serving Size:
1 medium apple

Exchanges:
3   Fruit

Calories 189
  Calories from Fat 7
Total Fat .... 1 g
  Saturated Fat .... 0 g

Cholesterol .... 0 mg
Sodium .... 4 mg
Carbohydrate .... 47 g
  Dietary Fiber .... 5 g
  Sugars .... 40 g

Protein .... 1 g

6 medium baking apples, cored
1 cup raisins
1/4 cup bourbon
1 tsp cinnamon
1 cup unsweetened grape juice

Preheat the oven to 350 degrees. Core each apple and cut about 1/4 inch of apple off the top. Soak the raisins in bourbon for 20 minutes. Stuff some of the raisins into each apple and sprinkle with cinnamon. Place the apples in a baking dish and pour grape juice over the apples. Bake for 40–50 minutes until apples are soft. Serve warm.

Healthy New Traditions

New, healthy holiday traditions are a gift that will last for many holidays. Start some new habits with the following ideas:

❊ Skim the fat from the juices that accumulate from the turkey, chicken, or roast. Serve the meat au jus, with no gravy.

❊ Use skim milk or evaporated skim milk when preparing mashed potatoes. Use herbs instead of salt to flavor them.

❊ Use small amounts of pineapple or apple juice for sweet potatoes instead of butter and brown sugar. Serve sweet potatoes for dessert instead of calorie-laden pies.

❊ Saute all vegetables used for stuffing in wine or broth rather than butter.

❊ Prepare as much of the menus as you can ahead of time, and budget some time for exercise and energetic family activities. Focus more on fun and less on food!

❊ Start your New Year's resolutions on Thanksgiving this year. It is never too early to begin living well and feeling better.

Caribbean Pork Kabobs

These kabobs go very well with grilled fruit.

Preparation Time:
10 minutes

6 Servings/Serving Size:
3–4 oz

Exchanges:
4   Very Lean Meat

Calories......................147
 Calories from Fat........37
Total Fat ....4 g
 Saturated Fat.............1 g

Cholesterol ....66 mg
Sodium....................48 mg
Carbohydrate...............2 g
 Dietary Fiber ....0 g
 Sugars........................2 g

Protein ....24 g

1 1/2 lb pork tenderloin, cut into 1-inch cubes
1/2 cup orange juice
1/4 cup lime juice
2 tsp brown sugar
1/2 tsp minced fresh thyme
1/2 tsp ground nutmeg
1/4 tsp ground cloves
1/4 tsp cayenne pepper

1. Combine all ingredients and place in a plastic bag. Let the pork cubes marinate in the refrigerator for at least 2 hours or up to 24 hours. If using wooden kabob skewers, soak 6 of them in warm water for 15 minutes. This prevents the skewers from catching on fire while the kabobs cook.

2. Prepare an outside grill with an oiled rack set 4 inches above the heat source. On a gas grill, set the heat to high. Remove the cubes from the bag and thread them on the skewers. Grill the kabobs for 12–15 minutes total until the pork is cooked through.

This adapted recipe is courtesy of the National Pork Producers.

*B*lack Beans and Rice

Try these spicy black beans served with pork, too.

Preparation Time:
20 minutes

---

6 Servings/Serving Size:
1/2 cup

Exchanges:
1 1/2   Starch

Calories.......................115
 Calories from Fat..........9
Total Fat ....1 g
 Saturated Fat.............0 g

Cholesterol ....0 mg
Sodium..................103 mg
Carbohydrate.............22 g
 Dietary Fiber ....5 g
 Sugars.......................2 g

Protein ....6 g

1/2 tsp olive oil
1/2 medium onion, chopped
1 garlic cloves, minced
1/3 cup short-grain white rice
3/4 cup low-fat, low-sodium chicken broth
1 tsp cumin
1/4 tsp cayenne pepper
1 3/4 cups canned black beans, drained and
  rinsed

Heat the oil in a stockpot over medium-high heat. Add the onion and garlic and saute for 4 minutes. Add the rice and saute for 2 more minutes. Add the chicken broth, bring to a boil, cover, lower the heat, and cook for 20 minutes. Add the spices and the black beans.

Cucumber Salad

This is a great salad served with chicken, too.

Preparation Time:	
15 minutes	

6 Servings/Serving Size:
1 cup

Exchanges:

1	Vegetable
1/2	Saturated Fat

Calories	52
Calories from Fat	23
Total Fat	3 g
Saturated Fat	2 g
Cholesterol	10 g
Sodium	39 mg
Carbohydrate	6 g
Dietary Fiber	2 g
Sugars	4 g
Protein	2 g

4 cups peeled, seeded, and chopped cucumber
1 cup shredded carrot
1 cup minced celery
3/4 cup low-fat sour cream
1 Tbsp minced fresh parsley
2 Tbsp apple cider vinegar
1 tsp minced fresh dill
1 tsp paprika

Combine the cucumber, carrot, and celery. Whisk together the remaining ingredients and add the dressing to the cucumber mixture. Mix well. Refrigerate for 1 hour before serving.

Tropical Mango Mousse

This light dessert can also be made with berries.

Preparation Time:
5 minutes

---

6 Servings/Serving Size:
1/2 cup

Exchanges:
1 1/2   Fruit

Calories 87
  Calories from Fat 3
Total Fat ....0 g
  Saturated Fat.............0 g

Cholesterol ....1 mg
Sodium ....23 mg
Carbohydrate...........21 g
  Dietary Fiber ....2 g
  Sugars.....................18 g

Protein ....2 g

2 small mangos, peeled and cubed
1 medium banana, peeled
2/3 cup plain nonfat yogurt
2 tsp honey
6 large ice cubes
1 tsp vanilla

In a blender, combine all ingredients until smooth. Refrigerate for 3 hours. Pour into individual dishes and serve.

Chicken Jubilee

Dark cherries give this dish its eye appeal.

Preparation Time:
15 minutes

6 Servings/Serving Size:
3–4 oz

Exchanges:

1	Fruit
4	Very Lean Meat

Calories	208
Calories from Fat	48
Total Fat	5 g
Saturated Fat	1 g

Cholesterol	69 mg
Sodium	258 mg
Carbohydrate	11 g
Dietary Fiber	0 g
Sugars	6 g

Protein	26 g

1 1/2 lb chicken cutlets
1/4 cup unbleached flour
1/2 tsp salt
1/2 tsp pepper
2 tsp canola oil
1 9-oz can dark cherries in water (reserve juice)
1 Tbsp cherry preserves
3 Tbsp brandy

In a plastic bag, combine the chicken cutlets with the flour, salt, and pepper. Shake to coat well. Heat the oil in a skillet over medium-high heat. Add the chicken cutlets and cook on each side for about 4–5 minutes. Add the cherries, cherry juice, preserves, and brandy. Bring to a boil and boil 1 minute. Spoon the cherry juice over the chicken and serve.

Orzo with Spinach and Feta Cheese

This dish is a great change from potatoes or rice.

Preparation Time:	
15 minutes	
6 Servings/Serving Size:	
1/2 cup	
Exchanges:	
2 1/2	Starch
Calories 204	
Calories from Fat 30	
Total Fat .... 3 g	
Saturated Fat .... 1 g	
Cholesterol .... 4 mg	
Sodium .... 82 mg	
Carbohydrate .... 37 g	
Dietary Fiber .... 2 g	
Sugars .... 4 g	
Protein .... 8 g	

1 1/2 cups dry orzo
2 tsp olive oil
1 medium onion, minced
1 10-oz package frozen chopped spinach, thawed
  and well drained
1/4 cup crumbled feta cheese
Fresh ground pepper to taste

Cook the orzo according to package directions. Drain. Heat the oil in a skillet over medium-high heat. Add the onion and saute for 5 minutes. Add the spinach and saute for 4 more minutes. Toss the onion spinach mixture with the hot orzo. Add the feta cheese and ground pepper and toss well. Serve immediately.

Sauted Cherry Tomatoes and Multicolored Peppers

This dish is a colorful accompaniment to any meal.

Preparation Time:
15 minutes

---

6 Servings/Serving Size:
1/2 cup

Exchanges:
1   Vegetable

Calories.......................33
  Calories from Fat........10
Total Fat ....1 g
  Saturated Fat.............0 g

Cholesterol ....0 mg
Sodium....................10 mg
Carbohydrate..............6 g
  Dietary Fiber ....1 g
  Sugars....................3 g

Protein ....1 g

1 medium red pepper, sliced in strips
1/2 each medium yellow and green peppers,
    sliced in strips
1/3 cup low-fat, low-sodium chicken broth
1 tsp olive oil
1 cup halved cherry tomatoes
2 Tbsp sliced scallions
Fresh ground pepper to taste

In a large pot of boiling water, add all the peppers. Blanch for 2 minutes. Drain and plunge the peppers in a bowl of ice water. Drain again. Heat the broth and oil in a large skillet over medium-high heat. Add the cherry tomatoes and scallions and saute for 4 minutes. Add the peppers, cover, and steam for 3 minutes. Serve.

Gingerbread Pudding with Ginger Vanilla Sauce

This creamy pudding is soaked in a real vanilla sauce.

Preparation Time:	
15 minutes	

6 Servings/Serving Size:
1/2 cup

Exchanges:

1	Starch
1/2	Fruit
1	Skim Milk

Calories	197
Calories from Fat	23
Total Fat	3 g
Saturated Fat	1 g

Cholesterol	74 mg
Sodium	215 mg
Carbohydrate	33 g
Dietary Fiber	1 g
Sugars	23 g

Protein	11 g

3 cups cubed whole-grain bread (preferably 1–2 days old)
2 eggs
2 egg whites
2 cups evaporated skim milk
1/4 cup sugar
2 tsp grated fresh ginger
1/4 cup raisins (soak in 1/2 cup boiling water for 10 minutes; drain and save raisin water for sauce)
1/2 cup water
1/2 cup reserved raisin water
2 Tbsp apple juice concentrate
1 vanilla bean, split
1 tsp grated fresh ginger
1 Tbsp cornstarch or arrowroot powder
2 Tbsp water

1. Preheat the oven to 325 degrees. To prepare the pudding, place the bread cubes in a baking dish. Combine the egg, egg white, skim milk, sugar, ginger, and raisins and mix well. Pour the mixture over the bread and let stand for 15 minutes. Bake for 45–60 minutes until pudding is set.

2. Meanwhile, combine all remaining ingredients except the cornstarch or arrowroot powder and 2 Tbsp water in a small saucepan. Bring to a boil, lower the heat, and simmer for 5 minutes. Mix the cornstarch or arrowroot powder with the water until smooth. Add to the sauce and cook until sauce is clear and thickened. Serve the sauce over warm pieces of bread pudding.

Pita Pizza Pizzazz

Kids love to help make these pita pizzas.

Preparation Time:
10 minutes

---

6 Servings/Serving Size:
1 oz bread with 2 oz meat
and 1/2 cup vegetables

Exchanges:

1	Starch
2	Vegetable
3	Very Lean Meat
1/2	Fat

Calories	258
Calories from Fat	56
Total Fat	6 g
Saturated Fat	3 g

Cholesterol	54 mg
Sodium	499 mg
Carbohydrate	23 g
Dietary Fiber	4 g
Sugars	5 g

Protein	26 g

3 whole-wheat pita breads, split
1 1/2 cups marinara sauce
1 cup sliced zucchini
1 cup chopped broccoli
1 cup diced red peppers
3/4 lb ground turkey (have your butcher grind
   this for you)
6 oz part-skim mozzarella cheese

1. Preheat the oven to 350 degrees. Spread
   some of the marinara sauce on each pita
   bread pizza. Place all pizzas on a cookie
   sheet. Heat the oil in a small skillet over
   medium-high heat. Add the zucchini, broccoli,
   and peppers and saute for 10 minutes.

2. Remove the vegetables from the skillet and
   place on all the pizzas. In the same skillet,
   brown the turkey meat until no pink remains.
   Divide the turkey evenly over each pizza.
   Sprinkle cheese on each pizza and bake for 5
   minutes until the cheese melts.

Chicken Nuggets

These nuggets are easy finger food to eat without fuss.

Preparation Time: 10 minutes	

6 Servings/Serving Size: 3 oz

Exchanges:

1	Starch
4	Very Lean Meat
1/2	Monounsaturated Fat

Calories	239
Calories from Fat	64
Total Fat	7 g
Saturated Fat	2 g
Cholesterol	71 mg
Sodium	275 mg
Carbohydrate	13 g
Dietary Fiber	1 g
Sugars	1 g
Protein	29 g

1 cup dry bread crumbs
1/4 cup Parmesan cheese
2 tsp dried oregano
2 tsp dried basil
1 tsp paprika
1/2 tsp dried thyme
1 1/2 lb boneless, skinless chicken breasts, cut
  into 2-inch cubes
1 Tbsp olive oil

1. Preheat the oven to 350 degrees. Combine all
    ingredients except chicken and oil in a plastic
    bag. Place chicken cubes in the bag and
    shake well.

2. Place the cubes on a nonstick cookie sheet.
    Drizzle olive oil over the cubes, or mist lightly
    with olive oil from a spray bottle. Bake the
    cubes for about 10 minutes until chicken is
    cooked through and tender. Serve cold.

Fun Veggies and Dips

Preparation Time:
25 minutes

6 Servings/Serving Size:
1 cup vegetables with 2
Tbsp cheese dip and 1
Tbsp peanut butter dip

Exchanges:

1	Starch
1	Vegetable
1	Medium-Fat Meat
1/2	Fat

Calories	193
Calories from Fat	79
Total Fat	9 g
Saturated Fat	2 g

Cholesterol	7 mg
Sodium	247 mg
Carbohydrate	19 g
Dietary Fiber	3 g
Sugars	10 g

Protein	12 g

Vegetables
1 cup baby carrots
1 cup cucumber slices
1 cup mixed red and yellow peppers
1 cup cherry tomatoes
1 cup raw zucchini slices
1 cup yellow squash slices

Cheese Dip
1/2 cup low-fat cottage cheese
1/4 cup part-skim ricotta cheese
2 Tbsp Parmesan cheese
1/4 cup low-fat buttermilk
1 tsp minced fresh chives
1 tsp garlic powder

Peanut Butter Dip
1/2 cup reduced-fat peanut butter
2 tsp honey
2 tsp wheat germ
1 Tbsp minced apple

Arrange the vegetables decoratively on a large platter. To make both dips, just combine well by hand in bowls. Let dips refrigerate for 1 hour. Serve the dips side by side with the vegetables.

Pineapple Sundaes

Layers of pineapple spiked with ginger complement creamy yogurt.

Preparation Time:
15 minutes

6 Servings/Serving Size:
1/2 cup fruit with 1/2 cup yogurt

Exchanges:
1	Fruit
1/2	Skim Milk

Calories.....................121
  Calories from Fat..........2
Total Fat ....0 g
  Saturated Fat.............0 g

Cholesterol ....3 mg
Sodium....................99 mg
Carbohydrate............24 g
  Dietary Fiber ....1 g
  Sugars......................22 g

Protein.........................7 g

1 1/2 cups pineapple chunks (canned or fresh)
1 1/2 cups mandarin oranges, packed in their own juice, drained
2 Tbsp minced crystallized ginger
3 cups plain nonfat yogurt
2 tsp vanilla
2 tsp sugar
Minced crystallized ginger

Combine the pineapple, oranges, and ginger and mix well. Combine the yogurt, vanilla, and sugar. In parfait glasses, layer the fruit and yogurt, ending with yogurt. Sprinkle with a little ginger to serve.

The intelligent want

self-control;

children want candy.

—Rumi

Spring

Cocktail Shrimp Balls

This is a great uncooked appetizer you can fix the night before
and set out when your guests arrive.

Preparation Time:
15 minutes

12 Servings/Serving Size:
2 pieces

Exchanges:

1	Vegetable
1	Very Lean Meat

Calories	61
Calories from Fat	8
Total Fat	1 g
Saturated Fat	0 g

Cholesterol	92 mg
Sodium	269 mg
Carbohydrate	3 g
Dietary Fiber	0 g
Sugars	2 g

Protein	10 g

1 lb cooked shelled medium shrimp
1/2 cup chili sauce
1 hard-boiled egg
4 Tbsp nonfat cream cheese
1/4 cup minced celery
1 1/2 Tbsp minced onion
1 tsp Worcestershire sauce
Fresh ground pepper and salt to taste
4 Tbsp minced fresh parsley

1. Process all ingredients except the parsley in a
    food processor until they are finely chopped,
    but not like a paste. The mixture should still
    be somewhat chunky.

2. Form the mixture into balls and roll in
    parsley. Place on a nonstick cookie sheet
    covered with wax paper and refrigerate
    overnight before serving.

Quick and Easy Chicken Pate

This elegant appetizer takes only minutes to prepare.

Preparation Time:
10 minutes

---

6 Servings/Serving Size:
2 oz

Exchanges:
1	Vegetable
2	Lean Meat

Calories.....................137
 Calories from Fat........39
Total Fat ....4 g
 Saturated Fat............1 g

Cholesterol ....50 mg
Sodium...................93 mg
Carbohydrate..............4 g
 Dietary Fiber ....1 g
 Sugars.......................2 g

Protein.......................17 g

---

1 medium onion, finely diced
1 celery stalk, finely diced
1/2 cup minced carrot
1/3 cup brandy
2 Tbsp low-fat, low-sodium chicken broth
1 tsp paprika
1 1/2 tsp curry
Fresh ground pepper and salt to taste
12 oz cooked chicken, cut into 1-inch cubes

1. Saute the onion, celery, and carrot in the brandy and broth for 10 minutes. Place the vegetables in a food processor and process until smooth. Add remaining ingredients and process until the mixture becomes a thick paste.

2. Press the mixture into a 9 x 5-inch pan covered with wax paper and refrigerate for 24 hours before serving. Slice and serve.

Turkey-Dill Meatballs

These turkey meatballs are reminiscent of Swedish meatballs, but they're lower in fat.

Preparation Time:
20 minutes

6 Servings/Serving Size:
3–4 oz

Exchanges:

1 1/2	Starch
5	Very Lean Meat

Calories	283
Calories from Fat	28
Total Fat	3 g
Saturated Fat	1 g

Cholesterol	148 mg
Sodium	292 mg
Carbohydrate	24 g
Dietary Fiber	1 g
Sugars	10 g

Protein	36 g

Meatballs
1 1/2 lb ground turkey (have your butcher grind this for you)
1/2 cup dry bread crumbs
2 eggs, beaten
3/4 cup minced onion
1/4 cup evaporated skim milk
1 Tbsp minced fresh dill
1/4 tsp cinnamon
1 tsp cumin
1 tsp Worcestershire sauce
Fresh ground pepper and salt to taste

Sauce
2 tsp paprika
1 cup nonfat sour cream
1 tsp minced garlic
1 cup evaporated skim milk
1/2 cup water
1 Tbsp cornstarch or arrowroot powder
2 Tbsp water

1. Preheat the oven to 350 degrees. Combine all meatball ingredients and shape into 2-inch rounds. Place in a baking dish and bake for 20–25 minutes until cooked through. Combine all sauce ingredients except the cornstarch or arrowroot powder and water in a medium saucepan. Cook over medium heat until smooth, about 5–6 minutes.

2. Mix together the cornstarch or arrowroot powder and the water. Add to the saucepan and cook about 1–2 more minutes until thickened. Remove the meatballs from the pan and serve with the sauce.

Spinach-Stuffed Jumbo Mushrooms

Your guests will love this classic recipe.

Preparation Time:
15 minutes

6 Servings/Serving Size:
2 mushrooms

Exchanges:
1/2	Starch
1/2	Monounsaturated Fat

Calories	67
Calories from Fat	29
Total Fat	3 g
Saturated Fat	1 g

Cholesterol	1 mg
Sodium	107 mg
Carbohydrate	8 g
Dietary Fiber	2 g
Sugars	2 g

Protein	3 g

12 jumbo mushrooms, caps cleaned and stems removed (reserve stems)
1 Tbsp olive oil
1/2 cup minced onion
2 garlic cloves, minced
1/2 cup frozen chopped spinach, thawed and well drained
2 Tbsp Parmesan cheese
1/4 cup dry bread crumbs
1/4 cup diced pimento
1 tsp oregano
Fresh ground pepper and salt to taste

Preheat the oven to 350 degrees. Chop the mushroom stems. Heat the oil in a skillet over medium-high heat. Add the stems, onion, and garlic and saute for 5 minutes. Add the spinach and saute for 2 minutes. Add the remaining ingredients and stir. Stuff each mushroom cap with some of the filling. Place all mushrooms in a baking dish and bake, uncovered, for 15 minutes.

Black Bean Salsa

This salsa is great with grilled fish, too.

Preparation Time:
10 minutes

18 Servings/Serving Size:
1/4 cup

Exchanges:
1   Vegetable

Calories.........................31
  Calories from Fat.........2
Total Fat ....0 g
  Saturated Fat............0 g

Cholesterol ....0 mg
Sodium...................31 mg
Carbohydrate..............6 g
  Dietary Fiber ....2 g
  Sugars......................2 g

Protein.......................2 g

1 15-oz can black beans, drained and rinsed
1/2 cup chopped red onion
1 jalapeno pepper, minced
2 Tbsp balsamic vinegar
1 Tbsp lime juice
1 tsp minced garlic
2 cups chopped tomatoes
1 cup chopped red pepper
1/2 cup minced fresh cilantro
2 Tbsp minced parsley

Combine all ingredients and refrigerate 2 hours before serving.

Warm Mexican Bean Dip

This is a great low-fat alternative to high-fat bean dips.

Preparation Time:
15 minutes

---

6 Servings/Serving Size:
about 1/4 cup

Exchanges:

1	Starch
1	Very Lean Meat
1	Saturated Fat

Calories	158
Calories from Fat	59
Total Fat	7 g
Saturated Fat	4 g

Cholesterol	21 mg
Sodium	574 mg
Carbohydrate	16 g
Dietary Fiber	5 g
Sugars	4 g

Protein	8 g

1 15-oz can nonfat refried beans
1 6-oz package low-fat cream cheese
1 4-oz can green chilies
1 14-oz can chopped tomatoes, drained
1/2 tsp onion powder
1/2 tsp garlic powder
1/4 cup shredded low-fat cheddar cheese
1 tsp chili powder

Mix together all ingredients in a saucepan until the cheese melts. Serve with low-fat tortilla chips.

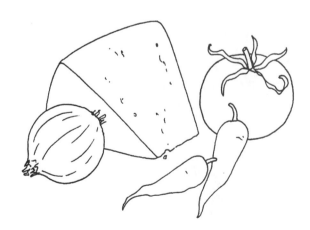

Spicy Corn Salsa

Serve this salsa with fresh, barbecued chicken or fish to add a southwestern flavor.

Preparation Time:
10 minutes

6 Servings/Serving Size:
1/2 cup

Exchanges:
1   Starch

Calories 69
  Calories from Fat 11
Total Fat ....1 g
  Saturated Fat.............0 g

Cholesterol ....0 mg
Sodium.....................4 mg
Carbohydrate............15 g
  Dietary Fiber ....2 g
  Sugars......................4 g

Protein ....2 g

2 cups corn kernels
1/4 cup diced ripe avocado
1/2 cup minced red onion
2 Tbsp minced tomato
2 Tbsp minced jalapeno pepper
2 Tbsp lime juice
2 tsp sugar
1 Tbsp red wine vinegar

Combine all ingredients and chill for several hours before serving.

Black Bean Spread

You can try this recipe as a sandwich spread, too.

Preparation Time:
5 minutes

---

12 Servings/Serving Size:
2 Tbsp

Exchanges:
1/2   Starch

Calories..........................42
 Calories from Fat..........2
Total Fat ....0 g
 Saturated Fat.............0 g

Cholesterol ....0 mg
Sodium..................107 mg
Carbohydrate...............7 g
 Dietary Fiber ....2 g
 Sugars......................1 g

Protein..........................3 g

1 15-oz can black beans, drained and rinsed
  (reserve 1 Tbsp liquid)
3 Tbsp hot salsa
2 scallions, minced
2 garlic cloves, minced
1/2 cup low-fat cottage cheese
1 tsp hot pepper sauce
2 tsp cumin
1 tsp coriander
Fresh ground pepper and salt to taste

Combine all ingredients in a blender and blend
until smooth, using bean liquid if necessary to
moisten.

 *Make changes slowly. Watch
Mother Nature. It takes her
months to change the seasons.
Why try to change the habits of a
lifetime in one day?*

Roasted Vegetable Spread

Roasting brings out all the natural flavors in vegetables, especially in eggplant and peppers.

Preparation Time:
10 minutes

6 Servings/Serving Size:
1/4 cup

Exchanges:
1   Vegetable
1/2 Monounsaturated Fat

Calories..........................56
  Calories from Fat........31
Total Fat.......................3 g
  Saturated Fat.............1 g

Cholesterol ....1 mg
Sodium....................20 mg
Carbohydrate..............6 g
  Dietary Fiber ....1 g
  Sugars........................3 g

Protein.........................1 g

1 medium eggplant, cut in half
1 Tbsp olive oil
1 large green pepper, cored, seeded, and cut in
  half
1 red pepper, cored, seeded, and cut in half
2 Tbsp lemon juice
1 Tbsp olive oil
1 Tbsp tomato paste
1 Tbsp Parmesan cheese

1. Preheat the oven to 500 degrees. Place the eggplant, cut side down, on a baking sheet and roast in the oven for 15–20 minutes. Brush with half the olive oil. Add the peppers to the pan and continue to roast for an additional 25 minutes, brushing with the rest of the oil.

2. Cool the vegetables and peel the eggplant. Drain the vegetables by placing them on a paper towel. Dry well. Place the vegetables in a food processor and blend. Then add the remaining ingredients and blend well. Refrigerate before serving.

The Herb Patch

You know spring is here by the scent of fresh herbs and flowers wafting through the air. Grocery stores now carry a year-round selection of many herbs, but you may enjoy planting and growing your own. If you prefer the convenience of store-bought herbs, follow these helpful tips:

✳ When you bring the herbs home, bundle them together like a bouquet of flowers and secure the ends with a rubber band or a twist tie. Place the herbs inside a glass of water filled to reach the top of the rubber band or tie. Place a loose plastic bag on top of the glass and set the herbs in the refrigerator. This helps keep them fresh.

✳ Basil has the shortest life after purchase—a matter of days—so use it quickly and replace it often! On the other hand, fresh dill and parsley, if stored in the above manner, will last for almost 2 weeks. Before you use basil, it is best to rub the basil leaf between your fingertips to extract the flavor.

✳ To use fresh herbs, simply snip them with a pair of scissors right into the cooking pot or serving dish. Be sure to use the flavorful stems too, except with rosemary and sage.

✳ Don't overwhelm your dish with the flavor of fresh herbs. Taste carefully throughout the cooking process, and decide how much herbs you want to add in small batches. Your recipes should not taste like a jumble of strong herbs.

✳ Try using fresh herbs instead of ground as often as you can. You will notice a much better taste and fresher flavor. If a fresh herb is unavailable, use half the amount of the ground herb. Buy ground herbs in the smallest quantities possible and use them within a year.

Grilled Caribbean Chicken Breasts

Imagine tropical breezes and an ocean sunset accompanying this Caribbean chicken.

Preparation Time:
10 minutes

6 Servings/Serving Size:
3–4 oz

Exchanges:	
4	Very Lean Meat

Calories	154
Calories from Fat	41
Total Fat	5 g
Saturated Fat	1 g

Cholesterol	69 mg
Sodium	61 mg
Carbohydrate	1 g
Dietary Fiber	0 g
Sugars	1 g

Protein	25 g

1/4 cup fresh squeezed orange juice
1 tsp orange peel
1 Tbsp olive oil
1 Tbsp lime juice
1 tsp minced ginger
2 garlic cloves, minced
1/4 tsp hot pepper sauce
1/2 tsp minced fresh oregano
1 1/2 lb boneless, skinless chicken breasts, halved

In a blender, combine all ingredients except the chicken. Pour the marinade over the chicken breasts and marinate in the refrigerator at least 2 hours or up to 48 hours. Grill or broil the chicken for about 6 minutes per side until no trace of pink remains.

This adapted recipe is courtesy of the National Broiler Council.

Grilled Chicken with Herbs

This chicken is also delicious served cold the next day.

Preparation Time:
10 minutes

6 Servings/Serving Size:
3–4 oz

Exchanges:
4   Very Lean Meat
1   Monounsaturated Fat

Calories.........................197
  Calories from Fat........87
Total Fat ....10 g
  Saturated Fat.............2 g

Cholesterol ....69 mg
Sodium......................78 mg
Carbohydrate...............1 g
  Dietary Fiber ....0 g
  Sugars........................1 g

Protein........................25 g

2 Tbsp minced fresh Italian parsley
2 tsp minced fresh rosemary
2 tsp minced fresh thyme
1 sage leaf
3 garlic cloves, minced
1/4 cup olive oil
1/2 cup balsamic vinegar
Fresh ground pepper and salt to taste
1 1/2 lb boneless, skinless chicken breasts,
    halved

In a blender, combine all ingredients except the chicken. Pour the marinade over the chicken breasts and marinate in the refrigerator at least 2 hours or up to 48 hours. Grill or broil the chicken for about 6 minutes per side until no trace of pink remains.

Chicken with Rosemary and Wine

Serve crusty bread to soak up this recipe's delicious juices.

Preparation Time:
20 minutes

6 Servings/Serving Size:
3–4 oz

Exchanges:
1	Starch
4	Very Lean Meat
1/2	Monounsaturated Fat

Calories	250
Calories from Fat	57
Total Fat	6 g
Saturated Fat	1 g
Cholesterol	69 mg
Sodium	541 mg
Carbohydrate	18 g
Dietary Fiber	5 g
Sugars	11 g
Protein	28 g

1 Tbsp olive oil
1 1/2 lb boneless, skinless chicken breasts, halved
1/4 cup dry white wine
3 garlic cloves, minced
1 medium onion, diced
1 cup diced carrot
1 28-oz can crushed tomatoes
2 tsp sugar
1 Tbsp minced fresh rosemary
1/2 cup minced fresh Italian parsley
1/4 cup sliced black olives
2 tsp capers
Fresh ground pepper and salt to taste
2 Tbsp Parmesan cheese

1. Heat the oil in a heavy skillet over medium-high heat. Add the chicken breasts and saute on both sides for a total of 10 minutes. Remove the chicken from the skillet. Add the wine and heat until boiling. Add the garlic and onion and saute for 5 minutes.

2. Add the carrot and saute for 5 more minutes. Add the tomatoes and sugar. Return the chicken breasts to the skillet. Simmer, uncovered, for 20 minutes. Add the rosemary, parsley, olives, capers, pepper, and salt. Simmer for 10 more minutes. Sprinkle with Parmesan cheese to serve.

Best Oven-Fried Chicken

All the crunch of good fried chicken without the fat!

Preparation Time:
15 minutes

---

6 Servings/Serving Size:
3–4 oz

Exchanges:

1	Starch
4	Lean Meat

Calories......................311
 Calories from Fat......120
Total Fat ....13 g
 Saturated Fat............3 g

Cholesterol ....142 mg
Sodium.................343 mg
Carbohydrate............14 g
 Dietary Fiber ....1 g
 Sugars......................1 g

Protein........................32 g

1 cup bread crumbs
1/4 cup Parmesan cheese
1 tsp garlic powder
1 tsp onion powder
1 tsp minced fresh thyme
1/2 tsp minced fresh oregano
1 tsp minced fresh basil
2 tsp paprika
Fresh ground pepper and salt to taste
2 eggs
2 egg whites
1 tsp hot pepper sauce
1 1/2 lb boneless, skinless chicken breasts, halved
3 Tbsp olive oil

1. Preheat the oven to 350 degrees. Combine the bread crumbs, Parmesan cheese, and spices in a plastic bag. In a shallow bowl, beat the eggs and egg whites. Add the hot pepper sauce. Dip each chicken breast into beaten eggs. Roll in the bread crumb mixture.

2. Spread the chicken breasts out on a cookie sheet. Drizzle olive oil on each chicken breast. Bake the chicken for 30–35 minutes until no traces of pink remain.

Mustard and Sesame Chicken

Dijon mustard adds a twist to this soy-based marinade.

Preparation Time:
10 minutes

6 Servings/Serving Size:
3–4 oz

Exchanges:
4   Very Lean Meat

Calories......................160
 Calories from Fat........35
Total Fat ....4 g
 Saturated Fat.............1 g

Cholesterol ....69 mg
Sodium..................581 mg
Carbohydrate..............4 g
 Dietary Fiber ....0 g
 Sugars......................3 g

Protein......................26 g

2 scallions, minced
3 garlic cloves, minced
2 shallots, minced
1/2 cup lite soy sauce
2 Tbsp Dijon mustard
1 Tbsp oyster sauce
1 Tbsp Hoisin sauce
2 tsp hot pepper sauce
1 cup low-fat, low-sodium chicken broth
2 tsp sesame oil
2 tsp honey
1 1/2 lb boneless, skinless chicken breasts,
   halved

In a blender, combine all ingredients except the chicken. Pour the marinade over the chicken breasts and marinate in the refrigerator at least 2 hours or up to 48 hours. Grill or broil the chicken for about 6 minutes per side until no trace of pink remains.

Spicy Indian Chicken

Serve tall goblets of cool water with this spicy dish!

Preparation Time:
10 minutes

6 Servings/Serving Size:
3–4 oz

Exchanges:
4   Very Lean Meat

Calories	143
Calories from Fat	26
Total Fat	3 g
Saturated Fat	1 g
Cholesterol	69 mg
Sodium	72 mg
Carbohydrate	2 g
Dietary Fiber	0 g
Sugars	1 g
Protein	26 g

1 1/2 cups plain nonfat yogurt
2 tsp cayenne pepper
2 small red chilies, minced
2 tsp minced ginger
1 tsp ground coriander
2 garlic cloves, minced
2 tsp cumin
2 tsp mustard seeds
1 tsp paprika
1/4 tsp allspice
1 1/2 lb boneless, skinless chicken breasts,
    halved

In a blender, combine all ingredients except the chicken. Pour the marinade over the chicken breasts and marinate in the refrigerator at least 2 hours or up to 48 hours. Grill or broil the chicken for about 6 minutes per side until no trace of pink remains.

* * * * * * * * * * * * * *

Treat yourself to a really nice set of measuring cups and spoons and an inexpensive food scale. These tools don't cost much. But they are vital for your good health. Unless you weigh or measure the food you eat, how will you know what size your servings are?

* * * * * * * * * * * * * *

Cajun Chicken with Orange Mustard Sauce

You can keep this Cajun seasoning mixture on hand for other uses.

Preparation Time:	
15 minutes	

6 Servings/Serving Size:
3–4 oz

Exchanges:

1 1/2	Carbohydrate
3	Very Lean Meat
1	Monounsaturated Fat

Calories	287
Calories from Fat	74
Total Fat	8 g
Saturated Fat	1 g

Cholesterol	69 mg
Sodium	317 mg
Carbohydrate	25 g
Dietary Fiber	0 g
Sugars	21 g

Protein	26 g

1 tsp paprika
1 tsp onion powder
1 tsp garlic powder
1 tsp cayenne pepper
1 tsp fresh basil leaves
1/2 tsp minced fresh thyme
Fresh ground pepper and salt to taste
1 1/2 lb boneless, skinless chicken breasts,
    halved and pounded to 1/4-inch thickness
2 Tbsp canola oil
1 1/2 cups low-sugar orange marmalade
6 Tbsp Dijon mustard

1. Prepare the Cajun seasoning mixture by combining the first seven ingredients. Sprinkle the chicken with the Cajun seasoning and place in the refrigerator for 30 minutes.

2. Heat the oil in a heavy skillet over medium-high heat. Add the chicken breasts. Saute on both sides for a total of 7–9 minutes. Combine the orange marmalade and mustard, add to the pan, and bring to a boil. Simmer for 3 more minutes.

This adapted recipe is courtesy of the National Broiler Council.

Springtime Cornish Hens

This delicious sauce is also great on pork.

Preparation Time:
10 minutes

6 Servings/Serving Size:
3 oz, no skin

Exchanges:
1/2	Fruit
2	Very Lean Meat

Calories.........................82
  Calories from Fat.......16
Total Fat ....2 g
  Saturated Fat.............0 g

Cholesterol ....47 mg
Sodium....................74 mg
Carbohydrate..............5 g
  Dietary Fiber ....0 g
  Sugars.......................4 g

Protein........................11 g

3 Cornish hens (about 3/4 lb each)
1 10-oz jar low-sugar apricot jam
1 Tbsp lemon juice
1 package low-sodium onion soup mix
1 Tbsp Dijon mustard

1. Preheat the oven to 350 degrees. Wash the hens inside and out. Remove the giblets and discard. Warm the jam in the microwave for 30 seconds until it melts. Add the remaining ingredients to the jam and stir. Reserve 1/4 of the sauce and keep warm.

2. Place the hens in a roasting pan and baste with the remainder of the sauce. Bake the hens for 45–60 minutes. Cut the hens in half, discard the skin, and serve with the reserved sauce.

Cathy's Marinated Chicken

This simple chicken is great served with rice pilaf and a crisp salad.

Preparation Time:
5 minutes

6 Servings/Serving Size:
3–4 oz

Exchanges:
4   Very Lean Meat
1/2   Monounsaturated Fat

Calories 175
  Calories from Fat 48
Total Fat ....5 g
  Saturated Fat.............1 g

Cholesterol ....73 mg
Sodium ....270 mg
Carbohydrate..............2 g
  Dietary Fiber ....0 g
  Sugars ....1 g

Protein ....27 g

1 cup dry white wine
1 cup fresh lemon juice
2 Tbsp olive oil
1/4 cup lite soy sauce
1 1/2 lb boneless, skinless chicken breast

Mix the marinade ingredients together and pour over the chicken. Marinate in the refrigerator overnight. Grill or broil the chicken 6 inches from the heat source on each side for 5–8 minutes until juices run clear.

Low-Fat Chicken Tostadas

Serve these tasty tostadas with some black bean soup and a chilled fruit dessert!

Preparation Time:
15 minutes

6 Servings/Serving Size:
3–4 oz chicken

Exchanges:

1 1/2	Starch
1	Vegetable
4	Very Lean Meat

Calories	292
Calories from Fat	57
Total Fat	6 g
Saturated Fat	2 g

Cholesterol	76 mg
Sodium	309 mg
Carbohydrate	23 g
Dietary Fiber	3 g
Sugars	4 g

Protein	33 g

1 1/2 lb cooked, boneless, skinless chicken breast, shredded
3 cups shredded romaine lettuce
1/2 cup chopped red pepper
1/2 cup chopped green pepper
1/2 cup chopped fresh tomatoes
6 6-in flour tortillas
6 Tbsp fat-free sour cream
6 Tbsp salsa
6 Tbsp low-fat cheddar cheese

Combine the chicken, lettuce, peppers, tomatoes, and onions in a large bowl. Heat the tortillas by placing them one at a time in a dry skillet and turning once until brown and puffy. To assemble the tostadas, place a tortilla on a plate, top with some of the chicken mixture, and garnish with sour cream, salsa, and cheese.

Great Wall of China Chicken Salad

Preparation Time:
20 minutes

6 Servings/Serving Size:
3–4 oz chicken with 1 cup vegetables

Exchanges:
1/2	Starch
2	Vegetable
5	Very Lean Meat
1/2	Fat

Calories	288
Calories from Fat	73
Total Fat	8 g
Saturated Fat	2 g

Cholesterol	96 mg
Sodium	565 mg
Carbohydrate	14 g
Dietary Fiber	4 g
Sugars	6 g

Protein	40 g

Salad

1 1/2 lb cooked boneless, skinless chicken breasts, cut into 2-inch strips
1 cup diagonally sliced celery
1/2 cup thinly sliced mushrooms
1 cup diagonally and thinly sliced carrots
1/2 cup thinly sliced red pepper
1 cup lightly steamed broccoli florets
1 cup fresh snow peas, trimmed
1 cup bean sprouts

Dressing

1 cup low-fat, low-sodium chicken broth
2 Tbsp low-calorie peanut butter
4 Tbsp lite soy sauce
3 garlic cloves, finely minced
1 tsp crushed red pepper
2 tsp minced ginger
1 Tbsp cornstarch or arrowroot powder
2 Tbsp water
2 Tbsp toasted sesame seeds
1/2 cup minced scallions

1. Combine all salad ingredients in a large salad bowl. Combine all dressing ingredients except for the cornstarch or arrowroot powder and water in a medium saucepan over medium heat. Bring to a boil, reduce the heat, and simmer for 5 minutes.

2. Combine the cornstarch or arrowroot powder and water. Add to the dressing, bring to a boil, then simmer until thickened, about 3 minutes. Pour the dressing over the salad. Garnish with sesame seeds and scallions and serve.

Sage Chicken with Peppers

This colorful, spicy dish dresses up any dinner table.

Preparation Time:
20 minutes

---

6 Servings/Serving Size:
3–4 oz

Exchanges:

1	Starch
1	Vegetable
4	Very Lean Meat

Calories	243
Calories from Fat	50
Total Fat	6 g
Saturated Fat	1 g

Cholesterol	69 mg
Sodium	431 mg
Carbohydrate	19 g
Dietary Fiber	4 g
Sugars	11 g

Protein	28 g

1 Tbsp olive oil
1 1/2 lb boneless, skinless chicken breasts, cut
   into 2-inch cubes
1 cup diced onion
3 garlic cloves, minced
1 each small red, yellow, green, and orange
   peppers, julienned
1 Tbsp minced fresh sage
1 28-oz can crushed tomatoes
2 Tbsp dry red wine
2 tsp crushed red pepper

1. Heat the oil in a heavy skillet over medium-high heat. Add the chicken and saute for 5–6 minutes. Remove the chicken from skillet. In the remaining pan drippings, saute the onion and garlic for 5 minutes. Add the peppers and saute for 5 more minutes.

2. Add the sage, tomatoes, wine, and crushed pepper and simmer for 20 minutes. Add the chicken and simmer for 10 more minutes. Serve over rice or pasta if desired.

Steamed Chicken with Chinese Barbecue Sauce

Steaming is the best way to keep fat at bay!

Preparation Time:
10 minutes

6 Servings/Serving Size:
3–4 oz

Exchanges:
4   Very Lean Meat

Calories.......................151
  Calories from Fat........28
Total Fat ....3 g
  Saturated Fat.............1 g

Cholesterol ....69 mg
Sodium..................374 mg
Carbohydrate..............4 g
  Dietary Fiber ....0 g
  Sugars.......................4 g

Protein.......................25 g

1 1/2 lb skinless, boneless chicken breasts,
    halved and pounded to 1/2-inch thickness
2 Tbsp lite soy sauce
1 Tbsp minced ginger
1/2 cup rice vinegar
1/3 cup barbecue sauce
2 garlic cloves, minced
1/2 tsp Chinese Five Spice
1/2 cup minced scallions

1. Arrange the chicken breasts on a heatproof
    plate. Sprinkle the chicken with soy sauce
    and ginger. Place a metal rack inside a deep
    wok, set the wok to high, and add 2–3 inches
    water to the bottom of the wok. Place the
    plate of chicken on the rack, cover the wok,
    and steam the chicken for about 10–15
    minutes, adding more water if necessary. (No
    trace of pink should remain. You may need to
    steam the chicken in two batches.)

2. While the chicken is steaming, heat the
    remaining ingredients in a saucepan over
    medium heat. Remove the steamed chicken
    from the wok and garnish chicken with
    scallions. Serve with hot barbecue sauce on
    the side.

Lemon-Lime Chicken

This is a great dish to serve for a light spring luncheon.

Preparation Time:
15 minutes

6 Servings/Serving Size:
3–4 oz

Exchanges:
4 Very Lean Meat
1/2 Monounsaturated Fat

Calories......................157
 Calories from Fat........47
Total Fat.....................5 g
 Saturated Fat.............1 g

Cholesterol.............69 mg
Sodium...................74 mg
Carbohydrate...............1 g
 Dietary Fiber.............0 g
 Sugars.......................1 g

Protein.......................25 g

2 Tbsp fresh lemon juice
2 Tbsp fresh lime juice
2 Tbsp olive oil
2 tsp sugar
2 tsp minced fresh thyme
1/4 cup low-fat, low-sodium chicken broth
Fresh ground pepper and salt to taste
1 1/2 lb chicken breasts, boned, skinned, and
 halved

In a blender, combine all ingredients except the chicken. Pour the marinade over the chicken breasts and marinate in the refrigerator at least 2 hours or up to 48 hours. Grill or broil the chicken for about 6 minutes per side until no trace of pink remains.

Lamb and Asparagus Dinner

Set some daffodils on your table to complement this spring meal!

Preparation Time:
25 minutes

6 Servings/Serving Size:
3 oz lamb with 1/2 cup asparagus

Exchanges:

2	Vegetable
3	Lean Meat

Calories	205
Calories from Fat	64
Total Fat	7 g
Saturated Fat	2 g

Cholesterol	75 mg
Sodium	112 mg
Carbohydrate	8 g
Dietary Fiber	2 g
Sugars	4 g

Protein	26 g

1/2 cup dry white wine
3 garlic cloves, minced
1 cup chopped red onion
1 1/2 lb boneless lamb, cut into cubes
3 cups lightly steamed, sliced, fresh asparagus
Fresh ground pepper and salt to taste

In a medium skillet over medium-high heat, add half the wine. Bring to a boil and add the garlic and onion. Saute for 5 minutes. Add the lamb and saute for 6 more minutes. Add the remaining wine and asparagus. Cook, covered, for 5–8 minutes until lamb is tender. Add pepper and salt to taste.

Marinated Lamb Chops

Red wine and raspberry vinegar add a fruity flavor to traditional lamb chops.

Preparation Time:
10 minutes

6 Servings/Serving Size:
3 oz

Exchanges:
2   Lean Meat
1/2   Fat

Calories........................135
  Calories from Fat........58
Total Fat ....6 g
  Saturated Fat.............2 g

Cholesterol ....56 mg
Sodium...................86 mg
Carbohydrate..............1 g
  Dietary Fiber ....0 g
  Sugars.......................1 g

Protein........................17 g

1/2 cup dry red wine
1/4 cup raspberry vinegar
2 Tbsp Dijon mustard
Fresh ground pepper and salt to taste
2 lb lamb chops

Combine the first four ingredients. Add the lamb chops and marinate in the refrigerator for 1–2 hours. Grill or broil the lamb chops until done as desired.

Every healer since Hippocrates has stated that food is our best medicine.

Mediterranean Grilled Lamb

Use bread or pasta to soak up the juices from this delicious dish.

Preparation Time: 15 minutes	
6 Servings/Serving Size: 3 oz	
Exchanges: 3 Lean Meat	
Calories................158	
Calories from Fat........77	
Total Fat.....................9 g	
Saturated Fat............3 g	
Cholesterol ....62 mg	
Sodium....................70 mg	
Carbohydrate..............1 g	
Dietary Fiber ....0 g	
Sugars.......................1 g	
Protein........................19 g	

1/3 cup minced red onion
2 Tbsp olive oil
1/4 cup balsamic vinegar
3 garlic cloves, minced
1 Tbsp minced fresh basil
Fresh ground pepper and salt to taste
6 4–5-oz lamb chops

Combine all ingredients except the lamb chops, then add the lamb chops and marinate in the refrigerator at least 3–5 hours. Grill or broil the lamb chops until done as desired.

Indian Kabobs

Serve these kabobs with saffron rice and crisp cucumbers for a royal meal.

Preparation Time:
20 minutes

6 Servings/Serving Size:
1 kabob

Exchanges:

1/2	Fruit
1	Vegetable
3	Lean Meat

Calories	231
Calories from Fat	72
Total Fat	8 g
Saturated Fat	3 g
Cholesterol	111 mg
Sodium	194 mg
Carbohydrate	11 g
Dietary Fiber	1 g
Sugars	8 g
Protein	28 g

1/2 cup low-fat cottage cheese
1 1/2 lb ground lamb
1 medium onion, minced
1/3 cup raisins
1 Tbsp curry powder
1 egg
2 tsp minced fresh parsley
2 tsp cumin
Fresh ground pepper and salt to taste
18 cherry tomatoes

1. Soak 6 wooden skewers in water. Blend the cottage cheese in a blender until smooth. Add the remaining ingredients except the cherry tomatoes. Mix until blended and then form the mixture into 24 meatballs.

2. Starting and ending with a meatball, alternately thread the meatballs and cherry tomatoes onto 6 wooden skewers. Oven broil the kabobs for about 10–15 minutes until the lamb is cooked through.

Roast Leg of Lamb

Celebrate the beginning of spring with this most elegant of spring dishes.

Preparation Time:	
15 minutes	

6 Servings/Serving Size:
4 oz

Exchanges:
4	Lean Meat
1/2	Monounsaturated Fat

Calories	241
Calories from Fat	120
Total Fat	13 g
Saturated Fat	4 g

Cholesterol	87 mg
Sodium	130 mg
Carbohydrate	1 g
Dietary Fiber	0 g
Sugars	1 g

Protein	27 g

2 Tbsp Dijon mustard
6 garlic cloves, minced
2 Tbsp olive oil
1 4-lb leg of lamb, trimmed of fat
Parsley

Preheat the oven to 325 degrees. Combine the mustard, garlic, and oil and rub over the lamb. Place the lamb in a roasting pan and roast for about 35 minutes per pound or until done as desired.

Greek Lamb Burgers with Cucumber Dill Sauce

Greek spices and a cool, creamy cucumber sauce make these burgers unique.

Preparation Time:	
15 minutes	

6 Servings/Serving Size:
3 oz lamb with 2 Tbsp sauce (Free Food)

Exchanges:

1	Starch
4	Lean Meat
1/2	Saturated Fat

Calories	313
Calories from Fat	129
Total Fat	14 g
Saturated Fat	6 g

Cholesterol	126 mg
Sodium	455 mg
Carbohydrate	16 g
Dietary Fiber	1 g
Sugars	3 g

Protein	29 g

Burgers
1 1/2 lb ground lean lamb (have your butcher grind this for you)
4 oz feta cheese
1/2 cup minced mint
1/2 minced onion
1 cup dry bread crumbs
1 Tbsp minced fresh oregano
1 garlic clove, minced
3 Tbsp red wine vinegar
2 eggs, beaten
Fresh ground pepper and salt to taste

Sauce
1/2 cup peeled, seeded, and diced cucumber
1 cup plain low-fat yogurt
1 Tbsp minced fresh dill
2 tsp minced fresh parsley
1 tsp minced fresh chives
2 tsp cider vinegar
Fresh ground pepper and salt to taste

Combine all burger ingredients, form into patties, and grill or broil over medium-high heat for 5–6 minutes per side. Combine all sauce ingredients and pour sauce over cooked burgers to serve.

Perky Pasta

Pasta is a staple of the American diet. With a little imagination, fresh herbs, and spring vegetables, you can turn plain pasta into something special! Here are a few tips to keep your pasta tasting its best:

✳ Purchase the best quality pasta you can afford. Look for imported Italian pastas made from hard, durum, semolina wheat.

✳ Buy either fresh or boxed pasta. The nice thing about fresh pasta is that it cooks in one minute! You need to use fresh pasta within 24 hours, or freeze it and use within 3 months.

✳ Make sure your pasta pot is big enough for the pasta to literally swim in it. You don't necessarily need to add oil. Just make sure the water is at a full rolling boil and the pasta is moving vigorously in the water.

✳ Cook your pasta only until it is al dente ("to the tooth"). Pasta should be slightly chewy.

✳ Do not rinse your pasta. Sauces adhere better when the wheat starch is left clinging to the pasta.

✳ Serve pasta at room temperature, as the Italians do. Despite ads that show steam wafting from a plate of pasta, it is more flavorful when eaten at room temperature.

Creamy Citrus Pasta

Try this pasta recipe by itself or with grilled seafood.

Preparation Time:
10 minutes

6 Servings/Serving Size:
1 cup

Exchanges:

3	Starch
1/2	Skim Milk

Calories 282
 Calories from Fat 38
Total Fat .... 4 g
 Saturated Fat .... 2 g

Cholesterol .... 10 mg
Sodium .... 182 mg
Carbohydrate .... 47 g
 Dietary Fiber .... 2 g
 Sugars .... 8 g

Protein .... 13 g

1 Tbsp butter
1 1/2 cups evaporated skim milk
1 1/2 Tbsp lemon juice
1/2 tsp orange extract
1/2 tsp lemon peel
1/2 tsp orange peel
1/4 cup grated Parmesan cheese
Fresh ground pepper and salt to taste
6 cups cooked penne pasta

In a nonstick skillet over medium heat, mix all ingredients except the cheese, pepper, salt, and pasta. Stir constantly until heated through. Add the cheese, pepper, and salt and heat a few more minutes. Add the sauce to the cooked pasta and serve.

Spicy Peanut Pasta

For variety, try adding cooked chicken or shrimp to this wonderfully creamy peanut sauce.

Preparation Time:
10 minutes

6 Servings/Serving Size:
1 cup

Exchanges:
3 1/2	Starch
1/2	Fat

Calories	299
Calories from Fat	57
Total Fat	6 g
Saturated Fat	1 g

Cholesterol	0 mg
Sodium	319 mg
Carbohydrate	50 g
Dietary Fiber	4 g
Sugars	6 g

Protein	11 g

1/3 cup lite crunchy peanut butter
1/4 tsp coconut extract
1 1/4 cups low-fat, low-sodium chicken broth
1/2 tsp crushed red pepper
2 garlic cloves, minced
1 tsp grated fresh ginger
2 Tbsp lite soy sauce
1/2 tsp hot pepper sauce
2 tsp sugar
Fresh ground pepper and salt to taste
1 Tbsp cornstarch or arrowroot powder
2 Tbsp water
6 cups fusilli pasta
1/4 cup sliced scallions

Combine all ingredients except cornstarch or arrowroot powder, water, and pasta in a medium saucepan. Cook over medium heat for 10–15 minutes. Combine the cornstarch or arrowroot powder with the water. Mix until smooth. Add to the sauce, and cook for 1 more minute until thickened. Pour the sauce over the pasta and garnish with scallions to serve.

Rosemary Pasta

Rosemary is a prized herb in Italian cooking.

Preparation Time:
20 minutes

6 Servings/Serving Size:
1 cup

Exchanges:
3	Starch
1	Vegetable
1	Very Lean Meat
1/2	Monounsaturated Fat

Calories	325
Calories from Fat	66
Total Fat	7 g
Saturated Fat	2 g

Cholesterol	8 mg
Sodium	461 mg
Carbohydrate	48 g
Dietary Fiber	4 g
Sugars	6 g

Protein	17 g

1 Tbsp olive oil
1 medium zucchini, halved and cut into 4-inch slices
1 medium yellow squash, halved and cut into 4-inch slices
8 medium mushrooms, sliced
1 4-oz can pitted black olives, drained and quartered
1 28-oz can plum tomatoes, drained and chopped
8 oz low-fat shredded cheddar cheese
1 tsp minced fresh rosemary
6 cups cooked rotini pasta

Preheat the oven to 350 degrees. In a large skillet, saute the zucchini and squash in oil over medium heat for 2 minutes. Place all ingredients in a 9 x 12-inch baking dish and mix well. Bake, uncovered, for 15 minutes.

Now

is the season of

   *butterfly mornings*

and

wildflower afternoons.

Tarragon Dill Pasta with Shrimp

This colorful dish is a complete meal in itself.

Preparation Time:
20 minutes

6 Servings/Serving Size:
1 1/2 cups

Exchanges:

3	Starch
1	Vegetable
2	Very Lean Meat
1/2	Monounsaturated Fat

Calories	372
Calories from Fat	62
Total Fat	7 g
Saturated Fat	1 g

Cholesterol	161 mg
Sodium	237 mg
Carbohydrate	50 g
Dietary Fiber	4 g
Sugars	6 g

Protein	26 g

2 Tbsp canola oil
1 garlic clove, minced
1 medium onion, chopped
2 small zucchini, julienned
1/2 small red or yellow pepper, julienned
2 small ripe plum tomatoes, diced
1 cup frozen peas, thawed
1/4 cup chopped fresh dill
2 Tbsp tarragon
3 Tbsp fresh lemon juice
1 1/2 lb peeled and deveined medium shrimp
1/4 tsp red pepper flakes
Fresh ground pepper and salt to taste
6 cups cooked small shells, radiatore, or penne

Heat the oil in a large skillet or wok over medium heat. Add the garlic and onion and saute for 1 minute. Add the zucchini and pepper and saute for 1 more minute. Add all remaining ingredients except the pasta and stir well. Cover and bring to a boil. Reduce heat and simmer for 2 minutes. Add the pasta and stir thoroughly.

Fettucine Verde

Serve this perky dish with a bright orange vegetable, such as carrots.

Preparation Time:
25 minutes

6 Servings/Serving Size:
1 cup

Exchanges:

2 1/2	Starch
1/2	Monounsaturated Fat

Calories	225
Calories from Fat	50
Total Fat	6 g
Saturated Fat	1 g

Cholesterol	47 mg
Sodium	118 mg
Carbohydrate	35 g
Dietary Fiber	2 g
Sugars	2 g

Protein	9 g

1 1/2 cups fresh spinach leaves
1/2 cup minced fresh parsley
1 Tbsp olive oil
1/2 cup low-fat, low-sodium chicken broth
1/2 cup dry white wine
2 tsp minced garlic
Fresh ground pepper and salt to taste
6 cups cooked fettucine
1/4 cup grated Parmesan cheese

Wash the spinach leaves, pat dry, and tear into pieces. Place all ingredients except the pasta and cheese in a skillet. Cook over medium heat until spinach is tender. Toss the spinach mixture with the cooked fettucine. Garnish with cheese to serve.

Gourmet Mushroom Pasta

Use any variety of wild mushrooms for this recipe, or try a combination of shiitake and regular white mushrooms for a fantastic taste.

Preparation Time:
15 minutes

---

6 Servings/Serving Size:
1 cup

Exchanges:
3	Starch
1	Vegetable
1/2	Monounsaturated Fat

Calories	282
Calories from Fat	42
Total Fat	5 g
Saturated Fat	1 g

Cholesterol	3 mg
Sodium	92 mg
Carbohydrate	48 g
Dietary Fiber	4 g
Sugars	6 g

Protein	11 g

1 Tbsp olive oil
1/2 cup chopped red onion
3 cups sliced mushrooms, stems removed
2 tsp garlic
1/2 cup evaporated skim milk
1/2 cup dry red wine
1/4 cup Parmesan cheese
2 tsp cornstarch or arrowroot powder
4 tsp water
6 cups cooked bow tie pasta
1/4 cup minced fresh parsley

1. Heat the oil in a medium skillet over medium-high heat. Add the onion and mushrooms and saute for 5 minutes. Add the garlic and saute for 1 more minute. Add the milk and wine and cook over medium heat for 3 minutes. Add the cheese and cook for 1 more minute.

2. Mix together the cornstarch or arrowroot powder and water. Add to the pan and cook until sauce is thickened. Toss the sauce with the pasta and garnish with parsley to serve.

Fusilli with Broccoli, Sun-Dried Tomatoes, and Garlic

The flavors in this dish blend wonderfully.

Preparation Time:
20 minutes

---

6 Servings/Serving Size:
1 cup pasta with 1/2 cup vegetables

Exchanges:

3	Starch
1	Vegetable

Calories	263
Calories from Fat	35
Total Fat	4 g
Saturated Fat	1 g

Cholesterol	0 mg
Sodium	213 mg
Carbohydrate	49 g
Dietary Fiber	5 g
Sugars	4 g

Protein	10 g

1 Tbsp olive oil
3 garlic cloves, minced
1/4 cup minced red onion
2 cups broccoli florets
1 cup chopped, rehydrated sun-dried tomatoes
1/2 cup low-fat, low-sodium chicken broth
6 cups cooked fusilli pasta
1 Tbsp grated Parmesan cheese

Heat the oil in a large skillet over medium-high heat. Add the garlic and onion and saute for 5 minutes. Add the broccoli and tomatoes and saute for 5 more minutes. Add the broth, cover, and steam for 3 minutes. Toss the vegetables with the pasta and garnish with cheese to serve.

Cool Radiatore with Melon

You'll like the flavor surprise of pasta, melon, and citrus together in this dish.

Preparation Time:
15 minutes

6 Servings/Serving Size:
1 cup pasta with 1/2 cup fruit

Exchanges:

2 1/2	Starch
1	Fruit

Calories 257
 Calories from Fat 24
Total Fat ....3 g
 Saturated Fat.............0 g

Cholesterol ....0 mg
Sodium...................14 mg
Carbohydrate............53 g
 Dietary Fiber ....3 g
 Sugars.....................19 g

Protein.........................7 g

1/2 cup limeade concentrate
2 tsp canola oil
1 tsp chili powder
1 1/2 cups honeydew chunks
1 1/2 cups cantaloupe chunks
1 medium cucumber, peeled, seeded, and cut into
    1/2-inch chunks
6 cups cooked radiatore pasta, rinsed under cold
    water

In a medium bowl, whisk together the limeade concentrate, oil, and chili powder. Add all remaining ingredients, toss well to coat with the dressing, and serve.

Mediterranean Fettucine with Shrimp

This quick dish tastes like it took hours to prepare!

Preparation Time: 15 minutes	

6 Servings/Serving Size:
2 oz shrimp with 1 cup pasta

Exchanges:

2 1/2	Starch
2	Very Lean Meat

Calories	279
Calories from Fat	46
Total Fat	5 g
Saturated Fat	2 g

Cholesterol	136 mg
Sodium	267 mg
Carbohydrate	39 g
Dietary Fiber	3 g
Sugars	5 g

Protein	20 g

6 cups cooked fettucine
12 oz peeled and deveined medium shrimp
1 10-oz package chopped frozen spinach, thawed
1 cup plain low-fat yogurt
1/4 cup crumbled feta cheese
2 garlic cloves, minced
1 Tbsp minced dill
Fresh ground pepper to taste

Three minutes before the pasta is finished cooking, add the shrimp and spinach to the pot. Drain completely. Toss with the remaining ingredients and serve.

Quick Ziti and White Bean Salad

You can whip up this salad in no time!

Preparation Time:	
10 minutes	

6 Servings/Serving Size:
1 cup

Exchanges:

3	Starch
1/2	Fat

Calories	281
Calories from Fat	45
Total Fat	5 g
Saturated Fat	1 g

Cholesterol	3 mg
Sodium	456 mg
Carbohydrate	48 g
Dietary Fiber	4 g
Sugars	5 g

Protein	11 g

1 15-oz can white beans (navy or cannellini), drained and rinsed
1/4 cup sliced green olives
2 Tbsp chopped fresh basil
2 cloves garlic, minced
2/3 cup low-fat Italian salad dressing
2 Tbsp grated Parmesan cheese
6 cups cooked ziti pasta

Combine all ingredients and serve at room temperature or chilled.

Grab Some Grains!

It's tough for major civilizations to develop in the absence of a basic cereal grain. Good for you (they're chock-full of B vitamins, iron, potassium, and fiber), easy to make, and satisfying to eat, grains are the perfect food in any season. There are three parts to a whole grain: the exosperm, rich in bran; the endosperm, principally starch; and the germ, rich in protein, polyunsaturated fatty acids, vitamins, and minerals. Whole grains are much more nutritious than refined products, such as bleached white flour, which have almost no fiber and retain very few vitamins and minerals.

Water or low-fat, low-sodium broths may be used as liquids for cooking grains. Be sure to tightly cover pots when cooking grains—they need all the steam they can get to properly swell. Do not stir while grains cook. Stirring loosens the starch and grains become gummy. Most of the grains below can be found in natural food stores and some major supermarkets. Buy them in bulk to save money, and store in glass containers in the refrigerator or in a cool, dry place.

Experiment freely with cooking the grains on the following list. For all of them, use 1 cup of dry grain per the amount of liquid specified, bring to a boil, then cover and cook over low heat for the time specified.

* Amaranth is an ancient staple of the Aztec civilization. It has very high-quality protein and nutty flavor. Use 2 cups of liquid and cook for 20–25 minutes for a yield of 2 cups.

* Barley is used most in Tibet, China, and Japan, and in this country in the brewing industry. Barley is less nutritious when pearled, but does take a shorter time to cook. Use 2 1/2 cups of liquid for pearled barley and cook for 45 minutes for a yield of 2 cups. Use 3 cups of liquid for hulled barley and cook for 90 minutes for a yield of 3 3/4 cups.

* Buckwheat is really a fruit, and is very good for people who are allergic to wheat. Roasted buckwheat is called kasha. Buckwheat is a great source of rutin, which benefits circulation. Use 2 cups of liquid and cook for 15 minutes for a yield of 2 cups.

* Corn, immensely popular in North and South America, is also called maize. To make polenta, use 4 cups of liquid for 1 cup of dry cornmeal and cook for 30 minutes for a yield of 2 cups. To make hominy, use 3 cups of liquid for 1 cup of dry cornmeal and cook for 2 1/2 hours for a yield of 2 cups.

* Millet is used as an alternative to rice in many countries, especially China, India, and Africa. It's preferred as a breakfast cereal, because it's very nutritious and easy to digest. Use 2 1/2 cups of liquid and cook for 30 minutes for a yield of 3 1/2 cups.

* Oats are a staple in northern Europe. They are easily digested and provide excellent protein and B vitamins. The bran of the oat has cholesterol-lowering properties. Use 2 3/4 cups of liquid and cook for 10 minutes for a yield of 2 1/2 cups.

* Quinoa is an ancient staple grain of the Incas. It is high in protein, calcium, and iron. Rinse 1 cup of grain thoroughly, use 2 cups of liquid, and cook for 15 minutes for a yield of 2 cups.

* Rice is a staple in China, Japan, and Africa—in fact, more rice is eaten in the world than any other grain. Rice freezes well, too. Be sure to rinse rice well before cooking it! Use 2 cups of liquid for 1 cup of white or brown rice and cook for 20 minutes (white) or 40–45 minutes (brown) for a yield is 2 1/2 cups. Use 3–4 cups of liquid for 1 cup of wild rice and cook for 55 minutes for a yield of 4 cups.

* Rye is popular in Eastern Europe, Russia, and Scandinavia. It was considered an unwanted seed for many centuries. It is the hardiest of the grains, often grown in cold climates and poor soils. It is similar to wheat nutritionally, but has less gluten. For 1 cup of rye berries, use 3 cups of liquid and cook for 2 hours for a yield of 2 1/2 cups.

* Wheat is a familiar staple, but try using other forms of it, such as couscous or bulgur wheat. To make couscous, use 3 cups liquid and pour over 1 cup of grain in a medium bowl. Allow the couscous to rehydrate for 5 minutes. Drain any excess water. The yield is 3 cups. To make bulgur wheat, follow the same directions but allow to rehydrate for 1 hour.

Parmesan Risotto

Risotto was meant to be eaten very fresh, so serve this dish immediately after cooking it.

Preparation Time:
15 minutes

---

6 Servings/Serving Size:
1/2 cup

Exchanges:
2 1/2	Starch
1/2	Monounsaturated Fat

Calories	226
Calories from Fat	55
Total Fat	6 g
Saturated Fat	2 g

Cholesterol	6 mg
Sodium	200 mg
Carbohydrate	36 g
Dietary Fiber	2 g
Sugars	4 g

Protein	8 g

1 Tbsp olive oil
1 1/2 cups minced onion
1 1/3 cup Arborio rice
1/2 cup dry white wine
4 cups low-fat, low-sodium chicken broth, hot
1/2 tsp turmeric
1/2 cup Parmesan cheese
1/2 cup minced fresh parsley

1. Heat the oil in a large stockpot. Add the onion and saute for 5–8 minutes. Add the rice and saute for 3 more minutes. Add the wine and cook until the wine is absorbed.

2. Add one cup of the hot chicken broth and stir until the rice has absorbed the broth. Continue to add cups of broth until the rice absorbs each cup. Add the turmeric during the last cup of broth. Add the cheese and parsley and serve.

Italian Rice Medley

This colorful rice dish goes well with any chicken entree.

Preparation Time:
15 minutes

6 Servings/Serving Size:
1/2 cup

Exchanges:
2 1/2	Starch
1	Vegetable

Calories	209
Calories from Fat	19
Total Fat	2 g
Saturated Fat	0 g

Cholesterol	0 mg
Sodium	122 mg
Carbohydrate	43 g
Dietary Fiber	2 g
Sugars	3 g

Protein	5 g

3 cups cooked long-grain rice
2 tsp olive oil
4 scallions, chopped
1 medium red pepper, chopped
1 14-oz can artichoke hearts, packed in water,
   drained and chopped
1 Tbsp minced fresh basil
1 Tbsp minced fresh oregano
1 Tbsp minced fresh Italian parsley
2 Tbsp balsamic vinegar

Heat the oil in a medium skillet over medium-high heat. Add the scallions and red pepper and saute for 5 minutes. Add the artichokes and herbs and saute for 3 more minutes. Add the rice and drizzle with vinegar to serve.

*Try keeping a diary of everything
you eat and drink for a week.*

*Some people who write down
what they eat lose weight faster.*

Basil Rice Salad

Basmati rice and basil team up for a light springtime salad.

Preparation Time:
20 minutes

6 Servings/Serving Size:
1/2 cup rice with 1/2 cup vegetables

Exchanges:

2	Starch
1	Vegetable
1 1/2	Monounsaturated Fat

Calories	254
Calories from Fat	86
Total Fat	10 g
Saturated Fat	1 g
Cholesterol	0 mg
Sodium	91 mg
Carbohydrate	37 g
Dietary Fiber	4 g
Sugars	6 g
Protein	6 g

3 cups cooked brown or white basmati rice (use regular brown or white rice if desired)
1 1/2 cups diced carrots
2 medium tomatoes, diced
1 cup canned kidney beans, drained and rinsed
2 scallions, minced
2 Tbsp lemon juice
2 Tbsp red wine vinegar
1/4 cup olive oil
1/4 cup minced fresh basil
2 Tbsp minced fresh Italian parsley
2 tsp sugar
Fresh ground pepper and salt to taste

Combine the rice, carrots, tomatoes, kidney beans, and scallions in a salad bowl. Whisk together the remaining dressing ingredients. Add the dressing to the salad and toss well. Chill for 1–2 hours before serving.

Wild Rice Seafood Salad

Be sure to rinse wild rice well before cooking it.

Preparation Time:	
15 minutes	

6 Servings/Serving Size:
1/2 cup rice with 3 oz seafood

Exchanges:

1 1/2	Starch
1	Vegetable
3	Very Lean Meat

Calories	250
Calories from Fat	27
Total Fat	3 g
Saturated Fat	0 g
Cholesterol	159 mg
Sodium	392 mg
Carbohydrate	27 g
Dietary Fiber	3 g
Sugars	5 g
Protein	29 g

1 6-oz package wild rice
1/2 lb halibut
1/4 cup low-fat mayonnaise
1/4 cup minced fresh parsley
1 Tbsp red wine vinegar
1 tsp lemon juice
2 Tbsp Dijon mustard
Fresh ground pepper and salt to taste
1 lb cooked medium shrimp, shelled and
   deveined
3/4 cup diced celery
1/2 cup sliced scallions
6 large romaine lettuce leaves
3 small tomatoes, cut into 12 wedges

1. Preheat the oven to 350 degrees. Cook the wild rice according to package directions. Drain and cool. Place the halibut on a baking sheet and bake for about 5–10 minutes until the fish is opaque. Let it cool slightly and cut the halibut into small pieces.

2. Whisk the next six ingredients together in a small bowl to make the dressing. Combine the cooled rice, halibut, shrimp, celery, and scallions in a salad bowl. Add the dressing to the salad and toss. To serve, place lettuce leaves on individual plates, top with wild rice seafood salad, and garnish with tomatoes.

Moroccan Salad

This is a delightful, crunchy version of tabouli salad.

Preparation Time:
30 minutes

6 Servings/Serving Size:
1/2 cup

Exchanges:

2	Starch
1	Vegetable
1/2	Monounsaturated Fat

Calories	207
Calories from Fat	50
Total Fat	6 g
Saturated Fat	1 g

Cholesterol	0 mg
Sodium	160 mg
Carbohydrate	35 g
Dietary Fiber	7 g
Sugars	3 g

Protein	6 g

1 cup dry bulgur wheat
2 cups boiling water
6 scallions, chopped
2 1/2 cups minced fresh parsley
1/2 cup minced mint
2 large tomatoes, diced
1 cup peeled, seeded, diced cucumber
1/4 cup olive oil
1/4 cup fresh lemon juice
2 tsp cumin
2 garlic cloves, minced
2 large rounds whole-wheat pita bread

1. Combine the bulgur wheat with the boiling water in a heat-proof bowl. Let stand 1 hour until the wheat has absorbed the water. Combine the remaining ingredients except the pita bread in a large salad bowl.

2. Cut the pita bread into triangles. Place the triangles on a cookie sheet and bake at 350 degrees until crisp, about 15 minutes. Remove from the oven and add to the salad bowl. Drain any excess water from the wheat. Add to the salad bowl and mix well. Refrigerate for 1–2 hours before serving.

Italian Polenta

Polenta, an Italian dish made with cornmeal, is so popular you can now buy ready-made mixes right in your grocery store.

Preparation Time:
20 minutes

6 Servings/Serving Size:
One 1-inch square with sauce

Exchanges:
1 1/2	Starch
1	Vegetable

Calories	138
Calories from Fat	3
Total Fat	0 g
Saturated Fat	0 g

Cholesterol	0 mg
Sodium	471 mg
Carbohydrate	29 g
Dietary Fiber	6 g
Sugars	6 g

Protein	5 g

1 6-oz box polenta mix
1 14-oz can artichoke hearts, packed in water, chopped
1 16-oz jar marinara sauce
2 Tbsp dry red wine
Nonstick cooking spray

1. Prepare the polenta according to package directions. Place polenta into a 6 x 6-inch baking dish and refrigerate until firm. To make the sauce, combine the remaining ingredients and bring to a boil. Lower the heat and let simmer for 20 minutes.

2. Cut the polenta into even squares. Place on a broiler pan sprayed with nonstick cooking spray and broil for 2–3 minutes. Turn and broil 1–2 more minutes. Serve hot with artichoke sauce on the side.

Fresh Peas with Tarragon

Fresh is always best, but you can use frozen and thawed peas in this recipe if you need to.

Preparation Time:
10 minutes

6 Servings/Serving Size:
1/2 cup

Exchanges:
1   Starch

Calories.........................89
  Calories from Fat........16
Total Fat.....................2 g
  Saturated Fat.............1 g

Cholesterol...............4 mg
Sodium..................181 mg
Carbohydrate............14 g
  Dietary Fiber.............5 g
  Sugars........................6 g

Protein.........................5 g

3 cups peas
1 Tbsp tarragon vinegar
2 tsp butter
1/2 cup pearl onions
1/2 cup low-fat, low-sodium chicken broth
1/4 tsp minced fresh tarragon

Combine all ingredients except tarragon in a saucepan and cook over medium heat until peas and onions are tender, about 5–8 minutes. (Allow a little more cooking time if you are using fresh shelled peas.) Add the tarragon, toss lightly, and serve.

Creamy Peas and Corn

This colorful combination is great served with grilled meats. Try using corn scraped right off the cob if you can.

Preparation Time:
15 minutes

6 Servings/Serving Size:
1/2 cup

Exchanges:
1 1/2   Starch

Calories......................124
 Calories from Fat........19
Total Fat ....2 g
 Saturated Fat.............0 g

Cholesterol ....2 mg
Sodium...................113 mg
Carbohydrate.............21 g
 Dietary Fiber ....3 g
 Sugars.......................7 g

Protein.........................7 g

1 1/2 cups peas
1 1/2 cups corn kernels
2 Tbsp low-calorie margarine
1/2 cup minced shallots
1/2 cup minced red pepper
1 cup evaporated skim milk
2 Tbsp sherry
1 Tbsp cornstarch or arrowroot powder
2 Tbsp water
2 Tbsp minced fresh parsley

1. Cook fresh peas in boiling water for 5 minutes and drain. If you are using frozen peas, cook according to package directions.

2. If you are using fresh corn, just scrape the kernels off the cob after removing the corn silks and boil gently for 1 minute. If you are using frozen corn, defrost it completely and drain.

3. Melt the margarine in a saucepan over medium-high heat. Add the shallots and red pepper and saute for 5 minutes. Add the milk and sherry and simmer for 5 more minutes. Combine the cornstarch or arrowroot powder and the water and add to the sauce. Cook over medium heat until bubbly. Add the corn and peas, and garnish with parsley to serve.

Indian Peas

Toasted peanuts and shredded coconut add great texture to this spicy dish.

Preparation Time:
15 minutes

---

6 Servings/Serving Size:
1/2 cup

Exchanges:
1/2	Starch
1/2	Monounsaturated Fat

Calories	73
Calories from Fat	25
Total Fat	3 g
Saturated Fat	1 g

Cholesterol	0 mg
Sodium	46 mg
Carbohydrate	10 g
Dietary Fiber	3 g
Sugars	4 g

Protein	3 g

2 cups peas
1/4 cup pearl onions
2 tsp canola oil
1 garlic clove, minced
1 Tbsp curry powder
1/4 tsp cinnamon
1/4 tsp ginger
1 medium tomato, diced
1 Tbsp chopped toasted peanuts, unsalted
1 Tbsp shredded coconut

Boil the peas and onions in a saucepan until tender, about 6–8 minutes. Drain. Heat the oil in a skillet over medium-high heat. Add the garlic and saute for 30 seconds. Add the curry, cinnamon, ginger, and tomato and cook for 3 minutes. Add the peas and onions and cook for 3 more minutes. Top with peanuts and coconut to serve.

*Eating is an adventure.
Try new tastes.
Try new varieties.
Try cooking your own.
Try growing your own.
The closer to the
earth it is,
the better your
food is going to be.*

Sugar Snap Peas and Peppers

The crunch of this dish is a welcome surprise.

Preparation Time:
15 minutes

6 Servings/Serving Size:
1/2 cup

Exchanges:
1   Vegetable
1/2 Monounsaturated Fat

Calories 40
  Calories from Fat 22
Total Fat ....2 g
  Saturated Fat ....0 g

Cholesterol ....0 mg
Sodium ....227 mg
Carbohydrate ....5 g
  Dietary Fiber ....1 g
  Sugars......................2 g

Protein........................1 g

1 Tbsp canola oil
1 1/2 cups sugar snap peas (do not shell)
1/2 cup each julienned red, yellow, and green
  peppers
2 Tbsp lite soy sauce
1 Tbsp lemon juice
Fresh ground pepper and salt to taste

Heat the oil in a skillet over medium-high heat. Add the peas and peppers and saute for 5 minutes. Sprinkle with soy sauce and lemon juice. Grind in pepper and salt to serve.

Tri-Colored Tortellini and Pea Salad

Try adding fresh crab or shrimp to this colorful pasta salad.

Preparation Time:
15 minutes

6 Servings/Serving Size:
1 cup

Exchanges:
3	Starch
1 1/2	Fat

Calories.......................320
  Calories from Fat........98
Total Fat ....11 g
  Saturated Fat.............3 g

Cholesterol ....38 mg
Sodium..................251 mg
Carbohydrate.............47 g
  Dietary Fiber ....3 g
  Sugars........................5 g

Protein.....................12 g

1/2 cup balsamic vinegar
2 Tbsp olive oil
2 tsp minced fresh chives
Fresh ground pepper and salt to taste
6 cups cooked tri-colored tortellini
1 cup diced red pepper
1 cup chopped plum tomatoes
1 cup chopped artichoke hearts, packed in water, drained
1/2 cup fresh corn
1/2 cup peas
2 Tbsp minced fresh parsley

Whisk together the first four ingredients to make the dressing. Combine all remaining ingredients in a large salad bowl. Add the dressing, toss well, and chill for several hours before serving.

Pea and Tomato Salad

Whip up this quick salad to accompany chicken or fish.

Preparation Time:
15 minutes

6 Servings/Serving Size:
1/2 cup

Exchanges:
1/2   Starch
1   Monounsaturated Fat

Calories 87
  Calories from Fat 44
Total Fat ....5 g
  Saturated Fat.............1 g

Cholesterol ....0 mg
Sodium ....61 mg
Carbohydrate..............9 g
  Dietary Fiber ....3 g
  Sugars.......................4 g

Protein.........................3 g

1 1/2 cups cooked peas
2 medium tomatoes, diced
1/2 tsp cumin
2 Tbsp olive oil
3 Tbsp white wine vinegar
1 Tbsp Dijon mustard
Fresh ground pepper and salt to taste

Combine all ingredients and toss well. Serve chilled.

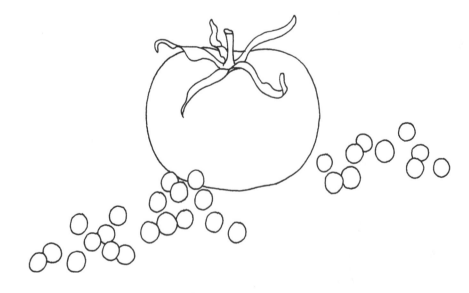

Corn and Pepper Saute

This corn medley can be served hot or cold.

Preparation Time:	
15 minutes	

6 Servings/Serving Size:
1/2 cup

Exchanges:

1	Starch

Calories	71
Calories from Fat	23
Total Fat	3 g
Saturated Fat	0 g
Cholesterol	0 mg
Sodium	29 mg
Carbohydrate	13 g
Dietary Fiber	2 g
Sugars	3 g
Protein	2 g

1 Tbsp canola oil
1/2 cup chopped onion
1 1/2 cups corn (scrape right off the cob, or use frozen and thawed)
1/2 cup diced red pepper
1/2 cup diced green pepper
1/2 cup halved cherry tomatoes
2 Tbsp fresh lemon juice
2 Tbsp minced fresh basil
Fresh ground pepper and salt to taste

Heat the oil in a large skillet over medium-high heat. Add the onion and saute for 5 minutes. Add the corn and peppers and saute for 5 more minutes. Add the cherry tomatoes and lemon juice. Cover and cook for 3 minutes. Add in basil, black pepper, and salt and cook 1 more minute.

Creamy Corn Pudding

Use fresh corn scraped right from the cob—corn pudding never tasted so good!

Preparation Time:
10 minutes

6 Servings/Serving Size:
1/2 cup

Exchanges:
1	Starch
1/2	Skim Milk
1/2	Fat

Calories	152
Calories from Fat	34
Total Fat	4 g
Saturated Fat	1 g

Cholesterol	73 mg
Sodium	151 mg
Carbohydrate	23 g
Dietary Fiber	2 g
Sugars	8 g

Protein	9 g

2 1/2 cups corn
2 eggs, beaten
1 12-oz can evaporated skim milk
1/4 tsp nutmeg
2 Tbsp low-calorie margarine
2 tsp sugar
Fresh ground pepper and salt to taste

Preheat the oven to 350 degrees. Combine all ingredients and pour into a glass casserole dish. Bake for 45 minutes until the center is firm and set.

Dilled Carrots

Carrots and dill make a wonderful pair.

Preparation Time:
10 minutes

6 Servings/Serving Size:
1/2 cup

Exchanges:
1	Vegetable
1/2	Monounsaturated Fat

Calories.........................46
  Calories from Fat........14
Total Fat ....2 g
  Saturated Fat.............0 g

Cholesterol ....0 mg
Sodium..................101 mg
Carbohydrate..............8 g
  Dietary Fiber ....2 g
  Sugars.......................3 g

Protein..........................1 g

3 cups sliced carrots or whole baby carrots
1/2 tsp lemon pepper
2 tsp minced fresh dill
2 tsp olive oil
Fresh ground pepper and salt to taste

Steam the carrots until tender, about 5–8 minutes. Combine with the other ingredients and serve.

✳✳✳✳✳✳✳✳✳✳✳✳✳✳✳✳✳✳

Try steaming! Steaming adds no fat to cooked foods, helps them stay moist, and is easy and fast. The best way to cook vegetables, steaming is the best way to reheat leftover rice and other grains and breathe new life into stale breads.

✳✳✳✳✳✳✳✳✳✳✳✳✳✳✳✳✳✳

Carrots and Shallots with Fresh Herbs

It's important that fresh herbs be added last in the cooking process. High heat may destroy their delicate flavors.

Preparation Time:
10 minutes

6 Servings/Serving Size:
1/2 cup

Exchanges:
1	Vegetable
1/2	Monounsaturated Fat

Calories	58
Calories from Fat	23
Total Fat	3 g
Saturated Fat	0 g
Cholesterol	0 mg
Sodium	79 mg
Carbohydrate	9 g
Dietary Fiber	3 g
Sugars	3 g
Protein	1 g

1 lb baby carrots
1 Tbsp olive oil
1/4 cup chopped shallots
1/2 cup low-fat, low-sodium chicken broth
1 tsp lemon juice
1/2 cup water
Fresh ground pepper and salt to taste
1 1/2 Tbsp minced fresh parsley
1/2 Tbsp minced fresh dill
1 tsp minced fresh rosemary

Combine all ingredients except the herbs in a saucepan and cook over medium heat until carrots are tender, about 5–8 minutes. Add the fresh herbs and toss well; cook for 1 more minute.

Raisin Carrots

This is a deliciously sweet vegetable dish.

Preparation Time:
10 minutes

6 Servings/Serving Size:
1/2 cup

Exchanges:
2	Vegetable
1/2	Monounsaturated Fat

Calories	62
Calories from Fat	21
Total Fat	2 g
Saturated Fat	0 g
Cholesterol	0 mg
Sodium	48 mg
Carbohydrate	10 g
Dietary Fiber	3 g
Sugars	5 g
Protein	1 g

1 Tbsp olive oil
2 Tbsp red wine vinegar
1 Tbsp minced fresh Italian parsley
2 tsp cumin
1/2 Tbsp minced fresh cilantro
2 Tbsp golden raisins
3 cups baby carrots, steamed until tender

Whisk together the dressing ingredients.
Combine with the cooked carrots and serve.

Vegetable Medley

This is a quick way to spice up frozen vegetables.

Preparation Time:
15 minutes

6 Servings/Serving Size:
1/2 cup

Exchanges:
1	Vegetable
1/2	Fat

Calories........................45
  Calories from Fat.......11
Total Fat ....1 g
  Saturated Fat.............0 g

Cholesterol ....0 mg
Sodium..................127 mg
Carbohydrate..............5 g
  Dietary Fiber ....1 g
  Sugars.......................3 g

Protein.........................1 g

1 1-lb bag frozen vegetable medley (including sugar snap peas, carrots, onions, and mushrooms)
1/2 cup low-fat, low-sodium chicken broth
1 Tbsp low-calorie margarine
1 Tbsp minced fresh herb of choice (try basil, oregano, thyme, or chervil)
1 tsp lemon pepper
Salt to taste

Steam the frozen vegetables in the broth until tender. Remove the vegetables and reduce the liquid in the pot to 2 Tbsp. Add the margarine, minced herb, and lemon pepper. Drizzle over the vegetables and serve.

Herbed Tomato Sauce with Sauted Vegetables

The secret to this tomato sauce is horseradish. Its unique flavor makes a vegetable side dish into a real crowd-pleaser. Or try serving the sauce over pasta or brown rice.

Preparation Time:
15 minutes

6 Servings/Serving Size:
1/2 cup

Exchanges:
1	Vegetable
1/2	Monounsaturated Fat

Calories	41
Calories from Fat	16
Total Fat	2 g
Saturated Fat	0 g

Cholesterol	0 mg
Sodium	11 mg
Carbohydrate	6 g
Dietary Fiber	2 g
Sugars	4 g

Protein	1 g

2 medium tomatoes, seeded and pureed in a blender
1 1/2 Tbsp prepared horseradish
2 Tbsp dry red wine
1 tsp sugar
2 tsp olive oil
2 garlic cloves, minced
1 tsp minced fresh basil
1/2 tsp minced fresh thyme
2 small zucchini, sliced into 1/4-inch-thick rounds
1/2 cup sliced fresh mushrooms
1/2 cup halved cherry tomatoes

1. In a small bowl, combine the pureed tomatoes, horseradish, wine, and sugar. Heat the oil in a large saucepan over medium-high heat. Add the garlic and saute for 30 seconds. Raise the heat slightly, add the basil and thyme, and stir-fry for 30 seconds.

2. Lower the heat slightly, add the zucchini and mushrooms, and saute for 2 minutes. Add the cherry tomatoes and pureed tomato mixture and cook, covered, over medium-low heat for 5 minutes.

This adapted recipe is courtesy of the Horseradish Information Council.

Fresh Tomato Herb Bisque

This bisque is simple, light, and fresh.

Preparation Time:
15 minutes

6 Servings/Serving Size:
1 cup

Exchanges:
| 1/2 | Skim Milk |
| 2 | Vegetable |

Calories	87
Calories from Fat	8
Total Fat	1 g
Saturated Fat	0 g
Cholesterol	3 mg
Sodium	146 mg
Carbohydrate	14 g
Dietary Fiber	1 g
Sugars	10 g
Protein	8 g

3 medium tomatoes, seeded
1 cup low-fat, low-sodium chicken broth
2 cups evaporated skim milk
2 tsp minced fresh basil
1 tsp minced fresh oregano
1 tsp minced fresh chives
Fresh ground pepper and salt to taste

Puree the tomatoes in a blender. Pour into a stockpot. Add the chicken broth and simmer for 1 hour. Add the milk and herbs and simmer for 20 minutes. Add the fresh ground pepper and salt.

Ma's Chicken Soup

Fresh peas and dill give this soup its springtime flavor.

Preparation Time:
15 minutes

---

6 Servings/Serving Size:
2 cups

Exchanges:
1/2	Starch
3	Very Lean Meat

Calories	142
Calories from Fat	32
Total Fat	4 g
Saturated Fat	1 g

Cholesterol	48 mg
Sodium	178 mg
Carbohydrate	9 g
Dietary Fiber	2 g
Sugars	4 g

Protein	21 g

3 cups low-fat, low-sodium chicken broth
1 1/2 lb boneless, skinless chicken breasts, cut
  into 2-inch cubes
1 cup chopped carrot
2 cups water
1 cup minced onion
1 cup chopped celery
2 tsp minced garlic
2 Tbsp minced fresh parsley
Fresh ground pepper and salt to taste
1 Tbsp minced fresh dill
1 cup fresh peas

Combine all ingredients except the dill and
peas in a large stockpot. Bring to a boil, then
simmer for 45 minutes. Add the dill and peas
and simmer for 5 more minutes.

Creamy Vegetable Soup

This soup is great served with crusty bread and fresh salad on a cool spring evening.

Preparation Time:
30 minutes

6 Servings/Serving Size:
1 cup

Exchanges:

1	Starch
1	Monounsaturated Fat

Calories	128
Calories from Fat	39
Total Fat	4 g
Saturated Fat	1 g

Cholesterol	5 mg
Sodium	275 mg
Carbohydrate	15 g
Dietary Fiber	2 g
Sugars	9 g

Protein	9 g

1 Tbsp olive oil
3 garlic cloves, minced
1 cup chopped cauliflower
1 cup chopped broccoli
1/2 cup chopped carrot
1/4 cup chopped celery
1/2 cup chopped onion
1 10-oz can low-fat, low-sodium chicken broth
2 Tbsp Dijon mustard
Fresh ground pepper and salt to taste
1 12-oz can evaporated skim milk
1 Tbsp minced fresh dill
2 tsp minced fresh parsley
1 Tbsp cornstarch or arrowroot powder
2 Tbsp water
1/4 cup Parmesan cheese

1. Heat the oil in a stockpot over medium heat. Add the garlic and saute for 30 seconds. Add the next five ingredients and saute for 10 minutes. Add in half the can of broth and bring to a boil. Simmer for 10 minutes. In batches, puree the contents of the stockpot in the blender. Set aside in a separate bowl.

2. In the same stockpot, heat remaining broth with the mustard, pepper, salt, and evaporated milk. Bring to a gentle simmer. Add the pureed vegetables and simmer on low for 5 minutes. Add the herbs and simmer for 2 more minutes. Mix together the cornstarch or arrowroot powder and the water. Add to the soup and cook for 2 minutes until thickened. Serve soup in bowls, garnished with Parmesan cheese.

Amazing Asparagus

When selecting asparagus, choose stalks that are neither too thick or thin, with tightly closed buds. Store upright in a shallow pan of water set in the refrigerator. This will help keep the asparagus fresh.

Asparagus steamers are fun to have—the asparagus cooks to perfection in this upright position. If not, a regular metal rack placed inside your steamer will still do nicely. Be sure to never overcook asparagus. A stalk should still be firm, not floppy, and retain its bright green color.

Creamy Tarragon Asparagus

Tarragon, a licorice-flavored herb, is very popular in French cuisine. It tastes great in this creamy sauce poured over freshly steamed asparagus.

Preparation Time:
15 minutes

6 Servings/Serving Size:
1/2 cup

Exchanges:	
2	Vegetable
1/2	Saturated Fat

Calories	78
Calories from Fat	28
Total Fat	3 g
Saturated Fat	2 g

Cholesterol	10 mg
Sodium	152 mg
Carbohydrate	8 g
Dietary Fiber	2 g
Sugars	5 g

Protein	6 g

2 1/2 lb fresh asparagus, ends snapped off
1/2 cup low-fat sour cream
1/4 cup Parmesan cheese
1 Tbsp low-fat mayonnaise
1 Tbsp tarragon
1 Tbsp lemon juice
1/2 cup evaporated skim milk
Fresh ground pepper and salt to taste

1. Rinse the asparagus and pat dry. Steam the spears in an asparagus steamer or in a metal steamer over boiling water for 8 minutes until tender-crisp.

2. Meanwhile, combine all remaining ingredients in a saucepan. Bring to a boil, lower the heat, and simmer for 5 minutes. Pour the sauce over the asparagus and serve.

Asparagus Vinaigrette

Delightfully crunchy, asparagus also tastes great cold.

Preparation Time:
15 minutes

6 Servings/Serving Size:
1/2 cup

Exchanges:
1   Vegetable
1   Monounsaturated Fat

Calories 60
  Calories from Fat 44
Total Fat ....5 g
  Saturated Fat ....1 g

Cholesterol ....0 mg
Sodium ....73 mg
Carbohydrate ....4 g
  Dietary Fiber ....1 g
  Sugars ....2 g

Protein ....2 g

1 1/2 lb fresh asparagus
1/3 cup balsamic vinegar
2 Tbsp low-fat, low-sodium chicken broth
2 Tbsp olive oil
2 tsp lemon juice
2 Tbsp Dijon mustard
2 Tbsp minced fresh parsley
2 tsp minced fresh tarragon
1 Tbsp minced fresh chives

Snap the tough ends off the asparagus. Steam the asparagus in a metal steamer over boiling water for 5–8 minutes, until asparagus is tender-crisp and bright green. Drain the asparagus and splash cold water over it to stop the cooking process. Set aside. Combine all remaining ingredients to make the vinaigrette, pour the vinaigrette over the asparagus, and serve.

Asparagus Soufflé

Serve this soufflé with fresh rolls and a sliced tomato salad for a perfect spring luncheon.

<table>
<tr><td>

Preparation Time:
25 minutes

---

6 Servings/Serving Size:
1 cup

Exchanges:

1	Vegetable
2	Lean Meat
1/2	Fat

Calories	154
Calories from Fat	79
Total Fat	9 g
Saturated Fat	3 g

Cholesterol	89 mg
Sodium	351 mg
Carbohydrate	5 g
Dietary Fiber	2 g
Sugars	2 g

Protein	15 g

</td></tr>
</table>

2 1/2 lb fresh asparagus, trimmed and cut into
  1-inch pieces
2 eggs, beaten
1 cup grated low-fat Swiss cheese
1 cup diced cooked low-fat turkey bacon
2 tsp canola oil
2 Tbsp Parmesan cheese
1 Tbsp cornstarch or arrowroot powder
1/4 cup low-fat, low-sodium chicken broth
2 egg whites, beaten until stiff

1. Preheat the oven to 350 degrees. Steam the asparagus in a metal steamer over boiling water for 5–6 minutes. Drain. Combine the asparagus with the eggs, Swiss cheese, turkey bacon, oil, and Parmesan cheese.

2. Combine the cornstarch or arrowroot powder with the chicken broth and stir until smooth. Add to the asparagus mixture. Fold in the beaten egg whites until they disappear. Pour the mixture into a greased soufflé dish and bake for 25–30 minutes until puffed and firm.

Asparagus and Cashews

Toasted cashews give crunch and flavor to fresh asparagus.

Preparation Time:
10 minutes

6 Servings/Serving Size:
1/2 cup

Exchanges:

1	Vegetable
1/2	Fat

Calories	51
Calories from Fat	34
Total Fat	4 g
Saturated Fat	1 g

Cholesterol	0 mg
Sodium	8 mg
Carbohydrate	4 g
Dietary Fiber	1 g
Sugars	1 g

Protein	2 g

1 1/2 lb fresh asparagus, trimmed and cut into 2-inch pieces
1 Tbsp sesame oil
3 Tbsp fresh lemon juice
1/2 tsp marjoram
2 Tbsp chopped toasted cashews, unsalted

Steam the asparagus in a metal steamer over boiling water for about 6–7 minutes. Drain. Combine asparagus with remaining ingredients and serve.

Asparagus and Roasted Red Pepper Salad

This colorful salad is delicious served for brunch.

Preparation Time:
15 minutes

6 Servings/Serving Size:
1/2 cup

Exchanges:
| 1 | Vegetable |
| 1 | Monounsaturated Fat |

Calories	67
Calories from Fat	45
Total Fat	5 g
Saturated Fat	0 g
Cholesterol	0 mg
Sodium	102 mg
Carbohydrate	5 g
Dietary Fiber	2 g
Sugars	3 g
Protein	2 g

2 cups steamed, sliced, fresh asparagus
1/2 cup diced roasted red pepper
1/2 cup sliced artichoke hearts
2 Tbsp olive oil
3 Tbsp fresh lemon juice
2 Tbsp red wine vinegar
1 tsp minced fresh dill
1 Tbsp minced fresh Italian parsley

Combine the asparagus, red pepper, and artichoke hearts in a salad bowl. Whisk together the remaining ingredients to make the dressing and pour over the salad. Chill and serve cold.

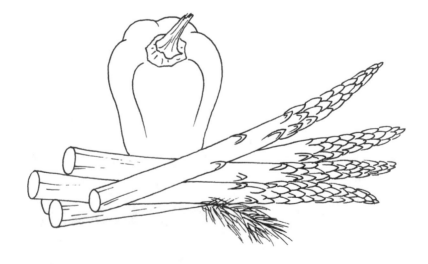

Asparagus Frittata

This frittata is delicious with fresh, warm rolls.

Preparation Time:
20 minutes

6 Servings/Serving Size:
2 eggs with 1/2 cup
vegetables

Exchanges:
2   Vegetable
2   Very Lean Meat
1/2 Monounsaturated Fat

Calories 138
  Calories from Fat 25
Total Fat ....3 g
  Saturated Fat ....0 g

Cholesterol ....0 mg
Sodium ....247 mg
Carbohydrate ....12 g
  Dietary Fiber ....3 g
  Sugars ....7 g

Protein ....17 g

3 cups diagonally sliced fresh asparagus
1 Tbsp olive oil
1/2 cup minced red onion
2 garlic cloves, minced
12 egg substitutes, beaten
1/4 cup evaporated skim milk
2 Tbsp minced fresh chives
12 thin slices tomato

1. Preheat the oven to 350 degrees. Steam the
    asparagus in a metal steamer over boiling
    water for 5–6 minutes. Drain and splash with
    cold water. Set aside. Heat the oil in a large
    oven-proof skillet (cast iron works well) over
    medium heat. Add the red onion and garlic
    and saute for 5 minutes.

2. Combine the egg substitutes with the
    evaporated skim milk. Add the chives. Pour
    over the onions and garlic and cook the
    underside for 10–12 minutes, lifting
    occasionally to let the top flow to the bottom
    and checking that the underside does not
    burn. The bottom should be golden in color
    and almost set.

3. Place the cooked asparagus on top of the egg
    and top with sliced tomatoes. Place the
    skillet in the oven and bake until the frittata
    is completely set, about 6–8 minutes. Set
    temperature to broil and broil the top for 2
    minutes. Remove the frittata from the oven
    and cut in wedges to serve.

Mushroom and Asparagus Toss

For a more exotic flavor, try to use a different mushroom like shiitake or cremini in this recipe.

Preparation Time:
20 minutes

6 Servings/Serving Size:
1/2 cup

Exchanges:
1   Vegetable
1/2 Monounsaturated Fat

Calories	50
Calories from Fat	31
Total Fat	3 g
Saturated Fat	0 g
Cholesterol	0 mg
Sodium	38 mg
Carbohydrate	4 g
Dietary Fiber	2 g
Sugars	1 g
Protein	2 g

1 Tbsp olive oil
2 garlic cloves, minced
1/4 cup minced scallions
1 1/2 cups sliced fresh asparagus
1 1/2 cups sliced mushrooms
1/2 cup low-fat, low-sodium chicken broth
Fresh ground pepper and salt to taste
1 Tbsp chopped toasted walnuts

Heat the oil in a skillet over medium-high heat. Add the garlic and scallions and saute for 30 seconds. Add the asparagus and mushrooms and saute for 5 minutes. Add the broth, cover, and steam for 3 minutes. Season with ground pepper and salt and garnish with toasted walnuts to serve.

Roasted Asparagus and Garlic

You may want to roast this aromatic vegetable dish at the same time as your dinner meat.

Preparation Time:
10 minutes

---

6 Servings/Serving Size:
1/2 cup

Exchanges:
| 1 | Vegetable |
| 1 | Monounsaturated Fat |

Calories	72
Calories from Fat	43
Total Fat	5 g
Saturated Fat	1 g

Cholesterol	0 mg
Sodium	34 mg
Carbohydrate	6 g
Dietary Fiber	2 g
Sugars	3 g

Protein	3 g

12 garlic cloves
2 Tbsp olive oil
1/4 cup dry white wine
3 cups sliced fresh asparagus
6 fresh thyme sprigs
Fresh ground pepper and salt to taste

Preheat the oven to 350 degrees. Tear off 6 large pieces aluminum foil. Divide all the ingredients on each piece of foil. Fold over each foil packet to seal it. Place the packets on a baking sheet and roast in the oven for 25–30 minutes until the asparagus is tender.

Asparagus, Orange, and Endive Salad

Raspberry vinegar is the key ingredient in this fruity-tasting salad.

Preparation Time:
15 minutes

6 Servings/Serving Size:
1 cup

Exchanges:

1/2	Fruit
1	Vegetable
1	Monounsaturated Fat

Calories	98
Calories from Fat	46
Total Fat	5 g
Saturated Fat	0 g

Cholesterol	0 mg
Sodium	35 mg
Carbohydrate	13 g
Dietary Fiber	3 g
Sugars	9 g

Protein	3 g

2 1/2 cups diagonally sliced fresh asparagus
2 cups torn endive leaves
2 small oranges, peeled, sliced into rings, and
  seeded
1 small red onion, very thinly sliced
1/3 cup raspberry vinegar
2 Tbsp canola oil
1 Tbsp orange juice
1 Tbsp sugar
Fresh ground pepper and salt to taste

1. Add the asparagus to a large pot of boiling water and blanch for 1 minute. Drain and plunge the asparagus into a bowl of cold water. Drain again. Dry the asparagus. Combine the asparagus with the endive, oranges, and red onion.

2. Whisk together the remaining dressing ingredients. Add the dressing to the asparagus-endive mixture, toss well, and serve.

Spring Menus

April Fool's Dinner

Scallops with Tarragon Mustard Sauce

Quick Vegetable Medley

Broccoli Slaw

Chocolate Mocha Torte

189–192

Easter Celebration

Spinach Poppers

Honey Lamb Chops

Roasted Potato and Carrot Salad

Bananas Flambé

193–196

A Day in Bermuda

Piña Coladas

Tropical Chicken Salad

Citrus Rice

Coconut Pudding Squares

197–200

Cinco de Mayo

Spicy Salsa

Crispy Chips

Mexican Roll-Ups

Zesty Mexican Cauliflower

*Sliced Mangoes and Papayas
with Lime*

201–205

Mother's Day
Brunch

Elegant Leek Soup

Herbed Crab Sandwiches

*Raspberry Poppy Seed
Dressing*

Chocolate Mint Cheesecake

206–209

On the
Italian Riviera

Tomato Crostini

*Mediterranean Game
Hens*

Orzo with Herbs

Amaretto Rice Pudding

210–213

Scallops with Tarragon Mustard Sauce

This subtle sauce is a great complement to the flavor of fresh scallops.

Preparation Time:
35 minutes

6 Servings/Serving Size:
3 oz

Exchanges:

1/2	Starch
1	Skim Milk
3	Very Lean Meat

Calories	245
Calories from Fat	38
Total Fat	4 g
Saturated Fat	2 g
Cholesterol	47 mg
Sodium	611 mg
Carbohydrate	20 g
Dietary Fiber	0 g
Sugars	15 g
Protein	30 g

1/2 cup dry white wine
1/2 cup low-fat, low-sodium chicken broth
2 shallots, minced
2 12-oz cans evaporated skim milk
1/4 cup smooth Dijon mustard
1/4 cup coarse Dijon mustard
1 Tbsp butter
1 1/2 lb sea scallops
1/4 cup finely minced fresh parsley

1. In a skillet over medium-high heat, heat the wine, broth, and shallots until the liquid is reduced by one-third. Add the milk, lower the heat, and reduce again by one-third. Add the mustard and stir until smooth. Do not boil.

2. In another skillet, melt the butter. Add the scallops and cook about 3–4 minutes until scallops turn opaque. Place the scallops on plates and spoon the sauce over them. Garnish with parsley.

Quick Vegetable Medley

This is a quick accompaniment to fish or chicken.

Preparation Time:
10 minutes

6 Servings/Serving Size:
1/2 cup

Exchanges:	
1	Vegetable

Calories	26
Calories from Fat	0
Total Fat	0 g
Saturated Fat	0 g

Cholesterol	0 mg
Sodium	40 mg
Carbohydrate	3 g
Dietary Fiber	1 g
Sugars	1 g

Protein	1 g

3 cups mixed vegetables, frozen and thawed
   (include broccoli, cauliflower, and carrots)
1 cup white wine
1 Tbsp minced fresh dill
1 tsp minced garlic
1 Tbsp fresh lemon juice
Fresh ground pepper and salt to taste

Combine all ingredients in a saucepan and cook over medium-high heat for 5–6 minutes. Remove the vegetables with a slotted spoon and keep warm. Bring the liquid remaining in the pot to a boil. Lower the heat and reduce by one-third. Pour over the cooked vegetables and serve.

Season vegetables with herbs, spices, or lemon juice instead of butter.

Broccoli Slaw

Often just tossed away, nutrition-providing broccoli stems are put to good use in this slaw.

Preparation Time:
20 minutes

6 Servings/Serving Size:
1/2 cup

Exchanges:
1	Vegetable
1	Monounsaturated Fat

Calories	59
Calories from Fat	42
Total Fat	5 g
Saturated Fat	1 g

Cholesterol	0 mg
Sodium	14 mg
Carbohydrate	5 g
Dietary Fiber	1 g
Sugars	3 g

Protein	1 g

1 1/2 cups shredded broccoli stems (peel the broccoli stems until smooth; shred by hand or in a food processor with a shredder or julienne blade)
1 cup shredded carrot
1/2 cup diced red and yellow pepper
1/4 cup balsamic vinegar
2 Tbsp olive oil
1 Tbsp minced fresh basil
1/2 Tbsp minced fresh oregano
1 Tbsp minced scallions
2 Tbsp lemon juice

In a large salad bowl, combine the first three ingredients. In a blender, combine all remaining ingredients for the dressing. Blend until smooth. Pour the dressing over the slaw and toss well. Serve immediately, or refrigerate before serving.

Chocolate Mocha Torte

This dessert is an elegant way to end the meal.

Preparation Time:
20 minutes

12 Servings/Serving Size:
1 custard cup

Exchanges:

2	Carbohydrate
1	Fat

Calories	204
Calories from Fat	68
Total Fat	**8 g**
Saturated Fat	4 g

Cholesterol	**16 mg**
Sodium	**262 mg**
Carbohydrate	**26 g**
Dietary Fiber	1 g
Sugars	12 g

Protein	**8 g**

5 Tbsp low-calorie margarine
1/4 cup chopped nuts (any variety)
2 tsp cinnamon
1 cup white flour
8 oz low-fat cream cheese
3 Tbsp sugar
1 1/2 cups lite nondairy whipped topping
2 tsp instant coffee
1 package artificially sweetened, low-fat, instant
   vanilla pudding
1 package artificially sweetened, low-fat, instant
   chocolate pudding
3 cups evaporated skim milk

1. Preheat the oven to 375 degrees. Mix together the margarine, nuts, cinnamon, and white flour. Press into a baking dish and bake until lightly brown. Remove from oven and let cool. Break into pieces and divide into custard cups.

2. Blend together the cream cheese, sugar, and 1 cup of the nondairy whipped topping. Add the coffee and cinnamon and beat well. Pour over the crust in each custard cup. Mix together the puddings and evaporated milk until thick. Spread on top of the cream cheese mixture in each custard cup. Place a dollop of the remaining nondairy topping over each cup to serve.

Spinach Poppers

Have your guests snack on these appetizers while the rest of the Easter dinner is cooking. You need mini-muffin tins for this recipe!

Preparation Time: 15 minutes	

6 Servings/Serving Size:
2–3 poppers

Exchanges:

2	Vegetable
1	Medium-Fat Meat

Calories	121
Calories from Fat	52
Total Fat	6 g
Saturated Fat	3 g
Cholesterol	86 mg
Sodium	272 mg
Carbohydrate	8 g
Dietary Fiber	2 g
Sugars	3 g
Protein	10 g

1 15-oz can artichoke hearts, drained and chopped
1 10-oz package chopped spinach, thawed and drained
1 cup part-skim ricotta cheese
2 eggs, beaten
1 garlic clove, minced
1/4 cup minced red onion
1/2 tsp minced fresh oregano
1/4 cup shredded part-skim mozzarella cheese
Fresh ground pepper and salt to taste
Nonstick cooking spray

Preheat the oven to 350 degrees. Mix all ingredients together in a large bowl. Spray mini-muffin tins with nonstick cooking spray and fill with popper batter. Bake for 25–30 minutes, remove from the oven, and serve.

Honey Lamb Chops

Mustard and honey gently flavor these lamb chops.

Preparation Time:
10 minutes

6 Servings/Serving Size:
2–3 oz

Exchanges:

1/2	Carbohydrate
2	Lean Meat

Calories 139
  Calories from Fat 54
Total Fat ....6 g
  Saturated Fat.............2 g

Cholesterol ....52 mg
Sodium...................45 mg
Carbohydrate...............5 g
  Dietary Fiber ....0 g
  Sugars.......................5 g

Protein........................16 g

2 Tbsp honey
2 Tbsp fresh lemon juice
2 Tbsp minced fresh rosemary
1/2 tsp Dijon mustard
1 tsp minced garlic
1 tsp onion powder
1/2 tsp dry mustard
6 5-oz lamb chops, trimmed of fat
6 sprigs fresh mint

Combine all ingredients except the lamb chops and mint in a small bowl and microwave for 1 minute. Brush the mixture on the chops and broil or grill, turning frequently, according to the following guidelines: 12 minutes for rare, 15 minutes for medium, and 18 minutes for well done. Garnish with mint and serve.

Roasted Potato and Carrot Salad

Roasting carrots and potatoes brings out all their natural sugars.

Preparation Time:
20 minutes

6 Servings/Serving Size:
1/2 cup

Exchanges:
1	Starch
1/2	Monounsaturated Fat

Calories	107
Calories from Fat	41
Total Fat	5 g
Saturated Fat	1 g

Cholesterol	0 mg
Sodium	31 mg
Carbohydrate	14 g
Dietary Fiber	3 g
Sugars	3 g

Protein	2 g

1 1/2 cups diced red potatoes, unpeeled
1 1/2 cups thickly sliced carrots
4 shallots, minced
3 garlic cloves, minced
1 Tbsp lemon juice
2 Tbsp olive oil
1 cup dry white wine
1 tsp cumin
Romaine lettuce leaves

Place all ingredients except the lettuce in a large roasting pan. Toss lightly to coat the vegetables well and roast, covered, for 45–60 minutes until the potatoes and carrots are very tender. Remove the vegetables from the oven and chill. To serve, place the lettuce in a large salad bowl or platter and top with the roasted vegetables.

Bananas Flambé

This holiday classic is great served this time of year.

Preparation Time:
5 minutes

6 Servings/Serving Size:
1 banana with 1/2 cup yogurt

Exchanges:
2 1/2   Carbohydrate

Calories 195
 Calories from Fat 20
Total Fat ....2 g
 Saturated Fat.............0 g

Cholesterol ....0 mg
Sodium....................97 mg
Carbohydrate............37 g
 Dietary Fiber ....2 g
 Sugars......................17 g

Protein..........................5 g

6 small ripe bananas, peeled and sliced
2 Tbsp low-calorie margarine
1 Tbsp brown sugar
1/2 tsp allspice
2 oz dark rum
3 cups sugar-free, low-fat, vanilla frozen yogurt

Melt the margarine in a skillet. Add the bananas and sprinkle with the sugar and allspice. Saute until bananas are browned. Add the rum and ignite with a long match. When the flames die down, serve bananas with vanilla yogurt.

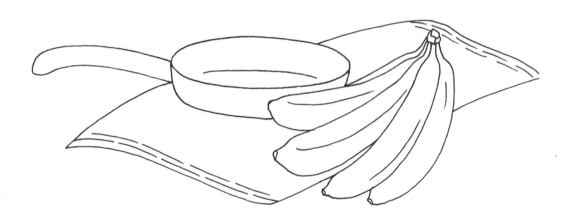

Piña Coladas

This is the perfect tropical drink for warm spring nights.

Preparation Time:
5 minutes

6 Servings/Serving Size:
1 cup

Exchanges:
1	Fruit
1/2	Skim Milk

Calories..........................99
  Calories from Fat..........4
Total Fat ....0 g
  Saturated Fat.............0 g

Cholesterol ....2 mg
Sodium....................64 mg
Carbohydrate.............20 g
  Dietary Fiber ....1 g
  Sugars.....................16 g

Protein.........................5 g

2 medium bananas
1 cup diced pineapple
1 tsp coconut extract
2 Tbsp lime juice
3 tsp sugar
3 cups skim milk
1 cup ice cubes

Place the bananas in a blender and puree. Add the remaining ingredients and puree until smooth.

Tropical Chicken Salad

Crunchy and sweet, this salad can't be beat!

Preparation Time:
10 minutes

6 Servings/Serving Size:
1 cup

Exchanges:

1	Fruit
1	Very Lean Meat
1/2	Fat

Calories	156
Calories from Fat	27
Total Fat	3 g
Saturated Fat	1 g

Cholesterol	42 mg
Sodium	143 mg
Carbohydrate	17 g
Dietary Fiber	2 g
Sugars	14 g

Protein	16 g

2 cups diced cooked chicken breast
1/2 cup sliced celery
1/2 cup chopped mango
1/4 cup sliced water chestnuts
2 cups diced pineapple, canned and drained or fresh
1 cup mandarin oranges, packed in their own juice and drained
1/4 cup low-fat mayonnaise
2 Tbsp low-fat sour cream
1 tsp coconut extract

Combine all ingredients and refrigerate for 1–2 hours before serving.

Citrus Rice

Cooking rice in chicken broth instead of water guarantees instant flavor.

Preparation Time:
15 minutes

12 Servings/Serving Size:
1/2 cup

Exchanges:
1 1/2   Starch

Calories........................114
  Calories from Fat........14
Total Fat ....2 g
  Saturated Fat.............0 g

Cholesterol ....0 mg
Sodium....................44 mg
Carbohydrate............23 g
  Dietary Fiber ....1 g
  Sugars........................2 g

Protein........................3 g

3 1/2 cups low-fat, low-sodium chicken broth
1 1/2 cups raw basmati rice, rinsed
2 tsp olive oil
1/4 cup minced onion
1/2 cup each diced red and yellow peppers
2 Tbsp chopped scallions
1/2 cup mandarin oranges, packed in their own juice
2 Tbsp orange juice
1 Tbsp lemon juice
Fresh ground pepper and salt to taste

1. In a large pot, bring the broth to a boil. Slowly add the rice and return to a boil. Cover, reduce heat to low, and cook for 15–20 minutes until the rice has absorbed the broth.

2. Meanwhile, heat the oil in a medium skillet over medium-high heat. Add the onion and peppers and saute for 5 minutes. Add the scallions and saute for 3 more minutes. Add the oranges and orange juice and cook for 5 minutes. Add the cooked rice, lemon juice, pepper, and salt and toss well to serve.

Coconut Pudding Squares

You can use a different-flavored extract in these creamy squares
if you wish.

Preparation Time:
15 minutes

12 Servings/Serving Size:
One 3/4-inch square

Exchanges:
2   Carbohydrate

Calories	160
Calories from Fat	22
Total Fat	2 g
Saturated Fat	1 g

Cholesterol	3 mg
Sodium	231 mg
Carbohydrate	27 g
Dietary Fiber	1 g
Sugars	16 g

Protein	7 g

15 graham crackers
1 package artificially sweetened, low-fat, instant
vanilla pudding
1 package artificially sweetened, low-fat, instant
coconut pudding
2 cups low-fat whipped topping
4 cups evaporated skim milk
1/4 tsp almond extract
1 cup chopped peaches, canned or fresh
1 cup mandarin oranges, packed in their own
juice, drained

Place half the graham crackers in a 9-inch
square pan. Mix together the remaining
ingredients except for the mandarin oranges.
Pour the pudding mixture over the graham
crackers. Add another layer of graham
crackers. Top with pudding mixture, garnish
with oranges, and chill for 4 hours. Cut into 12
servings and serve.

Spicy Salsa

A Mexican meal is incomplete without salsa and chips!

Preparation Time:
20 minutes

12 Servings/Serving Size:
1/4 cup

Exchanges:
1   Vegetable

Calories 20
  Calories from Fat 2
Total Fat ....0 g
  Saturated Fat.............0 g

Cholesterol ....0 mg
Sodium.....................7 mg
Carbohydrate.............5 g
  Dietary Fiber ....1 g
  Sugars.......................3 g

Protein.........................1 g

6 small tomatoes, peeled, seeded, and chopped
1/2 cup diced red onion
1/4 cup diced yellow onion
3 serrano peppers, minced
1/4 cup minced cilantro
1/2 cup minced fresh parsley
3 garlic cloves, minced
3 Tbsp red wine vinegar

Combine all ingredients and chill in the refrigerator for several hours before serving.

When talking,

some people throw stones;

others spread flowers.

Crispy Chips

Make your own chips without the fat!

Preparation Time:	
5 minutes	

6 Servings/Serving Size:
8 chips

Exchanges:

1/2	Starch

Calories	56
Calories from Fat	6
Total Fat	1 g
Saturated Fat	0 g

Cholesterol	0 mg
Sodium	41 mg
Carbohydrate	12 g
Dietary Fiber	1 g
Sugars	0 g

Protein	1 g

6 corn (blue or yellow) tortillas
Water
Chili powder

Preheat the oven to 450 degrees. Dip each tortilla quickly in water (this helps to crisp the chip). Stack the tortillas on top of each other. Cut the stack into 8 triangles. Lay the triangles on a nonstick cookie sheet. Sprinkle the chips with chili powder. Bake in the oven for 5–8 minutes until crisp.

Mexican Roll-Ups

These roll-up sandwiches are easy to make and fun to eat!

Preparation Time:
15 minutes

6 Servings/Serving Size:
3 oz roast beef in a 12-inch tortilla

Exchanges:

2	Starch
1	Vegetable
4	Lean Meat
1/2	Monounsaturated Fat

Calories	426
Calories from Fat	147
Total Fat	16 g
Saturated Fat	4 g

Cholesterol	86 mg
Sodium	475 mg
Carbohydrate	34 g
Dietary Fiber	2 g
Sugars	3 g

Protein	33 g

6 12-inch whole-wheat flour tortillas
6 large romaine lettuce leaves
1 1/4 lb thinly sliced cooked roast beef
1 cup diced tomatoes
1 cup diced red and yellow peppers
2 Tbsp olive oil
3 Tbsp red wine vinegar
2 tsp cumin

1. For each roll-up, tear off about a 15-inch piece of either waxed paper or aluminum foil. Place the tortilla flat on the paper or foil. Place a romaine lettuce leaf on top of the tortilla. Add 3 oz beef on top of the lettuce. Divide the tomatoes, peppers, oil, vinegar, and cumin over the beef for each roll-up.

2. Begin rolling the paper or foil over the tortilla to encase the filling. Roll until the sandwich is completely rolled up. Fold the excess paper or foil over the top and bottom of the roll-up. To eat, peel back the paper or foil.

Zesty Mexican Cauliflower

The sauce in this recipe is great over a baked potato, too.

Preparation Time:
15 minutes

6 Servings/Serving Size:
1/2 cup

Exchanges:

1	Starch

Calories	77
Calories from Fat	21
Total Fat	2 g
Saturated Fat	1 g

Cholesterol	8 mg
Sodium	129 mg
Carbohydrate	12 g
Dietary Fiber	2 g
Sugars	3 g

Protein	4 g

1 1/2 cups cauliflower florets
1/2 cup low-fat sour cream
1 Tbsp low-fat mayonnaise
1 tsp hot pepper sauce
1/2 cup salsa
1/4 cup low-fat shredded Cheddar cheese
1 1/2 cups cooked fresh corn

Cook the cauliflower florets by steaming them over boiling water for 5 minutes until tender. Drain and set aside. Combine all sauce ingredients in a large saucepan and cook over medium heat until bubbly, stirring constantly. Add the cooked cauliflower and corn. Toss well and serve.

Sliced Mangoes and Papayas with Lime

Cool down this spicy meal with this refreshing fruit.

Preparation Time:	
10 minutes	

6 Servings/Serving Size:
1/2 cup

Exchanges:

1 1/2	Fruit

Calories	87
Calories from Fat	3
Total Fat	0 g
Saturated Fat	0 g
Cholesterol	0 mg
Sodium	3 mg
Carbohydrate	23 g
Dietary Fiber	3 g
Sugars	18 g
Protein	1 g

1 medium papaya, peeled and thinly sliced
2 medium mangoes, peeled and cut into 2-inch
    cubes
1/4 cup fresh lime juice
2 tsp sugar

On a platter, place the papaya slices in a circular fan pattern. Pile the mango chunks in the center of the papayas. Combine the lime juice and sugar and stir until the sugar is dissolved. Sprinkle the mixture over the papayas and mangoes and serve.

The smile you show the world comes back.

Elegant Leek Soup

Be sure to thoroughly wash the leeks before using them in this soup. They tend to collect a lot of dirt within their leaves.

Preparation Time:
25 minutes

6 Servings/Serving Size:
1 cup

Exchanges:
1/2	Starch
1	Skim Milk
1/2	Saturated Fat

Calories	156
Calories from Fat	22
Total Fat	2 g
Saturated Fat	1 g

Cholesterol	7 mg
Sodium	186 mg
Carbohydrate	24 g
Dietary Fiber	2 g
Sugars	10 g

Protein	10 g

1 tsp butter
2 shallots, chopped
1 1/2 cups cleaned, chopped leeks (bottoms only)
1 cup blush wine
2 medium potatoes, peeled and diced
2 cups low-fat, low-sodium chicken broth
1 1/2 cups skim milk
1 1/2 cups evaporated skim milk
2 Tbsp crumbled blue cheese

Melt the butter in a stockpot over medium-high heat. Add the shallots and leeks and cook for 10 minutes. Add the wine, potatoes, and broth, bring to a boil, and cook until potatoes are soft. Add all other ingredients except the cheese and heat through, but do not boil. To serve, top individual bowls of soup with blue cheese.

Herbed Crab Sandwiches

Crab and cream cheese are a great combination. (These sandwiches are relatively high in sodium.)

Preparation Time:
15 minutes

---

6 Servings/Serving Size:
1 English muffin, 3 oz crab

Exchanges:

2	Starch
3	Lean Meat

Calories 326
 Calories from Fat 97
Total Fat ....11 g
 Saturated Fat..............5 g

Cholesterol ....163 mg
Sodium..................703 mg
Carbohydrate............32 g
 Dietary Fiber ....2 g
 Sugars.......................7 g

Protein........................24 g

1 1/2 lb lump crab meat
1/4 cup low-fat mayonnaise
1 Tbsp minced fresh parsley
1 Tbsp minced fresh tarragon
2 Tbsp minced scallions
6 oz low-fat cream cheese
2 eggs, beaten
1 tsp Dijon mustard
6 English muffins, split and toasted
6 slices tomato

Combine the crab, mayonnaise, parsley, tarragon, and scallions in a medium bowl. In a separate bowl, beat together the cream cheese, eggs, and mustard. Spread the crab mixture over the English muffins. Spread the cream cheese mixture on top, and broil the muffins 6 inches from the heat source for 3 minutes. Add the tomato slices and broil again for 2 more minutes.

Raspberry Poppy Seed Dressing

Serve this dressing with a crisp spinach salad.

Preparation Time:
5 minutes

12 Servings/Serving Size:
2 Tbsp

Exchanges:
1/2	Carbohydrate
1/2	Monounsaturated Fat

Calories	47
Calories from Fat	26
Total Fat	3 g
Saturated Fat	0 g

Cholesterol	0 mg
Sodium	9 mg
Carbohydrate	6 g
Dietary Fiber	0 g
Sugars	5 g

Protein	0 g

2 Tbsp sugar
1 1/2 tsp Dijon mustard
1 cup raspberry vinegar
1 garlic clove, minced
1 tsp onion powder
1 1/2 tsp poppy seeds
2 Tbsp canola oil
1 cup water
1 tsp unflavored gelatin

Whisk all ingredients together in a medium bowl and microwave for 2 minutes on high. Chill before serving.

Chocolate Mint Cheesecake

This special dessert is a perfect ending to any meal.

Preparation Time:
20 minutes

12 Servings/Serving Size:
1/12th of cake

Exchanges:
1 1/2	Carbohydrate
2	Saturated Fat

Calories	209
Calories from Fat	107
Total Fat	12 g
Saturated Fat	7 g

Cholesterol	65 mg
Sodium	248 mg
Carbohydrate	22 g
Dietary Fiber	2 g
Sugars	12 g

Protein	6 g

1 1/4 cups graham cracker crumbs
1 Tbsp butter, melted
1 Tbsp water
2 Tbsp cocoa powder
16 oz low-fat cream cheese
1/4 cup sugar
1/4 cup peppermint schnapps
2 eggs, beaten
3/4 cup cocoa
1 tsp vanilla

1. Preheat the oven to 325 degrees. To make the crust, combine the first four ingredients. Press into the bottom of a springform pan and bake for 5 minutes. Remove crust from oven and let cool.

2. Combine the cream cheese and sugar and beat well. Add the remaining ingredients and pour over the crust. Raise the oven temperature to 375 degrees and bake for 40 minutes until set. Cool before serving.

Tomato Crostini

Fresh tomatoes are delicious in the spring and summer.

Preparation Time:
10 minutes

6 Servings/Serving Size:
2 slices bread

Exchanges:
2 1/2   Starch
1/2 Monounsaturated Fat

Calories......................230
 Calories from Fat........46
Total Fat ....5 g
 Saturated Fat.............1 g

Cholesterol ....1 mg
Sodium..................438 mg
Carbohydrate.............39 g
 Dietary Fiber ....2 g
 Sugars.......................4 g

Protein.........................6 g

12 slices Italian bread (about 1 1/2 inches thick)
2 garlic cloves, cut in half
1 Tbsp olive oil
1 cup finely diced, seeded tomatoes
2 tsp capers
2 tsp minced black olives
2 tsp minced fresh basil
1 tsp minced fresh oregano
Fresh ground pepper and salt to taste

Preheat the oven to 350 degrees. Rub each slice of Italian bread with the garlic and brush with some of the olive oil. Place the bread slices on a cookie sheet and toast in the oven for 3–4 minutes. Combine the remaining ingredients in a small bowl. Place a spoonful of the tomato mixture on each bread slice and serve.

Mediterranean Game Hens

Classic Italian seasonings are best for these hens.

Preparation Time:
10 minutes

6 Servings/Serving Size:
1/2 hen without skin

Exchanges:
2   Very Lean Meat

Calories.........................68
 Calories from Fat........22
Total Fat ....2 g
 Saturated Fat.............1 g

Cholesterol ....47 mg
Sodium.....................30 mg
Carbohydrate...............1 g
 Dietary Fiber ....0 g
 Sugars........................0 g

Protein........................10 g

3 Cornish game hens
3 lemons, sliced
24 fresh rosemary sprigs
6 garlic cloves
6 tsp olive oil

1. Preheat the oven to 375 degrees. Wash and dry the game hens inside and out and remove the giblets. With poultry shears, cut each hen in half.

2. In the bottom of a large roasting pan, place the lemons, rosemary sprigs, and garlic. Place the hens on top and brush them with oil. Roast the hens in the oven for 40–45 minutes until they are tender and their juices run clear.

Orzo with Herbs

Fresh herbs will make this orzo especially flavorful.

Preparation Time:
10 minutes

---

6 Servings/Serving Size:
1 cup

Exchanges:
3   Starch
1/2 Monounsaturated Fat

Calories 254
  Calories from Fat 49
Total Fat ....5 g
  Saturated Fat.............1 g

Cholesterol ....0 mg
Sodium....................25 mg
Carbohydrate............44 g
  Dietary Fiber ....1 g
  Sugars.......................3 g

Protein..........................7 g

6 cups hot cooked orzo
2 Tbsp minced fresh basil
1 Tbsp minced fresh rosemary
1 tsp minced fresh oregano
1/2 tsp minced fresh thyme
1/2 tsp minced fresh sage
2 Tbsp minced fresh Italian parsley
2 Tbsp olive oil
1 Tbsp balsamic vinegar
1 tsp lemon juice
Fresh ground pepper and salt to taste

Combine all ingredients and serve at room temperature.

* * * * * * * * * * * * * *

Luck may
sometimes help;
work always does.

* * * * * * * * * * * * * *

Amaretto Rice Pudding

Amaretto is the secret ingredient in this smooth rice pudding.

Preparation Time:
20 minutes

6 Servings/Serving Size:
1/2 cup

Exchanges:
3 1/2	Carbohydrate
1/2	Saturated Fat

Calories	312
Calories from Fat	33
Total Fat	4 g
Saturated Fat	2 g
Cholesterol	81 mg
Sodium	234 mg
Carbohydrate	54 g
Dietary Fiber	3 g
Sugars	33 g
Protein	17 g

1/2 cup chopped dried peaches
1/4 cup Amaretto
1/2 cup uncooked white rice
4 cups evaporated skim milk
2 tsp butter
1/4 cup sugar
2 eggs, beaten
Cinnamon
Nutmeg

1. Soak the peaches in the Amaretto for 10 minutes. Set aside. Combine the rice, milk, butter, and sugar in a saucepan. Bring to a boil, lower the heat, and cook until the rice has absorbed the milk but the mixture is creamy, about 15–20 minutes. Stir constantly so the milk does not curdle.

2. Add the peaches and cook 1 more minute. Remove from the heat and add eggs. Return to the heat and cook for about 5 minutes until the mixture is creamy. To serve, sprinkle individual dishes of rice pudding with cinnamon and nutmeg.

Summer

Fire Up the Grill!

Grilling fresh meats, vegetables, and fruits is an ideal way to add tremendous flavor without much fuss—and cooking outdoors is easy, fun, and great for entertaining! With a little practice, almost anyone can become a grill master. Here are some tips to help you become proficient.

✤ Choose the type of grill that best fits your lifestyle. A charcoal kettle grill will impart a great, smoky flavor to food, but it is slow to start and messier to deal with because of the briquettes. Choices of fuel for charcoal kettles include standard briquettes and instant lighting briquettes. The former take longer to heat up, and the latter start quickly, but are more expensive. A gas grill is easy to start, but delivers a less authentic smoky flavor. You can achieve a desired flavor with good recipes and specialty wood chips, however. Electric grills are easy to use and deliver very predictable cooking results, but they are getting harder to find, and you also need to use wood chips to flavor the food.

✤ Set your cooking temperature carefully! Charcoal grills will generally be ready after 25–30 minutes. Gas grills have their own temperature controls, so simply set to the desired heat level. If your grill has lava rocks, they need about 15 minutes to heat. You'll need some practice to find the best temperature for different recipes on an electric grill.

Cooking techniques for best grilling results

☼ Allow any marinated food to come to room temperature before grilling it. Otherwise, the food may stick to the grill.

☼ Before cooking, brush the grill with oil using a long-handled grill brush, or spray the rack with cooking spray. This will also prevent sticking and help the food achieve even grill marks.

☼ Avoid pressing down on burgers as they cook, or piercing meats to see if they're done. This causes the natural, flavorful juices of the food to be lost.

☼ Buy long barbecue mitts that come up to your elbows to protect yourself against the intense heat of the fire. Also, wear suitable clothing, such as a large apron, and be sure to avoid loose sleeves.

☼ Purchase all long-handled barbecue equipment. A basting brush, spatula, and tongs should all be part of your set. A wire grill brush is also a must for easy clean-up. Use drip pans underneath the food to catch any excess fat.

☼ Never use gasoline to ignite a charcoal grill, and never add lighter fluid to an existing fire!

Marinades

All of the following liquid marinades yield 2 cups and can be used on 1 1/2 lb of meat. (The marinade contributes about 1/2 Fat Exchange, 2 1/2 grams of fat, and 22 1/2 calories to the average recipe, depending on the type of oil used.)

White Wine Marinade
1 1/2 cups dry white wine
2 Tbsp olive oil
1 small onion, sliced
1 small carrot, sliced
1 Tbsp chopped fresh basil
1 tsp crushed black peppercorns

Sesame Soy Marinade
1 1/2 cups low-fat, low-sodium
  chicken broth
3 Tbsp lite soy sauce
1 Tbsp sesame oil
2 tsp toasted sesame seeds
2 Tbsp orange juice

Garlic Herb Marinade
1/2 cup minced mixed fresh herbs
  (try basil, rosemary, or thyme)
1 cup dry white wine
5 garlic cloves, crushed
1 Tbsp black peppercorns
1/2 cup low-fat, low-sodium chicken
  broth
1 Tbsp olive oil

Spicy Marinade
1/2 cup sherry vinegar
1 cup low-fat, low-sodium chicken
  broth
2 Tbsp olive oil
1 jalapeno pepper, minced
2 garlic cloves, minced

Sweet Red Wine Marinade
1 1/2 cups dry red wine
2 Tbsp canola oil
1 tsp cinnamon
1/4 tsp ground ginger
1/4 tsp cloves
2 tsp sugar

Dry Rubs

Dry rubs are mixtures of dry herbs and spices rubbed on meat. They can be prepared and stored in a shaker bottle for easy use. You can also use them to wake up vegetables and salads. Rub the meat with a little flavored oil before adding the spices to help them adhere.

Zippy Barbecue Rub
2 Tbsp each garlic and onion powder
2 tsp chili powder
2 tsp ground oregano
2 tsp dried thyme
3 tsp paprika
1/2 tsp cayenne pepper

Rosemary Blend
1/4 cup dried rosemary
2 Tbsp garlic powder
2 tsp onion powder
1 tsp cayenne pepper
2 Tbsp dried thyme

Cinnamon Blend
1/4 cup cinnamon
2 Tbsp nutmeg
1 Tbsp ground ginger
2 tsp cloves

Garlic-Stuffed Sirloin Steak

The flavors of mellow garlic and juicy beef mingle in every bite!

Preparation Time:
20 minutes

6 Servings/Serving Size:
3–4 oz

Exchanges:
4   Lean Meat

Calories......................220
  Calories from Fat........80
Total Fat ....9 g
  Saturated Fat.............3 g

Cholesterol ....88 mg
Sodium....................91 mg
Carbohydrate..............3 g
  Dietary Fiber ....0 g
  Sugars.......................2 g

Protein ....31 g

1 Tbsp olive oil
1/4 cup finely chopped garlic
1/2 cup minced scallions
Fresh ground pepper and salt to taste
2 1/2 lb boneless top sirloin steak, cut 2 inches
  thick

1. Heat the oil in a medium skillet over medium
    heat. Add the garlic and saute for 5 minutes.
    Add the scallions and cook for 5 more
    minutes. Add the pepper and salt. Remove
    from the heat and let cool. Prepare an outside
    grill with an oiled rack set 6 inches above the
    heat source. On a gas grill, set the heat to
    medium.

2. Trim the excess fat from the steak. Make a
    horizontal slice through the center of the
    steak, parallel to the surface of the meat,
    about 1 inch from each side. Cut to, but not
    through, the opposite side. Spoon the stuffing
    into the pocket, spreading evenly. Secure the
    opening with toothpicks. Grill the steak,
    turning once, according to the following
    guidelines: 15–20 minutes for rare, 25–30
    minutes for medium, or 35–40 minutes for
    well done. Remove the toothpicks and slice to
    serve.

This adapted recipe is courtesy of the Beef Board and Veal Committee/Beef Industry Council.

Old-Fashioned Barbecued Sirloin

Instead of slapping on commercial barbecue sauce, let this sirloin marinate overnight for an authentic smoky taste.

Preparation Time:
10 minutes

6 Servings/Serving Size:
3–4 oz

Exchanges:
4   Lean Meat

Calories......................227
  Calories from Fat........91
Total Fat.....................10 g
  Saturated Fat............3 g

Cholesterol............87 mg
Sodium...................77 mg
Carbohydrate..............3 g
  Dietary Fiber.............1 g
  Sugars......................1 g

Protein......................30 g

1 Tbsp chili powder
2 tsp minced ginger
2 garlic cloves, minced
1 small onion, minced
1/3 cup lemon juice
2 Tbsp olive oil
2 tsp paprika
2 lb boneless top sirloin steak, well trimmed

1. Combine all marinade ingredients, then add the sirloin and marinate in the refrigerator overnight. Prepare an outside grill with an oiled rack set 6 inches above the heat source. On a gas grill, set the heat to medium.

2. Grill the sirloin, turning once, according to the following guidelines: 15–20 minutes for rare, 25–30 minutes for medium, or 35–40 minutes for well done. Carve into thin slices to serve.

Grilled Filet Au Poivre

Try these tender filets on a special occasion.

Preparation Time:
10 minutes

6 Servings/Serving Size:
3–4 oz

Exchanges:

3	Lean Meat

Calories	166
Calories from Fat	91
Total Fat	10 g
Saturated Fat	3 g

Cholesterol	55 mg
Sodium	428 mg
Carbohydrate	0 g
Dietary Fiber	0 g
Sugars	0 g

Protein	18 g

4 5-oz filet mignon steaks
2 tsp olive oil
5 Tbsp coarsely cracked black peppercorns
1 tsp salt

1. Rub each filet with some of the olive oil. Place the peppercorns on a piece of waxed paper. Press the steaks into the peppercorns to coat.

2. Prepare an outside grill with an oiled rack set 6 inches above the heat source. On a gas grill, set the heat to medium. Grill the filets, turning once, according to the following guidelines: 10–12 minutes for rare, 12–15 minutes for medium, or 17–18 minutes for well done.

The
sun comes forth
and goes down in a
circle. The moon does the
same, and both are round.
Even the seasons form a great
circle in their changing, and
always come back again to
where they were.

—Black Elk
Oglala Sioux

Honey-Mustard Steak

The tang of spicy brown mustard and the sweetness of apple juice make this steak a stand-out.

Preparation Time:
5 minutes

6 Servings/Serving Size:
3–4 oz

Exchanges:
3   Lean Meat

Calories	158
Calories from Fat	51
Total Fat	6 g
Saturated Fat	2 g
Cholesterol	65 mg
Sodium	300 mg
Carbohydrate	2 g
Dietary Fiber	0 g
Sugars	2 g
Protein	23 g

1/2 cup spicy brown mustard
2 Tbsp apple juice concentrate
1 tsp cinnamon
1 Tbsp honey
1 1/2 lb boneless top sirloin steak, well trimmed

1. Prepare an outside grill with an oiled rack set 6 inches above the heat source. On a gas grill, set the heat to medium.

2. Mix the mustard sauce ingredients together and brush one side of the steak with the sauce. Grill the steak, turning once and brushing with more sauce, according to the following guidelines: 14 minutes for rare, 20 minutes for medium, or 26 minutes for well done. Carve into thin slices to serve.

Tenderloin Kabobs with Rosemary

Use rosemary stems as brushes to baste these kabobs with port wine and olive oil.

Preparation Time:
20 minutes

6 Servings/Serving Size:
3–4 oz beef plus vegetables

Exchanges:
1	Vegetable
3	Medium-Fat Meat

Calories	255
Calories from Fat	126
Total Fat	14 g
Saturated Fat	4 g

Cholesterol	66 mg
Sodium	55 mg
Carbohydrate	7 g
Dietary Fiber	2 g
Sugars	3 g

Protein	23 g

1 1/2 lb beef tenderloin, cut into 1-inch cubes
12 large mushroom caps (remove stems from mushrooms)
1 medium red pepper, cut into 1-inch pieces
1 medium green pepper, cut into 1-inch pieces
12 cherry tomatoes
1 cup port wine
2 Tbsp olive oil
3 garlic cloves, finely minced
2 tsp minced fresh thyme
3 or 4 long, fresh rosemary stems

1. If using wooden kabob skewers, soak 6 of them in warm water for 15 minutes. This prevents the skewers from catching on fire while the kabobs cook. Then thread the beef, mushrooms, peppers, and cherry tomatoes on the skewers. Prepare an outside grill with an oiled rack set 4 inches above the heat source. On a gas grill, set the heat to high.

2. Combine the next four ingredients in a small saucepan and heat until the wine simmers. Keep on low heat. Dip the rosemary stems into the basting sauce and brush on the kabobs. Grill, turning constantly, for about 8–10 minutes total, until the meat is done as desired. Let everyone baste their own kabobs with the rosemary stem for grilling fun!

Herbed Chuck Steaks

Red wine vinegar acts as the perfect tenderizer for beef chuck steaks.

Preparation Time:	
10 minutes	

6 Servings/Serving Size:
3–4 oz

Exchanges:
4	Lean Meat

Calories	225
Calories from Fat	89
Total Fat	10 g
Saturated Fat	3 g
Cholesterol	94 mg
Sodium	86 mg
Carbohydrate	1 g
Dietary Fiber	0 g
Sugars	1 g
Protein	31 g

1/3 cup red wine vinegar
1/3 cup water
1 Tbsp olive oil
1 Tbsp minced fresh thyme
1/2 tsp sugar
Fresh ground pepper and salt to taste
2 lb boneless beef chuck steak, well trimmed

1. Combine all marinade ingredients, then add the chuck steak and marinate in the refrigerator for 6 to 8 hours. Prepare an outside grill with an oiled rack set 6 inches above the heat source. On a gas grill, set the heat to medium. Remove the steak from the marinade and reserve the marinade.

2. Grill the steak, turning once and brushing with reserved marinade, according to the following guidelines: 14 minutes for rare, 20 minutes for medium, or 26 minutes for well done. Carve into thin slices to serve.

This adapted recipe is courtesy of the Beef Board and Veal Committee/Beef Industry Council.

Best Burgers

Here's a great way to keep the fat content of your burgers down, but great flavor in: purchase lean ground sirloin for beef burgers, but add 2 tablespoons of ice water to the meat so it still remains juicy. Handle the meat very gingerly while making patties. Overhandling of the meat will cause it to toughen. Avoid pressing the meat down with a spatula while it's grilling—you'll release all the tasty juices!

Stuff-A-Burger

A surprise awaits you in the center of a juicy burger.

Preparation Time:	
10 minutes	

6 Servings/Serving Size:
3–4 oz

Exchanges:

4	Very Lean Meat
1/2	Fat

Calories 163	
Calories from Fat 50	
Total Fat ....6.5 g	
Saturated Fat ....2 g	

Cholesterol ....65 mg	
Sodium ....175 mg	
Carbohydrate ....0 g	
Dietary Fiber ....0 g	
Sugars ....1 g	

Protein ....28 g

1 1/2 lb lean ground sirloin
2 Tbsp ice water
Fresh ground pepper and salt to taste

Choose from the following stuffings: (use 1 Tbsp or a combination equal to 1 Tbsp per burger):
    Hot salsa
    Parmesan cheese
    Chili sauce
    Minced jalapeno peppers
    Bleu cheese
    Teriyaki sauce
    Marinara sauce
    Minced sauteed mushrooms
    Hoisin sauce
    Minced smoked ham
    Minced roasted red pepper
    Feta cheese

1. Mix together the ground sirloin with the water, pepper, and salt. Form into 12 small patties. Place 1 Tbsp of desired filling in the center of each of 6 patties. Top each patty with one of the remaining patties. Seal edges to secure filling inside.

2. Prepare an outdoor grill with an oiled rack set 4 inches above the coals. On a gas grill, set heat to high. Grill the burgers on both sides according to the following guidelines: 5–6 minutes for rare, 7–9 minutes for medium, or 10–12 minutes for well done.

Combo Burgers

These burgers taste like classic meatloaf.

Preparation Time:
10 minutes

6 Servings/Serving Size:
3–4 oz

Exchanges:
1/2	Starch
4	Very Lean Meat

Calories	169
Calories from Fat	39
Total Fat	4 g
Saturated Fat	2 g
Cholesterol	76 mg
Sodium	227 mg
Carbohydrate	6 g
Dietary Fiber	1 g
Sugars	2 g
Protein	25 g

1 1/2 lb combination of lean ground sirloin, lean ground pork, and lean ground veal
2 Tbsp ice water
1/4 cup ground oats
1/4 cup bottled chili sauce
1 small onion, minced
2 tsp Worcestershire sauce
·Fresh ground pepper and salt to taste

Prepare an outside grill with an oiled rack set 4 inches above the heat source. On a gas grill, set the heat to high. Combine the meat with the remaining ingredients. Shape into 6 patties. Grill the burgers for 10 minutes until they are crusty outside and slightly pink inside.

Mexican Burgers

Crushed tortilla chips give this burger a great texture and an interesting bite!

<table>
<tr><td>

Preparation Time:
10 minutes

---

6 Servings/Serving Size:
3–4 oz

Exchanges:

4	Very Lean Meat

Calories	136
Calories from Fat	7
Total Fat	1 g
Saturated Fat	0 g

Cholesterol	75 mg
Sodium	78 mg
Carbohydrate	3 g
Dietary Fiber	1 g
Sugars	0 g

Protein	28 g

</td></tr>
</table>

1 1/2 lb ground turkey (have your butcher grind this for you)
2 Tbsp ice water
2 Tbsp hot salsa
1/4 cup finely crushed, low-fat tortilla chips
2 tsp ground cumin
1/2 tsp chili powder

Prepare an outside grill with an oiled rack set 4 inches above the heat source. On a gas grill, set the heat to high. Combine the meat with the remaining ingredients. Shape into 6 patties. Grill the burgers, turning once, for a total of 8–10 minutes until the turkey is white throughout.

Luscious Lamb Burgers

Serve this burger tucked in grilled pita bread, with grilled red onions and red peppers stuffed inside. (See the recipe for Grilled Red and Yellow Peppers, p. 254.)

Preparation Time:
10 minutes

6 Servings/Serving Size:
3–4 oz

Exchanges:
3 Medium-Fat Meat

Calories	227
Calories from Fat	139
Total Fat	15 g
Saturated Fat	6 g
Cholesterol	76 mg
Sodium	69 mg
Carbohydrate	1 g
Dietary Fiber	0 g
Sugars	1 g
Protein	20 g

1 1/2 lb ground lamb
2 Tbsp plain nonfat yogurt
2 tsp minced fresh oregano
1 tsp minced fresh thyme
2 Tbsp lemon juice
2 garlic cloves, finely minced

Prepare an outside grill with an oiled rack set 4 inches above the heat source. On a gas grill, set the heat to high. Combine the meat with the remaining ingredients. Shape into 6 patties. Grill the burgers, turning once, according to the following guidelines: 6 minutes for rare, 8 minutes for medium, or 10 minutes for well done.

Even if snow covered the world completely,

the sun could melt it with a glance.

—Rumi

Great Grains Burger

This is a delicious, no-meat, burger alternative.

Preparation Time:
20 minutes

6 Servings/Serving Size:
3–4 oz

Exchanges:

2	Starch
1/2	Monounsaturated Fat

Calories	171
Calories from Fat	43
Total Fat	5 g
Saturated Fat	1 g

Cholesterol	37 mg
Sodium	72 mg
Carbohydrate	27 g
Dietary Fiber	3 g
Sugars	2 g

Protein	5 g

1 Tbsp olive oil
1/2 cup minced mushrooms
1 small onion, minced
1/4 cup ground oats
3 cups cooked short-grain brown rice (this rice is stickier, so the burger holds together better on the grill)
1 egg, beaten
2 Tbsp Parmesan cheese
1 Tbsp Worcestershire sauce

1. Heat the oil in a small skillet over medium-high heat. Add the mushrooms and onions and saute until the mushrooms are dark and the onion is golden, about 6–7 minutes.

2. Prepare an outside grill with an oiled rack set 6 inches above the heat source. On a gas grill, set the heat to medium.

3. Combine the mushrooms and onions with the remaining ingredients. Form the mixture into 6 patties. Grill the burgers, turning once, for a total of 6–7 minutes until the outside is golden brown.

Poultry Pizzazz

Grill chicken and turkey quickly over high heat, but be careful not to undercook (always grill until the meat is white throughout) or overcook. If you want to feed a crowd and double or even triple a recipe, you can save time by first roasting the chicken or turkey in the oven for about 15 minutes and then finish it off on the grill for another 10–15 minutes. Grilled leftover poultry is delicious the next day in sandwiches, soups, and salads, so you might want to make extra!

Chicken Satay

A satay is a spicy Indian kabob.

Preparation Time:
15 minutes

6 Servings/Serving Size:
3–4 oz

Exchanges:
4	Very Lean Meat
1/2	Fat

Calories	162
Calories from Fat	43
Total Fat	5 g
Saturated Fat	1 g

Cholesterol	69 mg
Sodium	60 mg
Carbohydrate	3 g
Dietary Fiber	0 g
Sugars	3 g

Protein	25 g

1 Tbsp corn oil
3 Tbsp lime juice
3 garlic cloves
1 red chili, minced
1 Tbsp honey
1 tsp ground coriander seeds
1 1/2 lb boneless, skinless chicken breasts,
    cubed into 1-inch pieces

1. In a blender, combine all ingredients for the satay sauce. Place the chicken cubes in a bowl, cover with the sauce, and marinate in the refrigerator for 4 hours. Prepare an outside grill with an oiled rack set 4 inches above the heat source. On a gas grill, set the heat to high.

2. If using wooden kabob skewers, soak 6 of them in warm water for 15 minutes. This prevents the skewers from catching on fire while the kabobs cook. Then thread the chicken cubes on the skewers. Grill the satays for about 4–5 minutes total, until the chicken is cooked through.

Spicy Salsa Chicken Grill

Liven up your grilled chicken with the spice of salsa!

Preparation Time:
15 minutes

6 Servings/Serving Size:
3–4 oz

Exchanges:
4   Very Lean Meat
1/2 Monounsaturated Fat

Calories 158
  Calories from Fat 47
Total Fat ....5 g
  Saturated Fat.............1 g

Cholesterol ....69 mg
Sodium ....78 mg
Carbohydrate..............1 g
  Dietary Fiber ....0 g
  Sugars ....1 g

Protein ....25 g

1/3 cup fresh lime juice
2 tsp minced fresh chives
2 tsp minced ginger
2 garlic cloves, minced
2 Tbsp olive oil
2 tsp chili powder
1 cup hot salsa
1 1/2 lb boneless, skinless chicken breasts

1. In a small saucepan, mix together the lime
    juice, chives, ginger, and garlic. Add the olive
    oil and chili powder and heat to boiling over
    medium heat. Stir in the salsa. Allow sauce to
    cool. Place the chicken in a plastic bag. Add
    the sauce and let marinate in the refrigerator
    for at least 2 hours or up to 24 hours.

2. Prepare an outside grill with an oiled rack set
    4 inches above the heat source. On a gas
    grill, set the heat to high. Grill the chicken
    breasts for 3–4 minutes on each side, turning
    once and basting with extra marinade, until
    the chicken is cooked through.

This adapted recipe is courtesy of the National Broiler Council.

Simply Great Grilled Chicken

You'll never find more moist grilled chicken!

Preparation Time:
10 minutes

6 Servings/Serving Size:
3–4 oz

Exchanges:	
4	Very Lean Meat
1/2	Fat

Calories	164
Calories from Fat	42
Total Fat	5 g
Saturated Fat	1 g

Cholesterol	69 mg
Sodium	665 mg
Carbohydrate	2 g
Dietary Fiber	0 g
Sugars	2 g

Protein	25 g

1/2 cup lite soy sauce
1/4 cup dry sherry
1 Tbsp canola oil
2 garlic cloves, minced
1 tsp minced ginger
1/4 tsp nutmeg
Fresh ground pepper to taste
1 1/2 lb boneless, skinless chicken breasts

1. Combine all marinade ingredients. Pour half the mixture over the chicken and set in the refrigerator to marinate for at least 2 hours or up to 24 hours. Save the remaining mixture for basting.

2. Prepare an outside grill with an oiled rack set 4 inches above the heat source. On a gas grill, set the heat to high. Grill the chicken breasts for 3–4 minutes on each side, turning once and basting with extra marinade, until the chicken is cooked through.

This adapted recipe is courtesy of the National Broiler Council.

Orange-Grilled Chicken with Herbs

Tucking fresh herbs under the skin of the chicken adds a wonderful flavor.

| **Preparation Time:** |
| 20 minutes |

6 Servings/Serving Size:
3–4 oz chicken without skin

Exchanges:

4	Very Lean Meat

Calories	138
Calories from Fat	26
Total Fat	3 g
Saturated Fat	1 g

Cholesterol	69 mg
Sodium	66 mg
Carbohydrate	1 g
Dietary Fiber	0 g
Sugars	1 g

| Protein | 25 g |

2 garlic cloves, minced
1 tsp grated orange peel
1/2 tsp minced fresh thyme
1/2 tsp minced fresh rosemary
Fresh ground pepper to taste
1 1/2 lb boneless chicken breasts, skin attached
1/2 cup fresh orange juice
2 Tbsp vinegar
1 Tbsp Worcestershire sauce

1. Combine the first five ingredients in a small bowl to make the herb mixture. Take each chicken breast and slip your fingers between the skin and flesh of the chicken, leaving the skin attached. Slide some of the herb mixture under the skin of each breast, pulling the skin back over each breast when finished.

2. Prepare an outside grill with an oiled rack set 4 inches above the heat source. On a gas grill, set the heat to high. Mix together the orange juice, vinegar, and Worcestershire sauce in a small bowl. Grill the chicken breasts for 3–4 minutes on each side, turning once and basting with the orange juice mixture, until the chicken is cooked through. Remove the skin before eating.

This adapted recipe is courtesy of the National Broiler Council.

Teriyaki Pineapple Chicken

Sweet pineapple rings top hot grilled chicken.

Preparation Time:
5 minutes

6 Servings/Serving Size:
3–4 oz

Exchanges:
4   Very Lean Meat

Calories 156
  Calories from Fat 28
Total Fat .... 3 g
  Saturated Fat .... 1 g

Cholesterol .... 73 mg
Sodium .... 309 mg
Carbohydrate .... 3 g
  Dietary Fiber .... 0 g
  Sugars .... 2 g

Protein .... 27 g

2 garlic cloves, minced
1/2 cup unsweetened pineapple juice
3 Tbsp Worcestershire sauce
1/4 cup teriyaki sauce
2 tsp hot pepper sauce
1 1/2 lb boneless, skinless chicken breasts

1. Combine all marinade ingredients in a plastic bag. Add the chicken breasts and marinate in the refrigerator at least 1 hour.

2. Prepare an outside grill with an oiled rack set 4 inches above the heat source. On a gas grill, set the heat to high. Grill the chicken breasts for 3–4 minutes on each side until the chicken is cooked through.

Raspberry Chicken

Using raspberry vinegar with chicken is a great way to add a burst of flavor.

| Preparation Time: |
| 15 minutes |

6 Servings/Serving Size:
3–4 oz

Exchanges:

| 4 | Very Lean Meat |

Calories	155
Calories from Fat	36
Total Fat	4 g
Saturated Fat	1 g

Cholesterol	69 mg
Sodium	72 mg
Carbohydrate	3 g
Dietary Fiber	0 g
Sugars	3 g

| **Protein** | 25 g |

3 Tbsp water
1/2 cup raspberry vinegar
1 Tbsp olive oil
2 Tbsp honey
1 tsp orange extract
1 tsp minced fresh rosemary
1/2 tsp nutmeg
Fresh ground pepper and salt to taste
1 1/2 lb boneless, skinless chicken breasts

1. Combine all ingredients except the chicken in a small bowl and microwave for 1 minute. Pour into a plastic bag. Add the chicken and marinate in the refrigerator at least 1 hour.

2. Prepare an outside grill with an oiled rack set 6 inches above the heat source. On a gas grill, set the heat to medium. Grill the chicken breasts for 6 minutes on each side until the chicken is cooked through.

Mango-Lime Chicken

This fruity chicken will remind you of tropical breezes.

Preparation Time:
10 minutes

6 Servings/Serving Size:
3–4 oz

Exchanges:
4   Very Lean Meat
1/2 Monounsaturated Fat

Calories 162
 Calories from Fat 38
Total Fat .... 4 g
 Saturated Fat .... 1 g

Cholesterol .... 73 mg
Sodium .... 71 mg
Carbohydrate .... 3 g
 Dietary Fiber .... 0 g
 Sugars .... 2 g

Protein .... 27 g

3 chicken breasts, boned, halved, and skinned
1/4 cup orange juice
2 Tbsp fresh lime juice
2 Tbsp mango chutney
2 tsp grated fresh ginger
1 Tbsp olive oil
1/2 tsp hot pepper sauce
1 tsp minced fresh oregano
2 garlic cloves, minced

1. Combine the chicken breasts with all remaining ingredients. Place in the refrigerator and marinate overnight.

2. The next day, prepare an outside grill with an oiled rack set 6 inches above the heat source. On a gas grill, set the heat to medium. Grill the chicken breasts for 6 minutes on each side until the chicken is cooked through.

Chicken in Fragrant Spices

Using a technique called scoring helps ensure that a marinade penetrates deep into the potentially tough chicken fibers.

Preparation Time:
10 minutes

6 Servings/Serving Size:
3–4 oz

Exchanges:
4   Very Lean Meat

Calories......................140
  Calories from Fat.......26
Total Fat ....3 g
  Saturated Fat.............1 g

Cholesterol ....69 mg
Sodium...................66 mg
Carbohydrate..............1 g
  Dietary Fiber ....0 g
  Sugars......................1 g

Protein ....26 g

1 1/2 lb boneless, skinless chicken breasts
3 garlic cloves, minced
2 Tbsp minced ginger
1 Tbsp cumin
1/2 tsp turmeric
1/4 cup plain nonfat yogurt, stirred until smooth

1. Make three diagonal slashes in the flesh of each chicken breast. Combine all remaining ingredients. Add the chicken breasts and coat well with the mixture. Marinate at least 8 hours or up to 48 hours.

2. Prepare an outside grill with an oiled rack set 4 inches above the heat source. On a gas grill, set the heat to high. Grill the chicken breasts for 3–4 minutes on each side until the chicken is cooked through.

Grilled Cornish Game Hens

Soy sauce gives these hens a delicate Asian flavor.

Preparation Time:
15 minutes

6 Servings/Serving Size:
1/2 hen without skin

Exchanges:
2   Very Lean Meat

Calories	64
Calories from Fat	16
Total Fat	2 g
Saturated Fat	0 g
Cholesterol	47 mg
Sodium	78 mg
Carbohydrate	1 g
Dietary Fiber	0 g
Sugars	1 g
Protein	10 g

3 Cornish game hens, split in half
3 garlic cloves
2 small shallots
2 tsp sugar
1 tsp cinnamon
2 Tbsp lite soy sauce
2 Tbsp dry sherry

1. Prepare the hens by washing them inside and out and discarding the giblets. With poultry shears, cut each hen in half. In a food processor, grind together the garlic, shallots, sugar, and cinnamon until the mixture is paste-like. Place in a bowl and stir in the soy sauce and sherry.

2. Rub the marinade over the Cornish hens and let them marinate in the refrigerator at least 2 hours or up to 48 hours. Then, prepare an outside grill with an oiled rack set 4 inches from the heat source. On a gas grill, set the heat to high. Grill the hens for 30 minutes, turning once, until juices run clear.

Grilled Turkey Paillards with Mediterranean Spices

Greek and Italian ingredients add a European touch to grilled turkey.

Preparation Time:
15 minutes

6 Servings/Serving Size:
3–4 oz

Exchanges:

1	Vegetable
4	Very Lean Meat
1	Saturated Fat

Calories	226
Calories from Fat	85
Total Fat	9 g
Saturated Fat	5 g

Cholesterol	100 mg
Sodium	432 mg
Carbohydrate	2 g
Dietary Fiber	0 g
Sugars	2 g

Protein	31 g

1 1/2 lb turkey breast, pounded to 1-inch thickness
2 Tbsp olive oil
1/4 cup fresh lemon juice
1 Tbsp minced fresh oregano
2 Tbsp minced fresh basil
2 tsp minced fresh thyme
1/2 cup white wine
3 Grilled Red and Yellow Peppers (see recipe, p. 254)
6 oz feta cheese, sliced thin
1/2 cup Greek olives

1. Combine turkey breast with all ingredients except the peppers, feta cheese, and olives. Marinate at least 2 hours or up to 48 hours. Prepare an outside grill with an oiled rack set 4 inches above the heat source. On a gas grill, set the heat to high.

2. Grill the turkey breast for 3–4 minutes on each side, turning once, until the turkey is white throughout. Place the turkey on a platter and surround it with grilled peppers, feta cheese, and olives. Serve with grilled pita bread if desired.

Tequila Turkey

Enjoy the flavors of this tipsy turkey.

Preparation Time:
10 minutes

---

6 Servings/Serving Size:
3–4 oz

Exchanges:
4   Very Lean Meat

Calories 151
  Calories from Fat........26
Total Fat ....3 g
  Saturated Fat.............1 g

Cholesterol ....75 mg
Sodium...................48 mg
Carbohydrate..............1 g
  Dietary Fiber ....0 g
  Sugars.....................1 g

Protein ....27 g

1 1/2 lb turkey breast filets
1/2 cup lemon juice
2 Tbsp olive oil
1/4 cup tequila
2 garlic cloves, minced
1 small onion, thinly sliced
1/4 cup minced red pepper

1. Combine the turkey with the marinade
    ingredients. Marinate for at least 2 hours or
    up to 48 hours.

2. Prepare an outside grill with an oiled rack set
    4 inches above the heat source. On a gas
    grill, set the heat to high. Grill the turkey for
    3–4 minutes on each side until it is white
    throughout.

Great Grilled Seafood

To grill fish easily, you may want to purchase a wire-hinged fish basket, so you can turn the fish without breaking it. Fish baskets are sold at all cookware shops, and are particularly good for small pieces of shrimp and scallops. Be sure to coat the inside of the basket with a little oil, so the seafood will not stick to the sides. You can also cover your grill with foil and poke small holes through it to keep your fish on the grill. Don't overcook seafood—keep it moist! When fish has just turned opaque, it's done.

Stuffed Whole Trout

Leave the head and tail on your trout for an authentic look.
The seafood department at the grocery store will clean and scale your fish
for you.

Preparation Time:
15 minutes

6 Servings/Serving Size:
3–4 oz

Exchanges:
1/2	Starch
2	Medium-Fat Meat

Calories	184
Calories from Fat	90
Total Fat	10 g
Saturated Fat	2 g

Cholesterol	46 mg
Sodium	87 mg
Carbohydrate	5 g
Dietary Fiber	0 g
Sugars	1 g

Protein	17 g

1 3-lb whole trout, cleaned, scaled, and slit open
   to form a pocket
2 cups soft bread crumbs
2 Tbsp olive oil
1 small onion, minced
1 Tbsp minced fresh dill

1. Prepare an outside grill with an oiled rack set
   6 inches above the heat source. On a gas
   grill, set the heat to medium. Rinse the fish
   inside and out with cool water. Pat dry. In a
   bowl, combine the remaining ingredients.
   Stuff the bread mixture into the cavity of the
   fish.

2. Either place the fish in an oiled fish basket
   and cook for about 25–30 minutes, turning
   every 10 minutes, or wrap the entire fish in a
   double thickness of aluminum foil and grill
   for 30–40 minutes, turning every 10 minutes.
   To serve, unwrap the fish from the foil or
   remove carefully from the basket. Place on a
   platter, remove the skin, and cut the fish into
   pieces. You may save the bones for making
   fish stock if you wish.

Grilled Salmon with Yogurt Dill Sauce

The flavors of sour cream, yogurt, and dill enhance fresh grilled salmon.

Preparation Time:
20 minutes

6 Servings/Serving Size:
3–4 oz with 2 1/2 Tbsp sauce

Exchanges:
1/2	Starch
3	Lean Meat
1/2	Monounsaturated Fat

Calories	241
Calories from Fat	106
Total Fat	12 g
Saturated Fat	2 g

Cholesterol	79 mg
Sodium	101 mg
Carbohydrate	5 g
Dietary Fiber	0 g
Sugars	3 g

Protein	26 g

1 1/2 lb salmon filets
1 Tbsp olive oil
2 Tbsp lemon juice
1 Tbsp minced fresh parsley
1/2 cup nonfat sour cream
1/2 cup plain low-fat yogurt
2 tsp sherry vinegar
1 Tbsp minced fresh dill
1 Tbsp minced scallions

1. Marinate the salmon in the oil, lemon juice, and parsley for 30 minutes. Prepare an outside grill with an oiled rack set 6 inches above the heat source. On a gas grill, set the heat to medium.

2. Grill the salmon for about 4–5 minutes on each side. Combine all ingredients for the sauce and serve it with the grilled salmon.

Citrus Swordfish with Tropical Salsa

This salsa is great served with any grilled fish or chicken. Try doubling this recipe and using the leftovers in Citrus Swordfish Salad (see recipe, p. 316).

Preparation Time:
25 minutes

6 Servings/Serving Size:
3–4 oz

Exchanges:
1	Fruit
3	Very Lean Meat
1/2	Monounsaturated Fat

Calories	195
Calories from Fat	52
Total Fat	6 g
Saturated Fat	1 g

Cholesterol	44 mg
Sodium	104 mg
Carbohydrate	12 g
Dietary Fiber	1 g
Sugars	10 g

Protein	23 g

Swordfish
1 1/2 lb swordfish steaks
1/2 cup fresh orange juice
1 Tbsp olive oil
1/4 tsp cayenne pepper
1 Tbsp pineapple juice concentrate

Salsa
1 medium orange, peeled, sectioned, and
   chopped into 1-inch pieces
1/2 cup diced pineapple chunks (use either fresh
   or packed in their own juice, juice drained)
1/4 cup diced mango
2 jalapeno peppers, minced
3 Tbsp orange juice
1 Tbsp diced red pepper
2 tsp sugar
1 Tbsp minced cilantro

1. Using a glass or ceramic bowl, marinate the swordfish in the orange juice, olive oil, cayenne pepper, and pineapple juice concentrate for 30 minutes. Prepare an outside grill with an oiled rack set 6 inches above the heat source. On a gas grill, set the heat to medium.

2. Grill the swordfish for about 6–7 minutes on each side until the swordfish is opaque in the center. Combine all ingredients for the salsa and serve it with the grilled swordfish.

Orange-Glazed Swordfish

These moist swordfish steaks are scented with ginger.

Preparation Time:	
10 minutes	

6 Servings/Serving Size:
3–4 oz

Exchanges:

3	Very Lean Meat
1	Fat

Calories	167
Calories from Fat	55
Total Fat	6 g
Saturated Fat	1 g

Cholesterol	44 mg
Sodium	304 mg
Carbohydrate	4 g
Dietary Fiber	0 g
Sugars	3 g

Protein	23 g

1 1/2 lb fresh swordfish steaks
1/2 cup fresh orange juice
1 Tbsp grated fresh ginger
2 tsp sesame oil
2 Tbsp lite soy sauce
1 Tbsp cornstarch or arrowroot powder
2 Tbsp water

1. Combine the swordfish with the orange juice, ginger, sesame oil, and soy sauce and marinate for 30 minutes. Prepare an outside grill with an oiled rack set 6 inches above the heat source. On a gas grill, set the heat to medium.

2. Drain and reserve the marinade. Grill the swordfish for about 6–7 minutes on each side until the swordfish is opaque in the center.

3. Place the reserved marinade in a saucepan and bring to a boil. Mix together the cornstarch or arrowroot powder with the water. Add to the sauce and cook for 1 more minute until thickened. Serve the orange sauce with the swordfish steaks.

Italian Grilled Tuna

Red peppers give this fresh tuna a festive look.

Preparation Time:
15 minutes

6 Servings/Serving Size:
3–4 oz

Exchanges:
4   Lean Meat

Calories	237
Calories from Fat	94
Total Fat	10 g
Saturated Fat	3 g
Cholesterol	69 mg
Sodium	52 mg
Carbohydrate	3 g
Dietary Fiber	0 g
Sugars	2 g
Protein	25 g

1 1/2 lb tuna steaks
2 Tbsp fresh lemon juice
1/2 cup diced roasted red peppers
1/2 cup sliced scallions
2 Tbsp minced fresh oregano
2 Tbsp minced fresh Italian parsley
1/3 cup balsamic vinegar
1 Tbsp olive oil
Fresh ground pepper and salt to taste

1. Combine the tuna steaks and lemon juice and marinate for 15 minutes. Prepare an outside grill with an oiled rack set 6 inches above the heat source. On a gas grill, set the heat to medium.

2. Grill or broil the tuna 6 inches from the heat source for 4–5 minutes on each side. Combine all remaining ingredients in a saucepan and bring to a boil. Pour the sauce over the tuna steaks to serve.

✿ ✿

Buy the best fish you can, preferably from Byzantium.

Sprinkle with marjoram. Wrap fish in fig leaves. Bake.

Have slaves serve it on silver platters.

—Archestratus, 330 BC

✿ ✿

Grilled Tuna with Chinese Five Spice Sauce

You can find Chinese Five Spice in the Asian section of your grocery store or in a specialty market. (This recipe is relatively high in sodium.)

Preparation Time:
20 minutes

6 Servings/Serving Size:
3–4 oz

Exchanges:

1	Starch
3	Very Lean Meat
1/2	Fat

Calories	218
Calories from Fat	58
Total Fat	6 g
Saturated Fat	2 g

Cholesterol	42 mg
Sodium	1264 mg
Carbohydrate	12 g
Dietary Fiber	1 g
Sugars	10 g

Protein	27 g

1 1/2 lb tuna steaks
2 tsp sesame oil
2 Tbsp lemon juice
1/2 cup lite soy sauce
1/2 cup Hoisin sauce
1 Tbsp honey
2 garlic cloves, minced
2 tsp Chinese Five Spice

1. Marinate the tuna steaks in the sesame oil and lemon juice for 30 minutes. Prepare an outside grill with an oiled rack set 6 inches above the heat source. On a gas grill, set the heat to medium.

2. While the tuna steaks are marinating, combine the remaining sauce ingredients and heat in a pan for 10 minutes over medium heat. Grill the tuna steaks for 6–7 minutes on each side, turning once, basting each side occasionally with the sauce. (Cook for a few minutes less if you like your tuna a little rarer.) Serve the tuna steaks with any remaining sauce on the side.

Grilled Red Snapper with Vera Cruz Sauce

Moist red snapper is livened up with a chili-spiked tomato sauce.

Preparation Time:	
25 minutes	

6 Servings/Serving Size:
3–4 oz with sauce

Exchanges:

2	Vegetable
3	Very Lean Meat
1/2	Monounsaturated Fat

Calories	173
Calories from Fat	45
Total Fat	5 g
Saturated Fat	1 g

Cholesterol	41 mg
Sodium	140 mg
Carbohydrate	8 g
Dietary Fiber	2 g
Sugars	4 g

Protein	24 g

1 1/2 lb red snapper filets
2 tsp chili powder
2 tsp olive oil
Fresh ground pepper to taste
2 tsp olive oil
1/2 cup minced onion
2 garlic cloves, minced
3 medium tomatoes, seeded and diced
1/4 cup fresh lime juice
2 tsp cinnamon
1 can (4 1/2 oz) green chilies
Fresh ground white pepper to taste

1. Rub the red snapper filets with the chili powder and olive oil. Grind black pepper over each filet. Let sit for 30 minutes. Heat the oil in a medium skillet over medium-high heat. Add the onion and garlic and saute for 3–4 minutes. Add the diced tomatoes and lime juice. Bring to a boil, lower the heat, and simmer for 10 minutes. Add the cinnamon, green chilies, and white pepper and simmer for 5 minutes. Keep sauce on low heat.

2. Prepare an outside grill with an oiled rack set 6 inches above the heat source. On a gas grill, set the heat to medium. Grill the red snapper filets for 5 minutes on each side, turning once. Serve the filets with the Vera Cruz sauce on the side.

Scallop and Shrimp Kabobs

It is important not to overcook small pieces of shellfish like shrimp and scallops. Cook just until scallops turn opaque and shrimp turns pink, and immediately remove the kabob from the heat.

Preparation Time:
20 minutes

6 Servings/Serving Size:
3–4 oz seafood plus vegetables and fruit

Exchanges:

1/2	Fruit
1	Vegetable
2	Very Lean Meat

Calories	123
Calories from Fat	20
Total Fat	2 g
Saturated Fat	0 g

Cholesterol	118 mg
Sodium	403 mg
Carbohydrate	10 g
Dietary Fiber	1g
Sugars	7 g

Protein	17 g

1 lb shelled, peeled large shrimp (keep tails on)
1/2 lb scallops
1 medium red pepper, cut into 1-inch pieces
1 medium green pepper, cut into 1-inch pieces
12 2-inch wedges of fresh pineapple
1/2 cup rice vinegar
2 tsp sesame oil
2 tsp minced ginger
3 Tbsp lite soy sauce

1. If using wooden kabob skewers, soak 6 of them in warm water for 15 minutes. This prevents the skewers from catching on fire while the kabobs cook. Then thread the shrimp, scallops, peppers, and pineapple on the skewers.

2. Prepare an outside grill with an oiled rack set 4 inches above the heat source. On a gas grill, set the heat to high. Combine all remaining ingredients for the basting sauce. Place the skewers on the grill and baste with some of the sauce. Grill kabobs for about 5–6 minutes total, turning and basting with the sauce while grilling. Heat remaining basting sauce until warm and serve on the side.

Grilled Shrimp With Pasta And Pineapple Salsa

This is a light, refreshing main course with a tang of citrus.

Preparation Time:
20 minutes

6 Servings/Serving Size:
3 oz shrimp with 1 cup pasta

Exchanges:

3 1/2	Starch
3	Very Lean Meat

Calories	383
Calories from Fat	30
Total Fat	3 g
Saturated Fat	1 g

Cholesterol	170 mg
Sodium	170 mg
Carbohydrate	57 g
Dietary Fiber	4 g
Sugars	14 g

Protein	31 g

2 15-oz cans pineapple chunks, packed in their own juice, drained
1 large red pepper, chopped
1 large red onion, chopped
1 jalapeno pepper, minced
1/2 cup orange juice
1/3 cup lime juice
1 1/2 lb peeled and deveined large shrimp
6 cups cooked rotini pasta

In a large bowl, combine all salsa ingredients except the shrimp and pasta. Prepare an outside grill with an oiled rack set 4 inches above the heat source. On a gas grill, set the heat to high. Grill the shrimp on each side for 2 minutes. Toss the pasta with the salsa, arrange the shrimp on top, and serve.

Grilled Salmon with Rigatoni and Herbed Tomato Relish

Use this tasty relish to top grilled chicken, too.

Preparation Time:
20 minutes

6 Servings/Serving Size:
3 oz salmon with 1 cup pasta

Exchanges:

2 1/2	Starch
1	Vegetable
3	Very Lean Meat
1/2	Fat

Calories	356
Calories from Fat	62
Total Fat	7 g
Saturated Fat	2 g

Cholesterol	43 mg
Sodium	90 mg
Carbohydrate	39 g
Dietary Fiber	3 g
Sugars	5 g

Protein	33 g

1 1/2 lb fresh boneless salmon (you can also try tuna or monkfish)
4 large, ripe tomatoes, chopped
1 cup fresh basil leaves
1/2 cup fresh mint leaves
1 Tbsp lemon juice
Fresh ground pepper and salt to taste
6 cups cooked rigatoni pasta

Prepare an outside grill with an oiled rack set 4 inches above the heat source. On a gas grill, set the heat to high. Grill the salmon until it flakes easily, turning once, for a total of about 10 minutes. Combine the remaining ingredients in a bowl, toss lightly with the salmon, and serve.

Grilled Red and Yellow Peppers

If you don't have a grill, you can roast these peppers over a gas flame. Using a long-handled fork or tongs, place a whole pepper directly into the flame, turning it constantly until evenly charred. Then place the pepper in a plastic bag to cool. When cool, peel off the charred skin, cut the pepper open, and remove the seeds and membrane. You can serve the roasted pepper whole or sliced.

Preparation Time:
5 minutes

---

6 Servings/Serving Size:
1/2 pepper

Exchanges:
1	Vegetable
1/2	Monounsaturated Fat

Calories	45
Calories from Fat	21
Total Fat	2 g
Saturated Fat	0 g

Cholesterol	0 mg
Sodium	2 mg
Carbohydrate	6 g
Dietary Fiber	1 g
Sugars	2 g

Protein	1 g

2 red peppers
1 yellow pepper
1 Tbsp olive oil
1 garlic clove, minced

1. Prepare an outside grill with an oiled rack set 4 inches above the heat source. On a gas grill, set the heat to high. Cut each pepper in half and remove the seeds and membrane. Combine the oil with the garlic.

2. Place the peppers directly on the rack, skin side down. Do not turn. Brush with the flavored oil. Grill for about 10 minutes until peppers are slightly charred. Place the peppers inside a plastic bag to cool.

3. When the peppers are cool, remove the charred skin with your fingers. Rinse the peppers under warm water to remove any excess charred skin, but if a little remains, don't worry—it's delicious, and adds to the flavor of the peppers!

Garden on a Skewer

Make a whole meal on skewers: serve these vegetable kabobs
with one of the previous recipes.

Preparation Time:
25 minutes

6 Servings/Serving Size:
1/2 cup

Exchanges:
1/2	Starch
1	Vegetable
1/2	Monounsaturated Fat

Calories	78
Calories from Fat	26
Total Fat	3 g
Saturated Fat	0 g

Cholesterol	0 mg
Sodium	14 mg
Carbohydrate	13 g
Dietary Fiber	2 g
Sugars	4 g

Protein	2 g

1 large ear of corn, husk removed, cut into 2-inch
  pieces
12 large mushroom caps
1 medium red pepper, cut into 1-inch pieces
1 small zucchini, unpeeled, cut into 2-inch pieces
12 cherry tomatoes
1/2 cup lemon juice
2 Tbsp dry white wine
1 Tbsp olive oil
1 tsp cumin
2 tsp minced fresh chives
1 tsp minced fresh parsley
Fresh ground pepper to taste

1. Prepare an outside grill with an oiled rack set
   6 inches above the heat source. On a gas
   grill, set the heat to medium. If using wooden
   kabob skewers, soak 6 of them in warm
   water for 15 minutes. This prevents the
   skewers from catching on fire while the
   kabobs cook.

2. Thread the vegetables on the skewers.
   Combine all remaining ingredients for the
   basting sauce. Grill the vegetable kabobs for
   about 15–20 minutes total, basting constantly
   with the sauce, until the vegetables are
   slightly charred.

Grilled Portobello Sandwich with Red Peppers and Onions

Preparation Time:
20 minutes

6 Servings/Serving Size:
1 sandwich

Exchanges:

2	Starch
3	Vegetable
1	Monounsaturated Fat

Calories	278
Calories from Fat	71
Total Fat	8 g
Saturated Fat	1 g

Cholesterol	0 mg
Sodium	322 mg
Carbohydrate	50 g
Dietary Fiber	5 g
Sugars	12 g

Protein	9 g

6 medium portobello mushroom caps (portobello mushrooms are large, thick mushrooms with a meaty taste; they can be found in some major supermarkets, natural food stores, and gourmet shops)
1 Tbsp olive oil
1 medium red onion, sliced into 6 2-inch slices
6 2-oz whole wheat pita bread wedges, opened to form a pocket
1 recipe Grilled Red and Yellow Peppers (see p. 254)
1/2 cup low-fat mayonnaise
3 garlic cloves, finely minced
1 Tbsp fresh lemon juice
1 Tbsp capers
Fresh ground pepper to taste

1. Prepare an outside grill with an oiled rack set 4 inches above the heat source. On a gas grill, set the heat to high. Place the portobello caps and red onion slices directly on the grill and brush with the olive oil. Grill, turning once, for 10–20 minutes, until mushrooms are soft and onions are caramelized.

2. Remove the vegetables from the grill. Add the pita bread and grill, on both sides, for a total of 3–4 minutes. Slice the peppers into strips. Combine all remaining ingredients for garlic lemon mayonnaise. To assemble the sandwiches, spread 1 Tbsp garlic lemon mayonnaise inside each pita pocket. Stuff with the portobello mushroom cap, onions, and red peppers.

Ginger-Glazed Carrots

These carrots have a delicate Asian flavor.

Preparation Time:	
10 minutes	

6 Servings/Serving Size:
1 large carrot

Exchanges:
1 Vegetable

Calories	66
Calories from Fat	8
Total Fat	1 g
Saturated Fat	0 g
Cholesterol	0 mg
Sodium	234 mg
Carbohydrate	14 g
Dietary Fiber	4 g
Sugars	6 g
Protein	2 g

6 large carrots, peeled and sliced in half lengthwise
3 Tbsp lite soy sauce
3 Tbsp rice vinegar
2 garlic cloves, minced
2 tsp sesame oil
2 tsp minced ginger
1/4 tsp Chinese Five Spice

1. In a large pot of boiling water, add the carrots and parboil for 5 minutes. Drain and rinse with cold water. In a large glass dish, combine the remaining ingredients. Add the carrots and marinate for 30 minutes.

2. Prepare an outdoor grill with an oiled rack set 4 inches from the heat source. On a gas grill, set the heat to high. Using an oiled, wire-hinged vegetable basket or grilling directly on the rack (whichever you find easier), cook the carrots, turning constantly, for 10 minutes, until they are slightly charred.

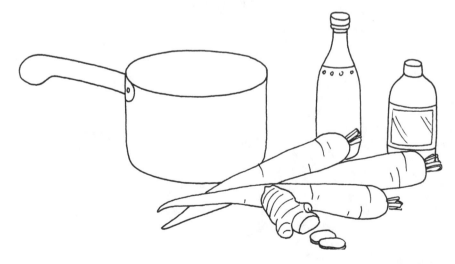

Herbed Russet Potatoes

You'll never want russet potatoes prepared any other way after
you try this recipe!

Preparation Time:	
15 minutes	

6 Servings/Serving Size:
1 medium potato

Exchanges:	
1 1/2	Starch

Calories	120
Calories from Fat	16
Total Fat	2 g
Saturated Fat	0 g
Cholesterol	0 mg
Sodium	10 mg
Carbohydrate	24 g
Dietary Fiber	4 g
Sugars	2 g
Protein	3 g

6 medium russet potatoes, washed, unpeeled,
   and cut in half lengthwise
1 Tbsp olive oil
1 Tbsp white wine
2 Tbsp low-fat, low-sodium chicken broth
2 tsp minced fresh thyme
1 tsp minced fresh rosemary
Fresh ground pepper to taste

1. Add the potatoes to a large pot of boiling
   water and boil for about 10–15 minutes, just
   until potatoes are slightly tender and not too
   soft. Drain. In a large glass dish, combine the
   remaining ingredients. Add the potatoes and
   marinate for 30 minutes.

2. Prepare an outside grill with an oiled rack set
   4 inches above the heat source. On a gas
   grill, set the heat to high. Grill each potato
   half directly on the rack or in an oiled, wire-
   hinged vegetable basket, turning constantly,
   for 15–17 minutes until the potatoes are
   cooked through.

Grilled Vegetable Basket

In this recipe, heaps of garden fresh vegetables are flavored with an herb marinade.

Preparation Time:
20 minutes

6 Servings/Serving Size:
1/2 cup

Exchanges:
1	Vegetable
1	Monounsaturated Fat

Calories 69
 Calories from Fat 42
Total Fat ....5 g
 Saturated Fat.............1 g

Cholesterol ....0 mg
Sodium....................52 mg
Carbohydrate..............6 g
 Dietary Fiber ....3 g
 Sugars.......................3 g

Protein ....1 g

Marinade
1/4 cup olive oil
1/4 cup balsamic vinegar
3 garlic cloves, minced
2 tsp minced fresh rosemary
1 tsp minced fresh basil
2 tsp lemon peel
Fresh ground pepper and salt to taste

Vegetables
1 fennel bulb, halved lengthwise
2 Belgian endives, halved lengthwise
1 small zucchini, sliced on the diagonal into 2-inch slices
1 small red onion, sliced into 6 slices, 2 inches thick

1. Puree the marinade ingredients in a blender until smooth. Set aside. In a large pot of boiling water, parboil the fennel for 5 minutes. Drain. Place all the vegetables in a glass dish, cover with the marinade, and marinate for 15 minutes.

2. Prepare an outside grill with an oiled rack set 4 inches above the heat source. On a gas grill, set the heat to high. Add the vegetables to an oiled, wired-hinged vegetable basket. Grill, turning constantly, for 15–20 minutes until the vegetables are slightly charred.

Honey-Grilled Vidalia Onions

Vidalia onions are so sweet they can be eaten like apples!

Preparation Time:
10 minutes

6 Servings/Serving Size:
1/2 onion

Exchanges:	
1	Starch

Calories	67
Calories from Fat	8
Total Fat	1 g
Saturated Fat	0 g

Cholesterol	0 mg
Sodium	205 mg
Carbohydrate	15 g
Dietary Fiber	1 g
Sugars	11 g

Protein	2 g

1 Tbsp honey
1/2 cup rice vinegar
2 Tbsp lite soy sauce
1 tsp sesame oil
3 large Vidalia onions

1. Combine the first four ingredients to make the honey sauce. Prepare an outside grill with an oiled rack set 6 inches above the heat source. On a gas grill, set the heat to medium.

2. Cut 3 6-inch pieces of aluminum foil. Place the onions on the foil. Brush each onion with the honey sauce. Fold the foil into a package around the onion and grill for about 30 minutes until the onions are soft. Remove the onions from the foil, cut in half, and serve.

Grannys on the Grill

These grilled apples are a great light dessert on a warm summer evening.

Preparation Time:	
10 minutes	

6 Servings/Serving Size:
1 medium apple

Exchanges:

2 1/2	Fruit
1	Monounsaturated Fat

Calories	188
Calories from Fat	48
Total Fat	5 g
Saturated Fat	0 g
Cholesterol	0 mg
Sodium	3 mg
Carbohydrate	38 g
Dietary Fiber	5 g
Sugars	32 g
Protein	1 g

6 medium Granny Smith apples, unpeeled, sliced
1/2 cup golden raisins
2 Tbsp canola oil
2 Tbsp brown sugar

1. Cut 6 8-inch pieces of aluminum foil. Prepare the apples and place each sliced apple on a square of foil. Sprinkle raisins, oil, and sugar over each apple.

2. Fold the foil into a package. Prepare an outside grill with an oiled rack set 6 inches above the heat source. On a gas grill, set the heat to medium. Grill the packets for about 30 minutes until the apples are tender. Remove from the foil and serve.

Good friends make you;
bad friends break you.

Peachy Skewers

These ginger-scented kabobs caramelize beautifully on the grill.

Preparation Time:
10 minutes

6 Servings/Serving Size:
1 small peach

Exchanges:

1	Fruit

Calories	63
Calories from Fat	18
Total Fat	2 g
Saturated Fat	0 g

Cholesterol	0 mg
Sodium	31 mg
Carbohydrate	12 g
Dietary Fiber	2 g
Sugars	10 g

Protein	1 g

6 small fresh peaches, cut into bite-sized pieces
2 tsp lemon juice
1 Tbsp finely minced ginger
2 Tbsp Amaretto
2 Tbsp low-calorie margarine

1. Marinate the peaches in all of the ingredients except the margarine for 20 minutes. Prepare an outside grill with an oiled rack set 6 inches above the heat source. On a gas grill, set the heat to medium.

2. Thread the peaches onto skewers (if you're using wooden skewers, be sure to soak them in water for at least 15 minutes first). Melt the margarine. Place the skewers on the grill and cook, turning constantly and basting with the margarine, for about 10 minutes until peaches are glazed and browned.

Tropical Kabobs

Peaches, nectarines, mangoes, and papayas contribute to this good-for-you treat.

Preparation Time:
10 minutes

6 Servings/Serving Size:
1/2 cup fruit

Exchanges:

1	Fruit

Calories	58
Calories from Fat	2
Total Fat	0 g
Saturated Fat	0 g

Cholesterol	0 mg
Sodium	2 mg
Carbohydrate	14 g
Dietary Fiber	2 g
Sugars	12 g

Protein	1 g

3 cups combined peaches, nectarines, mangoes, and papaya, all cut into bite-sized pieces
1 Tbsp lemon juice
1 Tbsp brandy
1 Tbsp honey
2 tsp cinnamon

Sprinkle the fruit with the remaining ingredients. Prepare an outside grill with an oiled rack set 6 inches above the heat source. On a gas grill, set the heat to medium. Thread the fruit onto skewers (if you're using wooden skewers, be sure to soak them in water for at least 15 minutes first). Grill, turning constantly, for 10 minutes until the fruit is caramelized.

Island-Grilled Bananas

These grilled bananas are deliciously flavored with coconut and rum.

Preparation Time:
10 minutes

6 Servings/Serving Size:
1 small banana

Exchanges:
1 1/2	Fruit

Calories	78
Calories from Fat	3
Total Fat	0 g
Saturated Fat	0 g

Cholesterol	0 mg
Sodium	2 mg
Carbohydrate	19 g
Dietary Fiber	2 g
Sugars	13 g

Protein	1 g

6 small bananas
3 Tbsp dark rum
1 1/2 tsp coconut extract
1 Tbsp brown sugar

1. Make a small slit into the skin of each banana. Cut through 1/4 inch of each banana and drizzle in some of the rum, extract, and sugar. Close up the skin with a toothpick. Prepare an outside grill with an oiled rack set 6 inches above the heat source. On a gas grill, set the heat to medium.

2. Grill the bananas in their skins for about 30–35 minutes until the skins are blackened and the bananas are hot. Slit each banana and push the ends in to fluff up. Eat like a baked potato, directly from the skin.

Better Salad-Making

Nothing tastes better than a cool, crisp salad in the summertime. Think beyond traditional iceberg and romaine lettuce by using some of the following interesting and healthy greens:

- Belgian endive is slightly bitter, with white, crunchy leaves. It's used in many French salads, and goes well with asparagus and fruits like oranges and strawberries. It can also be used as a "scoop" for ratatouille or salsa.

- Bibb lettuce has a small head with pale, tender leaves. It's a very mild-tasting lettuce.

- Bok choy cabbage has slightly bitter leaves attached to a white base. It's best to discard about 3–4 inches off the bottom and slice all the way to the top. Bok choy can be eaten raw or cooked. Look for baby bok choy—it has delicious, tender leaves.

- Boston lettuce has a buttery taste and soft leaves, and is good with seafood.

- Escarole is used in Italian cooking, and has green, curly leaves. Try it in salads, soups, or stews.

- Frisee is often included in mesclun mixtures (wild field green mixes). It has white curly leaves and a faintly bitter flavor.

- Green cabbage is traditionally used in coleslaw and as a casing for stuffing meat and rice. It can be stored up to two weeks in the refrigerator.

☼ Kale has a dark green or red leaf, and tastes great raw in salads or cooked until wilted and seasoned like spinach.

☼ Mache has sweet, tender leaves and is best in salads. It's also known as lamb's lettuce.

☼ Napa cabbage is often referred to as Chinese cabbage. It has very light green, curly leaves attached to a white base, and is more delicate in flavor than bok choy.

☼ Radicchio has bright purple leaves. It has a slightly bitter, peppery flavor and is used to make salads more colorful.

☼ Red cabbage is also used to add color to salads and coleslaw, and is delicious cooked with apples and spices during autumn.

☼ Spinach is best when used fresh. Buy loose spinach, not the type packaged in bags.

☼ Watercress has tiny, round, green leaves with a spicy, peppery flavor. Make the classic tea sandwiches for a special treat!

How to prepare the best salads

- Wash your greens in a salad spinner when you bring them home from the store. Pat dry, wrap the leaves in damp paper towels, then place the leaves in a vegetable bag with tiny breather holes. Lettuces lose their freshness quickly, so plan on shopping for them twice a week if you can.

- Always tear your greens when preparing a salad. Never cut greens with a knife, or their edges will turn brown.

- Pat your greens dry as thoroughly as you can prior to adding other ingredients and salad dressing. Otherwise, you'll end up with diluted flavor and small puddles in your salad bowl!

- Rub a wooden salad bowl with fresh-cut garlic prior to adding the ingredients for robust salads. The fresh garlic adds an extra flavor punch.

- When adding dressing, work like mad to incorporate the dressing (distribute it evenly throughout the salad). When preparing healthy dressing, you will often use less oil, so the yield of the dressing may be less than you are used to. A salad should have just enough dressing to enliven the greens, not saturate them with heavy oils or too many flavors.

- Use herbs like greens. Fresh mint, basil, chervil, and oregano can be used in greater quantities to make your salads unique.

- Go beyond your salad-making comfort zone! Try any or all of the many lettuces described here. Remember, the darker the leaves, the more nutritious they are.

California Walnut, Turkey, and Rice Salad

This crunchy salad is packed with good-for-you ingredients.

Preparation Time:
15 minutes

6 Servings/Serving Size:
1 cup

Exchanges:	
2	Starch
2	Lean Meat

Calories	262
Calories from Fat	52
Total Fat	6 g
Saturated Fat	1 g

Cholesterol	34 mg
Sodium	205 mg
Carbohydrate	33 g
Dietary Fiber	4 g
Sugars	6 g

Protein	20 g

Salad

3 cups cooked brown rice
2 cups diced cooked turkey (white meat)
1/2 cup diagonally sliced celery
1/4 cup pineapple chunks, drained
1/4 cup mandarin oranges, drained
1/4 cup water chestnuts, drained and thinly
    sliced
1/4 cup thinly sliced scallions
1/4 cup chopped walnuts
6 cups lettuce leaves (try romaine, spinach,
    Boston, or mache)

Dressing

1/2 cup low-fat lemon yogurt
1/2 cup low-fat mayonnaise
1 tsp grated lemon rind
1/2 tsp curry powder

Combine all salad ingredients except the lettuce leaves in a large bowl. Whisk together the dressing ingredients. Add the dressing to the salad mixture and toss to coat. Cover and refrigerate. To serve, spoon 1 cup of salad over 1 cup of the lettuce leaves.

This adapted recipe is courtesy of the Association for Dressings and Sauces.

Raspberry Turkey Salad

Drizzle this salad with Raspberry Poppy Seed Dressing (see recipe, p. 208) for a fresh summer main dish.

Preparation Time:
15 minutes

6 Servings/Serving Size:
3 oz turkey

Exchanges:

2	Vegetable
4	Very Lean Meat
1/2	Fat

Calories	212
Calories from Fat	52
Total Fat	6 g
Saturated Fat	2 g

Cholesterol	79 mg
Sodium	169 mg
Carbohydrate	9 g
Dietary Fiber	3 g
Sugars	5 g

Protein	31 g

4 cups fresh spinach, torn
3 cups romaine lettuce, torn
18 oz cooked, sliced turkey breast
3 oz part-skim mozzarella cheese
1/2 cup sliced raw mushrooms
1 cup sliced celery
1 medium red pepper, julienned
1 small cucumber, peeled and sliced
3/4 cup Raspberry Poppy Seed Dressing

Place the spinach and romaine on a large platter. Combine the remaining ingredients and toss lightly. Pile on top of the greens to serve.

Chuckwagon Tenderloin Salad

Wagon-wheel pasta and barbecued tenderloin brings a taste of the old Southwest to your backyard.

Preparation Time: 20 minutes	

6 Servings/Serving Size: 1/2 cup pasta with 4 oz beef

Exchanges:

1 1/2	Starch
2	Vegetable
4	Lean Meat

Calories	386
Calories from Fat	92
Total Fat	10 g
Saturated Fat	3 g
Cholesterol	101 mg
Sodium	476 mg
Carbohydrate	33 g
Dietary Fiber	4 g
Sugars	11 g
Protein	40 g

3 cups cooked wagon-wheel pasta (or use any other shaped pasta)
1 1/2 lb cold cooked beef, cut into 1 1/2 x 1/2-inch strips (use leftover lean sirloin)
1 small onion, very thinly sliced
1 green pepper, very thinly sliced
1 cup low-sodium barbecue sauce
1/4 cup Dijon mustard
3 cups red leaf lettuce
3 cups green leaf lettuce
2 large tomatoes, sliced

Combine the pasta, beef, onion, and green pepper in a salad bowl. Mix the barbecue sauce and Dijon mustard together in a separate bowl; add to the salad. Serve the salad over the mixed greens. Garnish with tomatoes.

This adapted recipe is courtesy of the Association for Dressings and Sauces.

Grilled Tuna and White Bean Salad

<table>
<tr><td>

Preparation Time:
20 minutes

6 Servings/Serving Size:
3–4 oz tuna with 1/2 cup beans

Exchanges:

2	Starch
1	Vegetable
4	Lean Meat
1/2	Monounsaturated Fat

Calories	423
Calories from Fat	151
Total Fat	17 g
Saturated Fat	3 g

Cholesterol	42 mg
Sodium	176 mg
Carbohydrate	35 g
Dietary Fiber	7 g
Sugars	10 g

Protein	34 g

</td></tr>
</table>

6 4-oz tuna steaks
1 Tbsp olive oil
Fresh ground pepper to taste
1 recipe Grilled Red and Yellow Peppers (see p. 254)
1/2 cup minced fresh Italian parsley
3 cups canned white beans (navy or cannellini) or garbanzo beans (chickpeas), drained and rinsed
1/2 cup minced red onion
1/4 cup diced celery
1/3 cup lemon juice
2 Tbsp olive oil
1 Tbsp minced scallions
1 Tbsp red wine vinegar
1 Tbsp sugar
Fresh ground pepper to taste
6 cups salad greens of choice

1. Prepare an outside grill with an oiled rack set 4 inches above the heat source. On a gas grill, set the heat to high. Brush the tuna with oil and pepper and grill, turning once, according to the following guidelines: 4–6 minutes for rare, 9–10 minutes for medium, or 12 minutes for well done). Then prepare a recipe of the Grilled Red and Yellow peppers.

2. Break the tuna into chunks and slice the peppers into strips. Combine the tuna and peppers in a large salad bowl with the parsley, beans, red onion, and celery. In a blender, add the lemon juice, olive oil, scallions, vinegar, sugar, and pepper and blend well. Pour the dressing over the tuna salad and chill for 1–2 hours. Serve the salad over the greens.

French Tuna Salad

Give ordinary tuna salad a twist with crunchy green beans.

Preparation Time:
10 minutes

6 Servings/Serving Size:
1 cup

Exchanges:

1/2	Starch
3	Very Lean Meat

Calories 146
  Calories from Fat 35
Total Fat ....4 g
  Saturated Fat ....1 g

Cholesterol ....161 mg
Sodium ....368 mg
Carbohydrate ....5 g
  Dietary Fiber ....2 g
  Sugars ....3 g

Protein ....21 g

Romaine lettuce leaves
1 10-oz package frozen French-style green
   beans, thawed and drained
1/2 cup chopped celery
1/2 cup chopped green onion
4 Tbsp fat-free Italian salad dressing
2 7 1/2-oz cans water-packed tuna, drained
4 hard-boiled eggs, sliced

Line individual salad plates with romaine lettuce leaves. Combine all remaining ingredients except the eggs and place on the lettuce leaves. Garnish with egg slices to serve.

*There
is nothing half
so much worth doing
as messing about in
boats.*

—*Kenneth Grahame,*
The Wind in the
Willows

Indian Potato Salad

Ground coriander and turmeric give this potato salad the richness of fine Indian cuisine.

Preparation Time:
15 minutes

6 Servings/Serving Size:
1/2 cup

Exchanges:
1	Starch
1/2	Monounsaturated Fat

Calories	118
Calories from Fat	31
Total Fat	3 g
Saturated Fat	1 g
Cholesterol	5 mg
Sodium	47 mg
Carbohydrate	18 g
Dietary Fiber	1 g
Sugars	7 g
Protein	5 g

1 lb russet potatoes, peeled and diced
1 Tbsp canola oil
1/2 cup diced onion
2 garlic cloves, minced
1 Tbsp ground coriander
2 tsp ground cumin
1/2 tsp turmeric
1 1/2 cups plain low-fat yogurt, stirred until smooth

1. In a pot of boiling water, cook the peeled and diced potatoes for about 15 minutes until tender. Drain and set aside. Heat the oil in a large skillet over medium-high heat. Add the onions and saute for 3 minutes.

2. Add the garlic and saute for 2 more minutes. Add the coriander, cumin, and turmeric and stir well. Add the cooked potatoes and cook for 2 minutes. Combine the potato mixture with the yogurt. Toss gently. Refrigerate for several hours before serving.

Italian Potato Salad

Grilled red and yellow peppers add flashes of color to this potato salad.

Preparation Time:
15 minutes

6 Servings/Serving Size:
1/2 cup

Exchanges:
1 1/2	Starch
1	Vegetable
1	Monounsaturated Fat

Calories	175
Calories from Fat	64
Total Fat	7 g
Saturated Fat	1 g

Cholesterol	0 mg
Sodium	73 mg
Carbohydrate	27 g
Dietary Fiber	3 g
Sugars	11 g

Protein	3 g

1 lb red potatoes, unpeeled and diced
1 recipe Grilled Red and Yellow Peppers (see
    p. 254), sliced
1/2 cup sliced scallions
1 Tbsp minced fresh basil
2 tsp minced fresh oregano
2 Tbsp minced fresh Italian parsley
2 Tbsp olive oil
1/4 cup red wine vinegar
1 Tbsp dry white wine
2 Tbsp Dijon mustard
1 Tbsp sugar

1. In a pot of boiling water, cook the potatoes in boiling water for about 15 minutes until tender. Drain. Add the peppers, scallions, basil, oregano, and parsley.

2. In a small bowl, whisk the remaining ingredients together by hand to make the dressing. Pour over the salad and serve immediately, or refrigerate for several hours before serving.

Ranch Potato Salad

Try this potato salad at your next picnic!

Preparation Time:
10 minutes

6 Servings/Serving Size:
1/2 cup

Exchanges:	
1 1/2	Starch

Calories	122
Calories from Fat	7
Total Fat	1 g
Saturated Fat	0 g

Cholesterol	0 mg
Sodium	352 mg
Carbohydrate	26 g
Dietary Fiber	2 g
Sugars	6 g

Protein	3 g

3 medium russet potatoes, peeled and cubed
1/4 cup low-fat mayonnaise
1/2 cup fat-free ranch salad dressing
3/4 cup diced celery
1/2 cup thawed frozen peas
1 tsp paprika
1/4 cup chopped scallions
Fresh ground pepper and salt to taste

Boil the potatoes for 10–15 minutes until done. Drain and set aside. Combine the remaining ingredients and toss well with the potatoes. Refrigerate for 1 hour before serving.

White Bean Salad

This pastel salad complements the golden colors of grilled foods.

Preparation Time:
15 minutes

6 Servings/Serving Size:
1/2 cup

Exchanges:
1	Starch
1	Monounsaturated Fat

Calories 132
  Calories from Fat........44
Total Fat ....5 g
  Saturated Fat.............1 g

Cholesterol ....0 mg
Sodium..................111 mg
Carbohydrate............18 g
  Dietary Fiber ....3 g
  Sugars......................2 g

Protein ....6 g

1 cup canned cannellini beans, drained and
  rinsed
1 cup canned navy beans, drained and rinsed
1/2 cup minced scallions
1/2 cup minced fresh Italian parsley
1/4 cup minced celery
1/4 cup balsamic vinegar
2 Tbsp olive oil
Fresh ground pepper to taste

In a large salad bowl, combine all ingredients.
Refrigerate for several hours before serving.

Garbanzo Bean and Barley Salad

Healthy, hearty barley gets a light lift from summer vegetables.

Preparation Time:
20 minutes

6 Servings/Serving Size:
1/2 cup

Exchanges:

2	Starch
1	Vegetable
1	Monounsaturated Fat

Calories	214
Calories from Fat	69
Total Fat	8 g
Saturated Fat	1 g

Cholesterol	0 mg
Sodium	28 mg
Carbohydrate	33 g
Dietary Fiber	7 g
Sugars	3 g

Protein	5 g

1 cup barley, rinsed
1/2 cup fresh green beans, trimmed and cut into
   2-inch pieces
2 small ripe tomatoes, diced
1/2 cup minced scallions
3 Tbsp red wine vinegar
3 Tbsp olive oil
1/2 cup canned garbanzo beans (chickpeas),
   drained and rinsed

In 2 cups of boiling water, add the rinsed barley. Bring to a boil, lower heat, cover, and simmer for 45 minutes until barley is tender. Set aside. In a large salad bowl, combine the remaining ingredients. Add the cooked barley and refrigerate for several hours before serving.

Green Bean Salad with Dill

This is a low-fat version of a popular side dish.

Preparation Time:
10 minutes

6 Servings/Serving Size:
1/2 cup

Exchanges:

1	Vegetable
1/2	Saturated Fat

Calories	57
Calories from Fat	29
Total Fat	3 g
Saturated Fat	2 g
Cholesterol	13 mg
Sodium	46 mg
Carbohydrate	6 g
Dietary Fiber	2 g
Sugars	4 g
Protein	2 g

1 10-oz package frozen green beans, thawed and drained
2 cups chopped, seeded, and peeled cucumber
1 cup low-fat sour cream
1 Tbsp minced fresh dill
2 tsp lemon juice
1/2 tsp white vinegar
1/4 tsp white pepper
Dash salt
Paprika

Combine the green beans and cucumbers together in a large bowl. Whisk together the remaining ingredients except the paprika and add to the vegetables. Toss well and refrigerate for 2 hours. Sprinkle the salad with paprika to serve.

Black Bean Jicama Salad

Crisp, crunchy, white cubes of jicama cool down this spicy salad.

| Preparation Time: |
| 20 minutes |

6 Servings/Serving Size:
1/2 cup

Exchanges:

| 1 | Starch |
| 1 1/2 Monounsaturated Fat | |

Calories	144
Calories from Fat	64
Total Fat	7 g
Saturated Fat	1 g

Cholesterol	0 mg
Sodium	4 mg
Carbohydrate	17 g
Dietary Fiber	5 g
Sugars	4 g

| Protein | 5 g |

1 1/2 cups canned black beans, drained and rinsed
1/4 cup corn kernels
1/4 cup diced red and yellow peppers
1/2 cup diced, peeled jicama
1/4 cup diced tomato
2 Tbsp minced red onion
3 jalapeno peppers, diced
3 garlic cloves, minced
2 Tbsp minced cilantro
3 Tbsp olive oil
3 Tbsp fresh lime juice
1 Tbsp cumin
2 Tbsp red wine vinegar

In a large salad bowl, combine all ingredients. Refrigerate at least 8 hours before serving.

Jicama Slaw

Jicama is the Mexican potato. Large, brown, and round, this vegetable, when shredded, makes a great slaw. You can find jicama in your supermarket produce section. Just peel off the tough brown skin and slice for salads, or shred by hand or in a food processor for this Southwestern slaw.

Preparation Time:
20 minutes

6 Servings/Serving Size:
1/2 cup

Exchanges:	
1	Vegetable
1	Monounsaturated Fat

Calories	63
Calories from Fat	4
Total Fat	5 g
Saturated Fat	1 g

Cholesterol	0 mg
Sodium	5 mg
Carbohydrate	6 g
Dietary Fiber	2 g
Sugars	3 g

Protein	1 g

1 1/2 cups shredded jicama
1/2 cup shredded carrot
1/2 cup shredded zucchini, unpeeled
1/4 cup very thinly sliced red onion
1/3 cup sherry vinegar
2 Tbsp olive oil
1 Tbsp cumin
1 tsp minced jalapeno or serrano peppers
2 garlic cloves, minced

In a large salad bowl, combine the first four ingredients. In a blender, combine all remaining ingredients for the dressing. Blend until smooth. Pour the dressing over the slaw and toss well. Serve immediately, or refrigerate before serving.

Apple Coleslaw

Children love this nutritious slaw because of its sweetness.

Preparation Time:
20 minutes

6 Servings/Serving Size:
1/2 cup

Exchanges:

1/2	Fruit
1	Vegetable
1/2	Polyunsaturated Fat

Calories	70
Calories from Fat	13
Total Fat	1 g
Saturated Fat	0 g

Cholesterol	0 mg
Sodium	219 mg
Carbohydrate	14 g
Dietary Fiber	1 g
Sugars	12 g

Protein	1 g

1 cup shredded red cabbage
1 cup shredded green cabbage
1/2 cup shredded carrot
1/4 cup diced Granny Smith apples
2 Tbsp raisins
2 Tbsp apple cider vinegar
3 Tbsp unsweetened apple juice concentrate
1/2 cup low-fat mayonnaise
Fresh ground pepper and salt to taste

In a large salad bowl, combine the first five ingredients. In a small bowl, combine all remaining ingredients for the dressing. Pour the dressing over the slaw and toss well. Cover and refrigerate for 30 minutes before serving.

Vinaigrette Salad Combos

Use this basic vinaigrette recipe as a start, then try some of
the variations over the different salad greens suggested here. (The nutrient
analysis does not include greens.)

Preparation Time:
10 minutes

6 Servings/Serving Size:
1 cup greens with 1 Tbsp
dressing

Exchanges:
1   Monounsaturated Fat

Calories.........................41
  Calories from Fat........41
Total Fat ....5 g
  Saturated Fat.............1 g

Cholesterol ....0 mg
Sodium.....................26 mg
Carbohydrate..............1 g
  Dietary Fiber ....0 g
  Sugars.......................1 g

Protein ....0 g

4 Tbsp red wine vinegar
1/4 tsp Dijon mustard
Fresh ground pepper and salt to taste
2 Tbsp olive oil

Mix together the red wine vinegar, mustard,
pepper, and salt. Whisk in the oil until smooth.

Variations
Herb: Add in 1 Tbsp minced fresh basil, dill,
  oregano, chives, thyme, or a combination of
  these to the basic recipe.
Garlic: Add in 1 Tbsp minced garlic.
Mustard: Add in an additional 1–2 tsp mustard.
Citrus: Substitute lemon or orange juice for part
  or all of the red wine vinegar.

Suggested Salad Combinations
Boston and Bibb
Mache and Radicchio
Romaine and Spinach
Frisee, Spinach, and Mache
Bok Choy and Chinese Cabbage

This adapted recipe is courtesy of the Olive Oil Association.

Italian Leafy Green Salad

Look for unique, delicious grapeseed oil in a gourmet or specialty market. (If you can't find it, use olive oil instead.)

Preparation Time:
15 minutes

6 Servings/Serving Size:
1 cup

Exchanges:

1	Vegetable
2	Polyunsaturated Fat

Calories	106
Calories from Fat	84
Total Fat	9 g
Saturated Fat	1 g

Cholesterol	0 mg
Sodium	35 mg
Carbohydrate	6 g
Dietary Fiber	2 g
Sugars	3 g

Protein	1 g

2 cups torn romaine lettuce
1 cup torn escarole
1 cup torn radicchio
1 cup torn red leaf lettuce
1/4 cup chopped scallions
1/2 each red and green pepper, sliced into rings
12 cherry tomatoes
1/4 cup grapeseed oil
2 Tbsp minced fresh basil
1/4 cup balsamic vinegar
2 Tbsp lemon juice
Fresh ground pepper and salt to taste

Combine the mixed greens, scallions, peppers, and tomatoes in a bowl, making sure the lettuce leaves are dry. Whisk together the remaining dressing ingredients. Pour the dressing over the salad and serve immediately.

Creamy Dill Salad

Snips of fresh dill add great flavor to this crisp salad.

Preparation Time:
15 minutes

6 Servings/Serving Size:
1/2 cup

Exchanges:

1/2	Carbohydrate
1	Vegetable

Calories	70
Calories from Fat	3
Total Fat	0 g
Saturated Fat	0 g

Cholesterol	0 mg
Sodium	61 mg
Carbohydrate	13 g
Dietary Fiber	3 g
Sugars	5 g

Protein	3 g

2 cups green beans, sliced into 2-inch pieces
1 cup sliced cucumbers, peeled
1 cup nonfat sour cream
1 Tbsp minced fresh dill
2 tsp lemon juice
1 tsp sugar
1/4 tsp fresh ground white pepper
1/2 tsp white wine vinegar
1/2 tsp paprika
6 cups salad greens of choice

1. Add the green beans to a large pot of boiling water and blanch for 30 seconds. Drain and plunge the beans into a bowl of ice water. Drain again and pat dry. Toss the green beans with the cucumbers.

2. Combine all remaining dressing ingredients except the salad greens. Toss the dressing with the green beans and cucumbers. Chill for 1–2 hours. Sprinkle paprika on top and serve the salad over the greens.

Beefsteak Tomato and Grilled Red and Yellow Pepper Salad

Roasted peppers and anchovies are crisscrossed on top of juicy beefsteak tomatoes.

Preparation Time:
20 minutes

6 Servings/Serving Size:
1 tomato round with 1 cup salad greens

Exchanges:
3	Vegetable
1 1/2	Monounsaturated Fat

Calories	138
Calories from Fat	65
Total Fat	7 g
Saturated Fat	1 g

Cholesterol	7 mg
Sodium	357 mg
Carbohydrate	16 g
Dietary Fiber	4 g
Sugars	8 g

Protein	5 g

6 cups salad greens of choice (try spinach, romaine, and red or green leaf lettuce)
1–2 beefsteak tomatoes, sliced into 6 6-inch rounds, each 2 inches thick
1 recipe Grilled Red and Yellow Peppers (see p. 254), sliced into thin strips
12 anchovy filets (drain as much of the oil as possible off the filets)
4 Tbsp red wine vinegar
1 1/2 Tbsp olive oil
2 tsp sugar
1 Tbsp Dijon mustard
1 Tbsp minced fresh basil
Fresh ground pepper to taste

Line a platter with the salad greens. Place the tomato slices on top. Divide the peppers and anchovies into 6 portions and crisscross them over the tomato rounds. Whisk together the remaining dressing ingredients. Sprinkle the dressing over the tomatoes and greens and serve.

Middle Eastern Stuffed Tomatoes

You can serve this dish as a light summer lunch or an evening appetizer.

Preparation Time:
20 minutes

6 Servings/Serving Size:
2 whole plum tomatoes

Exchanges:

1	Starch
1	Fruit
2	Vegetable
1/2	Monounsaturated Fat

Calories	206
Calories from Fat	37
Total Fat	4 g
Saturated Fat	1 g

Cholesterol	0 mg
Sodium	99 mg
Carbohydrate	41 g
Dietary Fiber	8 g
Sugars	15 g

Protein	7 g

1 cup dry bulgur wheat
2 cups low-fat, low-sodium chicken broth
2 Tbsp olive oil
1 cup diced red pepper
1/2 cup cooked green peas
1/4 cup minced fresh parsley
1/4 cup minced mint
1/2 cup golden raisins (plump first in 1 cup
    boiling water; let stand for 10 minutes; drain)
3 Tbsp lemon juice
Fresh ground pepper and salt to taste
12 plum tomatoes, halved and seeded
12 mint sprigs

1. In a heatproof bowl, add the dry bulgur wheat. Boil the chicken broth and pour over the bulgur wheat. Let stand 30 minutes to 1 hour until all liquid is absorbed. Drain off any excess liquid.

2. Meanwhile, combine remaining ingredients except the mint sprigs in a bowl. Add the bulgur wheat and mix well. Stuff the bulgur wheat mixture into the tomatoes. Garnish each tomato with a mint sprig and serve.

Strawberries with Balsamic Vinegar

A really good balsamic vinegar (well worth the extra pennies!) tastes more like wine than vinegar and is delicious over fresh strawberries.

Preparation Time:
10 minutes

6 Servings/Serving Size:
1 cup sliced strawberries

Exchanges:
1	Fruit

Calories.........................53
  Calories from Fat..........5
Total Fat ....1 g
  Saturated Fat.............0 g

Cholesterol ....0 mg
Sodium.....................2 mg
Carbohydrate.............13 g
  Dietary Fiber ....3 g
  Sugars.....................9 g

Protein ....1 g

6 cups stemmed and sliced strawberries
3 tsp sugar
3 tsp Balsamic vinegar

Toss the sliced strawberries with the sugar. Place the berries in individual dishes. Drizzle 1/2 tsp vinegar over each portion and serve.

You don't have to have small children in the house to celebrate the changing seasons. You deserve to see the decorations and color and symbols of the time of year, too.

Frozen Nectarine Yogurt

This frosty treat is the perfect ending to a hot summer day.

Preparation Time:	
10 minutes	

6 Servings/Serving Size:
1/2 cup

Exchanges

1 1/2	Carbohydrate

Calories	129
Calories from Fat	10
Total Fat	1 g
Saturated Fat	0 g
Cholesterol	3 mg
Sodium	30 mg
Carbohydrate	29 g
Dietary Fiber	2 g
Sugars	25 g
Protein	3 g

5 small nectarines, chopped
1 cup water
1/4 cup honey
1 Tbsp fresh lemon juice
1 tsp vanilla
1/4 cup unsweetened apple juice
1 cup plain low-fat yogurt

1. Combine the nectarines, water, and honey in a saucepan. Cook over medium heat until the nectarines are soft. Puree the mixture in a blender or food processor. Stir in the lemon juice, vanilla, and apple juice. Chill until cool.

2. Whisk the yogurt into the nectarine mixture. Pour into an 8 x 8-inch pan and freeze until crystals from around the edges, about 45 minutes. Stir the crystals into the middle of the pan and return to the freezer.

3. When the mixture is lightly frozen through, whip it until it is light in color. Spoon the mixture into a storage container and freeze until firm. Let soften at room temperature for 10 minutes before serving.

This adapted recipe is courtesy of the National Honey Board.

Blueberry Bake

Fresh-picked berries taste best in this tantalizing cobbler.

Preparation Time:
20 minutes

---

6 Servings/Serving Size:
1/2 cup berries with 1 small biscuit

Exchanges:
2 1/2   Carbohydrate

Calories	159
Calories from Fat	7
Total Fat	1 g
Saturated Fat	0 g

Cholesterol	1 mg
Sodium	194 mg
Carbohydrate	37 g
Dietary Fiber	4 g
Sugars	16 g

Protein	4 g

2 Tbsp honey
1 Tbsp sugar
1 Tbsp cornstarch or arrowroot powder
1 tsp cinnamon
1 cup water
2 Tbsp lemon juice
3 cups fresh blueberries or blackberries
1 cup whole-wheat pastry flour
1 tsp baking powder
1 Tbsp sugar
1/2 tsp baking soda
1/2 cup low-fat buttermilk

1. Preheat the oven to 400 degrees. In a large saucepan over medium heat, combine the honey, sugar, cornstarch or arrowroot powder, cinnamon, water, and lemon juice. Mix until smooth. Add the berries and cook over medium heat for about 10 minutes until thickened.

2. Combine the pastry flour, baking powder, sugar, and baking soda in a medium bowl. Add in the milk and stir until ingredients are combined. Pour the filling into a nonstick casserole dish. By tablespoons, drop the biscuit dough on top of the hot fruit. Bake in the oven for about 20 minutes until biscuits are slightly browned.

Tutti-Frutti Muffins

Use your favorite berry in this recipe.

Preparation Time:
15 minutes

12 Servings/Serving Size:
1 muffin

Exchanges:
2 Starch

Calories......................147
 Calories from Fat........21
Total Fat ....2 g
 Saturated Fat..............0 g

Cholesterol ....36 mg
Sodium...................137 mg
Carbohydrate............27 g
 Dietary Fiber ....2 g
 Sugars......................7 g

Protein.........................5 g

1 1/2 cups white flour
1 cup whole-wheat flour
2 tsp baking powder
1/2 tsp baking soda
2 eggs, beaten
1/4 cup sugar
1/2 cup unsweetened applesauce
1/2 cup evaporated skim milk
1 tsp vanilla
1/2 tsp orange extract
1 Tbsp canola oil
1/2 cup berries (try blueberries, strawberries, raspberries, or blackberries)

1. Preheat the oven to 350 degrees. Combine the flours, baking powder, and baking soda in a medium bowl. In a large bowl, combine the remaining ingredients except for the berries. Slowly add the dry ingredients to the large bowl and mix until blended. Do not overbeat. Fold in the berries.

2. Pour the batter into 12 nonstick muffin cups and bake for 25–30 minutes until done. Remove muffins from oven and let cool slightly. Remove muffins from pan and let cool completely.

Blackberry Muffins

Plump blackberries fill every bite of these moist muffins.

Preparation Time:
15 minutes

12 Servings/Serving Size:
1 muffin

Exchanges:

1	Starch
1/2	Fruit

Calories	97
Calories from Fat	12
Total Fat	1 g
Saturated Fat	0 g
Cholesterol	36 mg
Sodium	135 mg
Carbohydrate	19 g
Dietary Fiber	3 g
Sugars	7 g
Protein	4 g

2 cups whole-wheat pastry flour
2 tsp baking powder
1/2 tsp baking soda
2 tsp cinnamon
3 Tbsp sugar
1/2 cup unsweetened applesauce
2 eggs, beaten
1/2 cup low-fat buttermilk
2 cups fresh blackberries

1. Preheat the oven to 350 degrees. In a medium bowl, combine the flour, baking powder, baking soda, cinnamon, and sugar. In a separate bowl, combine the applesauce, eggs, and buttermilk.

2. Add the dry ingredients slowly to the wet ingredients. Mix gently until just combined. Carefully fold in the blackberries. Pour the batter into nonstick muffin cups until they are two-thirds full. Bake for 20–25 minutes until a toothpick comes out clean and muffins are lightly browned.

Fresh Fruit in Raspberry Grand Marnier Sauce

Use this raspberry sauce to whirl into plain yogurt or cottage cheese, too.

Preparation Time:
15 minutes

6 Servings/Serving Size:
1/2 cup

Exchanges:
1   Fruit

Calories 68
  Calories from Fat 4
Total Fat ....0 g
  Saturated Fat ....0 g

Cholesterol ....0 mg
Sodium......................2 mg
Carbohydrate...........16 g
  Dietary Fiber ....3 g
  Sugars....................12 g

Protein ....1 g

1 cup fresh raspberries
2 Tbsp orange juice
1 Tbsp lemon juice
1/4 tsp grated orange rind
1 1/2 cups sliced strawberries
1 1/2 cups green grapes
1 Tbsp Grand Marnier
1 Tbsp sugar

1. Puree the raspberries in the blender, using a little water if necessary. Strain to remove any seeds. Add the orange juice, lemon juice, and orange rind to the puree.

2. Toss the strawberries and grapes with the Grand Marnier and sugar. Let marinate for 1 hour. To serve, place the strawberries and grapes in six individual dessert dishes. Pour equal portions of raspberry sauce on top.

Fresh Berry Syrup

Try serving this delicious syrup warm over pancakes, waffles, or French toast.

Preparation Time:
10 minutes

8 Servings/Serving Size:
2 Tbsp

Exchanges:
1/2   Carbohydrate

Calories	38
Calories from Fat	1
Total Fat	0 g
Saturated Fat	0 g
Cholesterol	0 mg
Sodium	2 mg
Carbohydrate	10 g
Dietary Fiber	1 g
Sugars	8 g
Protein	0 g

1 cup fresh blueberries, blackberries, strawberries, or raspberries
1/2 cup unsweetened apple juice
1 1/2 tsp cornstarch or arrowroot powder
3 Tbsp sugar
1/2 tsp grated lemon peel
1 Tbsp lemon juice

Puree the berries with the apple juice. Transfer to a saucepan and add the cornstarch or arrowroot powder. Cook over medium heat until bubbly. Add in the sugar, lemon peel, and lemon juice.

Peaches and Raspberries with Champagne

Peaches and raspberries are layered with champagne-flavored vanilla yogurt.

Preparation Time:	
10 minutes	

6 Servings/Serving Size:
1/2 cup fruit

Exchanges:
1	Fruit

Calories	6
Calories from Fat	24
Total Fat	0 g
Saturated Fat	0 g
Cholesterol	1 mg
Sodium	32 mg
Carbohydrate	13 g
Dietary Fiber	3 g
Sugars	9 g
Protein	3 g

3 Tbsp champagne
1 cup plain nonfat yogurt
2 tsp vanilla
2 tsp sugar
1 1/2 cups sliced fresh peaches
1 1/2 cups fresh raspberries
Mint leaves

Combine the champagne with the yogurt, vanilla, and sugar. Mix well. Place a layer of fruit in each of six fluted champagne glasses. Spoon on champagne yogurt. Add more fruit. Repeat layering yogurt and fruit, ending with yogurt. Garnish each dessert with a mint sprig and serve.

Vanilla Peach Pudding

Instant vanilla pudding makes this dessert easy and quick to make!

Preparation Time:
15 minutes

6 Servings/Serving Size:
1 cup

Exchanges:
2 1/2   Carbohydrate

Calories 192
  Calories from Fat..........5
Total Fat ....1 g
  Saturated Fat.............0 g

Cholesterol ....6 mg
Sodium..................350 mg
Carbohydrate.............34 g
  Dietary Fiber ....2 g
  Sugars.....................21 g

Protein ....13 g

2 packages artificially sweetened, low-fat, instant vanilla pudding
4 cups cold evaporated skim milk
1 tsp cinnamon
1/2 tsp almond extract
2 cups diced fresh peaches
6 strawberries, sliced

In a metal bowl, whip together the pudding mix, cold milk, cinnamon, and almond extract. Mix until thick. Fold in the peaches and gently stir. Spoon pudding into six individual dishes and top with strawberries.

Sliced Peaches in Lime Rum Sauce

Dark rum and lime bring out the best in fresh summer peaches.

Preparation Time:
15 minutes

6 Servings/Serving Size:
1/2 cup

Exchanges:	
1	Fruit

Calories	72
Calories from Fat	1
Total Fat	0 g
Saturated Fat	0 g

Cholesterol	0 mg
Sodium	1 mg
Carbohydrate	18 g
Dietary Fiber	2 g
Sugars	14 g

Protein	1 g

1/2 cup fresh lime juice
1 Tbsp dark rum
2 Tbsp honey
1/4 cup water
Pinch cloves
2 tsp cornstarch or arrowroot powder
4 tsp water
3 cups sliced peaches

1. In a saucepan over medium heat, heat the lime juice, rum, honey, and water. Bring to a boil, lower the heat, and simmer for 5 minutes. Add the cloves.

2. Mix together the cornstarch or arrowroot powder and water. Add to the sauce. Add in the peaches and cook for about 10 minutes. Chill and serve in individual dishes.

Brandied Peaches

Fresh lemon thyme sweetens this dish—look for it in the produce section of a gourmet grocery store. Use regular thyme if lemon thyme is unavailable.

Preparation Time:
15 minutes

6 Servings/Serving Size:
1/2 cup

Exchanges:	
1	Fruit

Calories	81
Calories from Fat	1
Total Fat	0 g
Saturated Fat	0 g

Cholesterol	0 mg
Sodium	3 mg
Carbohydrate	16 g
Dietary Fiber	2 g
Sugars	12 g

Protein	1 g

1 1/2 cups sliced fresh peaches
1 1/2 cups fresh blueberries
1/4 cup brandy
2 Tbsp honey
6 sprigs lemon thyme

Combine the peaches and blueberries in a bowl. Mix together the brandy and honey. Pour the brandy-honey sauce over the fruit. Add the thyme sprigs and refrigerate for several hours. Serve chilled.

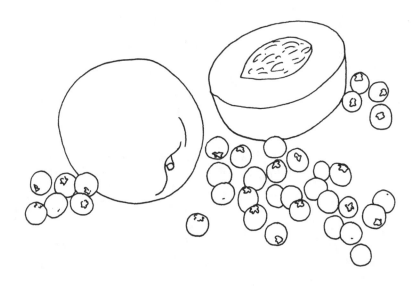

Purple Plums in Red Wine

Serve these succulent plums as a great finish to a
Mediterranean meal.

Preparation Time:
15 minutes

---

6 Servings/Serving Size:
1/2 cup

Exchanges:
| 1 1/2 | Fruit |

Calories	84
Calories from Fat	4
Total Fat	.......................0 g
Saturated Fat	.............0 g

Cholesterol	...............0 mg
Sodium	.....................1 mg
Carbohydrate	.............18 g
Dietary Fiber	.............2 g
Sugars	.....................11 g

Protein	.......................1 g

2 Tbsp sugar
1 cup dry red wine
1/2 tsp grated lemon rind
1/2 cup water
2 tsp cornstarch or arrowroot powder
4 tsp water
2 cups sliced plums
1 cup fresh sliced figs

Combine the sugar, wine, lemon rind, and 1/2
cup water in a saucepan and bring to a boil.
Lower heat and simmer for 5 minutes. Combine
the cornstarch and arrowroot powder with the
4 tsp water. Add to the syrup. Cook for 2
minutes until thickened. Pour the syrup over
the plums and figs and refrigerate for several
hours before serving.

Melon in Mint Sauce

A minty, low-fat sauce makes sweet melon even sweeter.

Preparation Time:
15 minutes

6 Servings/Serving Size:
1/2 cup

Exchanges:
1	Fruit
1/2	Saturated Fat

Calories 84
  Calories from Fat 30
Total Fat ....3 g
  Saturated Fat.............2 g

Cholesterol ....13 mg
Sodium...................24 mg
Carbohydrate............13 g
  Dietary Fiber ....1 g
  Sugars......................12 g

Protein ....1 g

1 cup low-fat sour cream
2 Tbsp minced mint
2 Tbsp sugar
1/4 tsp cardamom
1 cup cubed cantaloupe
1 cup cubed honeydew melon
1 cup cubed watermelon

Combine the first four ingredients in a small bowl and mix well. Add to the melon, toss lightly, and chill for several hours before serving.

....to
leave the world a
bit better, whether by
a healthy child, a garden
path, or a redeemed social
condition...this is to have
succeeded.

—Ralph Waldo
Emerson

Watermelon Nectar

This is a refreshing, healthy drink after a round of tennis or a
brisk walk.

Preparation Time:	
10 minutes	
6 Servings/Serving Size:	
1 cup	
Exchanges:	
1	Fruit
Calories	53
Calories from Fat	4
Total Fat	0 g
Saturated Fat	0 g
Cholesterol	0 mg
Sodium	2 mg
Carbohydrate	13 g
Dietary Fiber	1 g
Sugars	12 g
Protein	1 g

4 cups diced watermelon, seeds removed
2 cups water
2 Tbsp sugar
1/4 cup fresh lime juice
Shaved ice
Lime wedges

Puree half of the watermelon with 1 cup of the
water. Pour into a pitcher. Add the rest of the
fruit, water, sugar, and lime juice to the
blender and puree. Add this to the juice in the
pitcher. Pour over shaved ice and garnish each
glass with a lime wedge.

Summer Menus

Memorial Day Kickoff

Creamy Chive Dip

Vegetable Antipasto

Mussels Au Gratin

Chilled Melon and Berry Soup

303–306

Father's Day Dinner

Southwestern Bruschetta

South-of-the-Border Soup

Spicy Pita Pockets

Jeweled Fruit Tart

307–310

Fourth of July Extravaganza

White Bean Pate

Chunky Lobster Rolls

Sassy Sweet Potato Salad

Low-Fat Chocolate Mousse

311–314

Cooling Down the Heat

Tomatillo Gazpacho

Citrus Swordfish Salad

Artichoke Vinaigrette Salad

Giant Strawberries with Raspberry Dip

315–318

Beach Blanket Picnic

Seashore Shrimp Spread

Pasta, White Beans, and Tuna

Plum Bread

Mango and Papaya Salad with Orange Coconut Dressing

319–322

Labor Day Farewell

Ocean Crab Dip

Bow-Tie Pasta Alle Portofino

Garden Vegetable Stir-Fry

Adam's Fruit Popsicles

323–326

Creamy Chive Dip

Pack this dip in a crock or sturdy Tupperware container and pack it in your picnic basket, along with some crunchy vegetables or chewy pita bread wedges.

Preparation Time:
5 minutes

---

12 Servings/Serving Size:
2 Tbsp

Exchanges:
Free Food

Calories 22
 Calories from Fat 0
Total Fat ....0 g
 Saturated Fat.............0 g

Cholesterol ....2 mg
Sodium....................84 mg
Carbohydrate.............3 g
 Dietary Fiber ....0 g
 Sugars.......................1 g

Protein ....3 g

8 oz low-fat cottage cheese
1/2 cup nonfat sour cream
4 tsp garlic powder
4 tsp onion powder
3 Tbsp minced fresh chives

Mix all ingredients together by hand until smooth.

Vegetable Antipasto

These crisp, cool vegetables are refreshing to serve on a hot day.

Preparation Time:
25 minutes

6 Servings/Serving Size:
1 cup

Exchanges:
1	Vegetable
1	Monounsaturated Fat

Calories	73
Calories from Fat	44
Total Fat	5 g
Saturated Fat	1 g

Cholesterol	0 mg
Sodium	82 mg
Carbohydrate	7 g
Dietary Fiber	2 g
Sugars	4 g

Protein	2 g

1/2 cup red wine vinegar
2 Tbsp fresh lemon juice
2 Tbsp Dijon mustard
2 Tbsp olive oil
2 Tbsp minced fresh basil
2 tsp minced fresh rosemary
2 tsp minced fresh chives
2 Tbsp minced shallots
1 cup baby carrots
1 small red pepper, cored, seeded, and cut into strips
1 small yellow pepper, cored, seeded, and cut into strips
1 cup broccoli florets
1 cup cauliflower florets
1 cup zucchini chunks (2-inch chunks, unpeeled)

Place the carrots, peppers, broccoli, cauliflower, and zucchini in a bowl. Combine all remaining ingredients to make the vinaigrette. Add to the vegetables and toss well. Marinate the vegetables overnight and serve cold.

Mussels Au Gratin

Cracker crumbs and Parmesan cheese make these mussels golden and crusty!

Preparation Time:
25 minutes

6 Servings/Serving Size:
3–4 oz

Exchanges:
1	Starch
2	Very Lean Meat
1	Monounsaturated Fat

Calories	190
Calories from Fat	80
Total Fat	9 g
Saturated Fat	2 g

Cholesterol	27 mg
Sodium	467 mg
Carbohydrate	13 g
Dietary Fiber	1 g
Sugars	4 g

Protein	13 g

4 lb mussels
1/2 cup water
4 cloves garlic, minced
1 tsp ground pepper
2 Tbsp olive oil
3 Tbsp white wine
1/4 cup finely diced onion
1/2 cup finely minced fresh parsley
2 Tbsp fresh lemon juice
1 cup cracker crumbs
1/4 cup Parmesan cheese

1. Preheat the oven to 400 degrees. Scrub the mussels under running water; discard any that are not closed. Cut off beards (or you can have your seafood department do this for you). In a large pot, combine water, half of the garlic, and half of the pepper. Bring to a boil. Add the mussels and steam on medium heat until they open, about 7–10 minutes.

2. With a slotted spoon, transfer the mussels from the broth onto 2 rimmed baking sheets. Break off and discard the top halves of the shells and any unopened mussels. Heat the olive oil and wine in a medium skillet. Saute the remaining garlic and onion for 5 minutes. Add the parsley and lemon juice. Combine with the cracker crumbs and Parmesan cheese. Sprinkle the mixture over the mussels. Bake the mussels for 5 minutes until crumbs are lightly browned.

This recipe is courtesy of the National Fisheries Institute.

Chilled Melon and Berry Soup

This is a delicious way to drink a light dessert!

Preparation Time:
10 minutes

6 Servings/Serving Size:
1/2 cup

Exchanges:
1   Fruit

Calories.........................67
  Calories from Fat..........5
Total Fat ....1 g
  Saturated Fat.............0 g

Cholesterol ....1 mg
Sodium....................49 mg
Carbohydrate............13 g
  Dietary Fiber ....1 g
  Sugars.....................12 g

Protein ....2 g

1 cup cantaloupe chunks
1 cup honeydew chunks
1/4 cup dry white wine
2 Tbsp orange juice
2 Tbsp sugar
1 cup low-fat buttermilk
1/2 cup blueberries

In a food processor or blender, combine the melons, wine, juice, and sugar. Puree until almost smooth. Add the buttermilk and process again. Top each serving with blueberries.

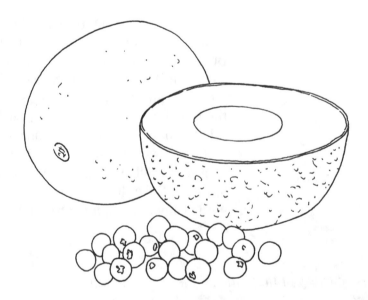

Southwestern Bruschetta

This is a wonderful way to begin a Southwestern meal.

Preparation Time:	
20 minutes	

6 Servings/Serving Size:	
2 slices	

Exchanges:	
3	Starch
1	Monounsaturated Fat

Calories	282
Calories from Fat	86
Total Fat	10 g
Saturated Fat	2 g

Cholesterol	1 mg
Sodium	411 mg
Carbohydrate	43 g
Dietary Fiber	3 g
Sugars	5 g

Protein	7 g

1 long loaf crusty French bread, cut into 12
   slices
3 Tbsp olive oil
1 1/2 Tbsp fresh lime juice
1 Tbsp minced cilantro
1/2 cup chopped plum tomatoes
1/2 cup frozen corn, thawed
1/2 cup minced green peppers
2 garlic cloves, minced
6–10 drops hot pepper sauce

Preheat the oven to 375 degrees. Brush each slice of bread with the oil and toast the bread slices on a cookie sheet in the oven for 5 minutes. Combine the remaining ingredients in a bowl and top each slice of bread with the bruschetta.

South-of-the-Border Soup

This is a spicy twist on traditional corn soup.

Preparation Time:
20 minutes

6 Servings/Serving Size:
1 cup

Exchanges:
1	Starch
1/2	Skim Milk
2	Vegetable
1/2	Monounsaturated Fat

Calories	203
Calories from Fat	38
Total Fat	4 g
Saturated Fat	1 g

Cholesterol	8 mg
Sodium	278 mg
Carbohydrate	32 g
Dietary Fiber	3 g
Sugars	13 g

Protein	14 g

2 tsp olive oil
1 cup diced onion
1 medium red pepper, chopped
2 jalapeno peppers, diced
2 1/2 cups low-fat, low-sodium chicken broth
2 cups evaporated skim milk
2 cups corn kernels
1 4-oz can green chilies
2 Tbsp cornstarch or arrowroot powder
4 Tbsp water
1/2 cup sliced scallions
1/2 cup low-fat Cheddar cheese

1. Heat the oil in a stockpot over medium-high heat. Add the onion and red pepper and saute for 5 minutes. Add the jalapeno peppers and saute for 5 more minutes. Add the chicken broth and bring to a boil. Lower the heat and simmer for 15 minutes. Add the milk, corn, and green chilies and simmer for 5–8 more minutes.

2. Mix together the cornstarch or arrowroot powder and water. Add to the soup and cook for about 5 minutes until thickened. Garnish each bowl of soup with scallions and cheese.

Spicy Pita Pockets

Give Dad something he can sink his teeth into!

Preparation Time:	
10 minutes	

6 Servings/Serving Size:
3–4 oz filling

Exchanges:

2	Starch
1	Vegetable
4	Lean Meat
1/2	Fat

Calories	422
Calories from Fat	148
Total Fat	16 g
Saturated Fat	8 g
Cholesterol	90 mg
Sodium	440 mg
Carbohydrate	36 g
Dietary Fiber	3 g
Sugars	5 g
Protein	36 g

1/2 cup fresh lime juice
2 Tbsp honey
2 Tbsp olive oil
2 garlic cloves, minced
1 tsp chili powder
1/2 tsp cumin
1 1/2 lb top sirloin steak, trimmed of all fat
6 large whole-wheat pita pockets
1 15-oz can Mexican-style chopped tomatoes, well drained
6 oz pepper jack cheese
12 romaine lettuce leaves

1. Combine the first six ingredients to make the marinade. Add the steak and marinate in the refrigerator for at least 6 hours. Then, prepare an outside grill with an oiled rack set 4 inches above the heat source. On a gas grill, set the heat to high.

2. Grill the steak until done as desired and cut into 24 thin slices. To assemble the sandwiches, open the pita bread to form a pocket. Add the steak to the pockets. Top with the tomatoes, cheese, and lettuce. Eat with a fork if necessary.

Jeweled Fruit Tart

Pack this dessert carefully into a picnic basket for a spectacular ending.

Preparation Time:
25 minutes

6 Servings/Serving Size:
1/6th of pie

Exchanges:
| 1/2 | Starch |
| 1 | Fruit |

Calories	115
Calories from Fat	12
Total Fat	1 g
Saturated Fat	0 g

Cholesterol	0 mg
Sodium	76 mg
Carbohydrate	25 g
Dietary Fiber	2 g
Sugars	15 g

| Protein | 2 g |

1 1/2 cups crushed graham crackers
1 Tbsp unsweetened apple juice concentrate
1 Tbsp honey
1 egg white
1 tsp lemon juice
2 tsp sugar
1 tsp cornstarch
1 Tbsp orange juice
1 cup sliced bananas
1 cup sliced strawberries
1 cup blueberries

1. Preheat the oven to 350 degrees. Mix the first four ingredients together to make the tart crust and press into the bottom of a 9-inch pan. Bake for 8–10 minutes. Remove from the oven and let cool.

2. To prepare the glaze, combine the lemon juice, sugar, cornstarch, and orange juice in a saucepan and bring to a boil. Lower heat and let cook for 1 minute until thick. Remove from heat.

3. To assemble the tart, arrange fruit in a decorative pattern over the crust. Spread glaze on top of the fruit. Chill 1 hour. Slice and serve.

White Bean Pate

This spread resembles the wonderfully aromatic French boursin cheese, but contains much less fat.

Preparation Time:
10 minutes

12 Servings/Serving Size:
2 Tbsp

Exchanges:
1/2   Starch

Calories....................... 49
 Calories from Fat 5
Total Fat .... 1 g
 Saturated Fat............ 0 g

Cholesterol .... 0 mg
Sodium................. 165 mg
Carbohydrate.............. 9 g
 Dietary Fiber ....2 g
 Sugars.......................1 g

Protein.........................3 g

1/2 cup minced scallions
3 garlic cloves, minced
1 15-oz can white beans (navy or cannelini)
2 tsp prepared Dijon mustard
1 Tbsp fresh lemon juice
1 tsp olive oil
2 Tbsp minced parsley
1 Tbsp minced basil
1 tsp minced thyme leaves
1 tsp minced dill
1 tsp minced tarragon
1/4 tsp nutmeg
Fresh ground pepper and salt to taste

Combine all ingredients in a blender or food processor. Process until smooth. Serve with crackers or pita bread.

Chunky Lobster Rolls

You can also try cooked jumbo shrimp in these tasty pita sandwiches. (This recipe is relatively high in sodium.)

Preparation Time:
15 minutes

6 Servings/Serving Size:
3 oz

Exchanges:
2 1/2	Starch
3	Very Lean Meat

Calories	294
Calories from Fat	32
Total Fat	4 g
Saturated Fat	0 g
Cholesterol	82 mg
Sodium	758 mg
Carbohydrate	39 g
Dietary Fiber	3 g
Sugars	8 g
Protein	30 g

1 1/2 lb cooked lobster meat, cartilage removed
3 garlic cloves, minced
1/2 cup low-fat mayonnaise
1/2 cup sliced celery
1/2 cup minced scallions
1 Tbsp lemon juice
1 cup shredded romaine lettuce
6 whole-wheat pita bread halves or whole-grain hamburger rolls

1. Mix together the cooked lobster with all ingredients except the lettuce and bread. If using pita bread, stuff ingredients into the pocket and serve.

2. If using hamburger rolls, scoop out some of the bread on one side of each roll to form a pocket. Place shredded lettuce in the hole. Pile on the lobster salad and top with remaining roll half.

Sassy Sweet Potato Salad

Grilled pineapple and sweet vidalia onions almost turn this salad into dessert!

Preparation Time:
25 minutes

6 Servings/Serving Size:
1/2 cup

Exchanges:
2 1/2   Starch

Calories 204
 Calories from Fat 38
Total Fat ....4 g
 Saturated Fat.............0 g

Cholesterol ....0 mg
Sodium ....339 mg
Carbohydrate............40 g
 Dietary Fiber ....4 g
 Sugars......................24 g

Protein ....3 g

3 medium sweet potatoes, peeled and diced into 2-inch pieces
1/2 recipe Honey-Grilled Vidalia Onions (1 1/2 large onions; see p. 260)
3 4-inch wedges fresh pineapple, peeled
1 Tbsp low-calorie margarine
2 Tbsp toasted walnuts
1/2 cup low-fat mayonnaise
1/2 cup nonfat sour cream
2 Tbsp cider vinegar
Fresh ground pepper to taste

1. In a pot of boiling water, cook the sweet potatoes for about 10–15 minutes until tender. Drain and place in a salad bowl. Prepare an outside grill with an oiled rack set 6 inches above the heat source. On a gas grill, set the heat to medium.

2. Grill the vidalia onions on one side of the grill. Place the wedges of pineapple on the other side of the grill. Melt the margarine and brush over the pineapple. Grill the pineapple for 10 minutes until it is caramelized.

3. Remove the onions and pineapple from the grill and dice. Add the grilled onions, pineapple, and walnuts to the cooked sweet potatoes. Set aside. In a small bowl, whisk the remaining ingredients together by hand to make the dressing. Add the dressing to the sweet potato mixture and toss. Refrigerate for several hours before serving.

Low-Fat Chocolate Mousse

This is a great low-fat version of a sinfully rich dessert.

Preparation Time:
15 minutes

6 Servings/Serving Size:
1/2 cup

Exchanges:	
2 1/2	Carbohydrate

Calories	192
Calories from Fat	13
Total Fat	1 g
Saturated Fat	1 g

Cholesterol	6 mg
Sodium	345 mg
Carbohydrate	31 g
Dietary Fiber	1 g
Sugars	17 g

Protein	14 g

2 1.4-oz packages artificially sweetened, low-fat, instant chocolate pudding and pie filling
4 cups evaporated skim milk
3/4 cup low-calorie whipped topping
Sliced strawberries

Mix the dry pudding with the evaporated milk for 1–2 minutes. Mix in the whipped topping. Place into individual dessert dishes and top with sliced strawberries.

✿ ✿

Don't overeat.

You seldom repent of having eaten too little.

—Thomas Jefferson

✿ ✿

Tomatillo Gazpacho

Tomatillos are small, green, Mexican tomatoes covered by thin husks. You can find them in the produce section. Buy small to medium ones, avoiding the large ones. To use, peel off the husk and wash the skin, then dice.

Preparation Time:
20 minutes

---

6 Servings/Serving Size:
1 cup

Exchanges:
2   Vegetable

Calories.......................52
  Calories from Fat........12
Total Fat ....1 g
  Saturated Fat............0 g

Cholesterol ....0 mg
Sodium..................271 mg
Carbohydrate............11 g
  Dietary Fiber ....2 g
  Sugars.......................6 g

Protein ....3 g

1 cup diced tomatillos
2 large red tomatoes, seeded and diced
1 small red pepper, diced
1/4 cup lime juice
2 cups low-fat, low-sodium chicken broth
1 1/2 cups spicy or regular tomato juice
2 garlic cloves, minced
1/2 cup diced, peeled cucumber
1/4 cup sliced scallions
1 Tbsp minced fresh thyme
1–2 tsp hot pepper sauce (taste first, then add as desired)

In a large bowl, combine all ingredients. This is a chunky soup rather than the pureed version. Puree half of the soup if you wish and add to the chunky mixture. Chill overnight or at least 8 hours. Serve in large wine goblets for an elegant touch.

Citrus Swordfish Salad

This recipe uses leftover portions of delicious grilled swordfish, for those too-hot-to-cook days!

Preparation Time:
15 minutes

6 Servings/Serving Size:
3–4 oz fish with 2 cups greens

Exchanges:
1	Fruit
4	Very Lean Meat
1/2	Fat

Calories	217
Calories from Fat	54
Total Fat	6 g
Saturated Fat	1 g

Cholesterol	44 mg
Sodium	124 mg
Carbohydrate	16 g
Dietary Fiber	4 g
Sugars	11 g

Protein	25 g

1 recipe Citrus Swordfish with Tropical Salsa (see p. 246), chilled and cut into chunks, salsa chilled
6 cups torn romaine lettuce
4 cups torn fresh spinach leaves
2 cups chopped red and yellow peppers

Toss the swordfish chunks lightly with the salsa. Place the greens and peppers in individual serving bowls. Top with portions of the salsa-tossed fish and serve.

Artichoke Vinaigrette Salad

This simple salad perfectly complements spicy food. Note that the artichokes need to marinate in the refrigerator overnight.

Preparation Time:
15 minutes

6 Servings/Serving Size:
1 cups

Exchanges:
1	Vegetable
1	Monounsaturated Fat

Calories	76
Calories from Fat	44
Total Fat	5 g
Saturated Fat	1 g

Cholesterol	0 mg
Sodium	510 mg
Carbohydrate	8 g
Dietary Fiber	3 g
Sugars	3 g

Protein	2 g

Dressing
2 Tbsp olive oil
2 Tbsp lemon juice
1/4 cup tarragon vinegar
2 tsp chili powder
1 tsp ground coriander
1/2 tsp cumin
1 tsp onion powder
1 tsp dry mustard
Fresh ground salt and pepper to taste

Salad
1 14-oz can artichoke hearts, drained and chopped
1 red pepper, chopped
1 cup seeded and peeled diced cucumber
6 cups torn romaine lettuce leaves

Whisk together all the dressing ingredients in a small bowl. Combine all the salad ingredients except the romaine lettuce. Add the dressing to the artichokes and marinate in the refrigerator overnight. Place the lettuce in a salad bowl and top with the marinated artichokes.

Giant Strawberries with Raspberry Dip

Try serving melon chunks with this festive berry dip, too.

Preparation Time:
10 minutes

6 Servings/Serving Size:
2 giant strawberries

Exchanges:
1	Fruit
1	Very Lean Meat

Calories	87
Calories from Fat	12
Total Fat	1 g
Saturated Fat	1 g

Cholesterol	10 mg
Sodium	195 mg
Carbohydrate	11 g
Dietary Fiber	2 g
Sugars	9 g

Protein	9 g

1 10-oz package frozen raspberries
1 cup low-fat cottage cheese
1/2 cup part-skim ricotta cheese
2 Tbsp evaporated skim milk
2 tsp almond extract
12 giant strawberries with stems intact

Puree the raspberries in a blender. Pour the puree into a bowl. Blend in the remaining ingredients (except the strawberries) by hand and mix well. Place the dip in a pretty bowl and chill for 2 hours. Serve dip surrounded by large strawberries.

Seashore Shrimp Spread

Pack this delicious dip into a crock or sturdy Tupperware container to carry down to the beach!

Preparation Time:	
5 minutes	

8 Servings/Serving Size:
1/4 cup

Exchanges:
| 1/2 | Starch |
| 1 | Very Lean Meat |

Calories	71
Calories from Fat	2
Total Fat	0 g
Saturated Fat	0 g
Cholesterol	18 mg
Sodium	304 mg
Carbohydrate	8 g
Dietary Fiber	0 g
Sugars	4 g
Protein	8 g

1 cup fat-free cream cheese
1 cup low-fat sour cream
2 tsp lemon juice
1/2 cup minced cooked shrimp
2 tsp lemon pepper

Combine all ingredients and mix together until smooth. Serve with raw vegetables or pita bread wedges.

Don't worry.
Most things you worry about never happen.

—*Thomas Jefferson*

Pasta, White Beans, and Tuna

White beans add a little extra fiber and protein to this nutritious salad.

Preparation Time:
20 minutes

6 Servings/Serving Size:
1 cup pasta with 2 oz tuna and 1/4 cup beans

Exchanges:
3 1/2	Starch
1	Vegetable
1/2	Monounsaturated Fat
2	Very Lean Meat

Calories	405
Calories from Fat	65
Total Fat	7 g
Saturated Fat	1 g

Cholesterol	17 mg
Sodium	429 mg
Carbohydrate	58 g
Dietary Fiber	7 g
Sugars	6 g

Protein	28 g

Salad
12 oz canned white meat tuna, drained and flaked
3 cups cooked, sliced, fresh asparagus
1 1/2 cups canned white beans (navy or cannellini), drained and rinsed
8 large black olives, pitted and sliced
1/2 cup diced roasted red pepper
6 cups cooked corkscrew pasta

Dressing
1/3 cup balsamic vinegar
2 Tbsp olive oil
2 tsp lemon juice
1 Tbsp Dijon mustard
2 Tbsp minced red onion
Fresh ground pepper and salt to taste

Combine all ingredients for the salad. Whisk together all dressing ingredients. Pour the dressing over the salad and refrigerate for 1 hour before serving.

Plum Bread

This slightly tart bread is delicious toasted.

Preparation Time:
15 minutes

9 Servings/Serving Size:
1 1-inch slice

Exchanges:
2 1/2   Starch
1/2   Monounsaturated Fat

Calories........................235
  Calories from Fat........44
Total Fat ....5 g
  Saturated Fat.............1 g

Cholesterol ....48 mg
Sodium...................129 mg
Carbohydrate.............41 g
  Dietary Fiber ....3 g
  Sugars.....................12 g

Protein..........................8 g

1 1/2 cups unbleached white flour
1 cup whole-wheat flour
2 tsp baking powder
2 eggs, beaten
1/4 cup sugar
1/2 cup unsweetened applesauce
2 Tbsp canola oil
1 cup evaporated skim milk
1 tsp lemon extract
2 tsp lemon peel
1 cup finely diced plums
Nonstick cooking spray
2 plums, seeds removed, cut into thin slices

1. Preheat the oven to 350 degrees. In a medium bowl, combine the flours and baking powder. Set aside. In a large bowl, combine the eggs, sugar, applesauce, oil, milk, extract, and lemon peel. Mix well. Slowly add the dry ingredients to the large bowl and mix well. Fold in the plums.

2. Pour the batter into a loaf pan that has been sprayed with nonstick cooking spray. Lay the plum slices on top. Bake for 40–45 minutes until a toothpick comes out clean. If necessary, cover the top loosely with foil so the plum slices do not overbake. Remove cake from oven and let cool for 10 minutes in the pan. Remove cake from pan and let cool completely.

Mango and Papaya Salad with Orange Coconut Dressing

You can also try using mixed berries in this tropical salad.

Preparation Time:	
10 minutes	

6 Servings/Serving Size:
1/2 cup

Exchanges:

1	Fruit
1	Saturated Fat

Calories	113
Calories from Fat	30
Total Fat	3 g
Saturated Fat	2 g

Cholesterol	16 mg
Sodium	127 mg
Carbohydrate	17 g
Dietary Fiber	2 g
Sugars	14 g

Protein	5 g

1 cup low-fat sour cream
1/2 cup fat-free cream cheese, softened
2 Tbsp orange juice
2 tsp coconut extract
1 tsp grated orange rind
3 cups combined diced papayas and mangoes

Mix together the first five ingredients until smooth and toss with the fruit. Chill before serving.

Make it a goal to eat 5 to 9 servings of fruits and vegetables a day.

Ocean Crab Dip

This dip tastes rich, but is surprisingly low in fat.

Preparation Time:
10 minutes

6 Servings/Serving Size:
2 Tbsp

Exchanges:
1   Lean Meat

Calories 60
  Calories from Fat 18
Total Fat ....2 g
  Saturated Fat ....0 g

Cholesterol ....14 mg
Sodium ....212 mg
Carbohydrate..............4 g
  Dietary Fiber ....0 g
  Sugars........................2 g

Protein ....6 g

1/2 cup fat-free cream cheese
1/4 cup fat-free mayonnaise
1/2 tsp lemon juice
1/4 tsp Worcestershire sauce
Dash cayenne pepper
1/2 cup lump crab meat, any shells or cartilage
    removed
3 Tbsp slivered almonds

1. Preheat the oven to 300 degrees. In a bowl,
   beat the cream cheese until light and fluffy.
   Add the mayonnaise, lemon juice,
   Worcestershire sauce, and cayenne pepper.
   Beat until smooth.

2. Fold in the crab and almonds. Place in a
   small casserole dish and bake for 10 minutes.
   Serve with crackers or raw vegetables.

Bow-Tie Pasta Alle Portofino

Fresh arugula is great in the summer.

Preparation Time:
20 minutes

6 Servings/Serving Size:
1 cup pasta, 3 oz shrimp

Exchanges:

3	Starch
1	Vegetable
2	Lean Meat

Calories	376
Calories from Fat	75
Total Fat	8 g
Saturated Fat	1 g
Cholesterol	214 mg
Sodium	362 mg
Carbohydrate	49 g
Dietary Fiber	4 g
Sugars	5 g
Protein	27 g

1 1/2 lb medium shelled and deveined shrimp
12 sun-dried tomatoes, rehydrated
8 fresh plum tomatoes, cubed
2 cups torn arugula
2 Tbsp minced fresh parsley
1/2 cup fresh Italian parsley
1/2 cup chopped fresh basil
2 Tbsp olive oil
1/4 cup fresh lemon juice
Fresh ground pepper and salt to taste
6 cups cooked bow-tie pasta

1. Prepare an outside grill with an oiled rack set 6 inches above the heat source. On a gas grill, set the heat to high. Place the shrimp in an oiled vegetable basket. Grill, turning constantly, for about 5 minutes. Remove shrimp from grill.

2. Combine the grilled shrimp with the remaining ingredients. Toss well and serve.

Garden Vegetable Stir-Fry

The whole garden's in this fiber-packed side dish!

Preparation Time:
15 minutes

6 Servings/Serving Size:
1/2 cup

Exchanges:
2   Vegetable

Calories 45
  Calories from Fat 6
Total Fat ....1 g
  Saturated Fat.............0 g

Cholesterol ....0 mg
Sodium ....355 mg
Carbohydrate.............9 g
  Dietary Fiber ....3 g
  Sugars.......................4 g

Protein ....3 g

1 cup low-fat, low-sodium chicken broth
2 garlic cloves, minced
2 tsp minced ginger
2 scallions, minced
1 cup broccoli florets
1 cup cauliflower florets
2 medium carrots, peeled and diagonally sliced
1 small red pepper, cored, seeded, and sliced
   thin
3 Tbsp lite soy sauce
2 Tbsp lemon juice

Heat the broth in a wok or heavy skillet over medium-high heat. Add the garlic, ginger, and scallions and stir-fry for 3 minutes. Add the broccoli, cauliflower, and carrots and stir-fry for 5 minutes. Add the red pepper, soy sauce, and lemon juice. Cover and steam for 5 minutes.

Adam's Fruit Popsicles

Enjoy those long, hot summer days with this refreshing treat.

Preparation Time:
5 minutes

6 Servings/Serving Size:
1 popsicle (1/2 cup)

Exchanges:
1 1/2   Fruit

Calories	78
Calories from Fat	1
Total Fat	0 g
Saturated Fat	0 g
Cholesterol	0 mg
Sodium	5 mg
Carbohydrate	19 g
Dietary Fiber	0 g
Sugars	18 g
Protein	1 g

1 1/2 cups white grape juice
1 1/2 cups red grape juice
2 Tbsp lemon juice

Combine all ingredients and pour into popsicle molds. Insert wooden or plastic popsicle sticks and freeze until firm.

Fall

Chicken Noodle Tetrazzini

This is a wonderfully comforting dish on a chilly night.

Preparation Time:
20 minutes

---

6 Servings/Serving Size:
1 cup pasta with 3 oz chicken

Exchanges:

4	Starch
4	Very Lean Meat
1/2	Fat

Calories	496
Calories from Fat	74
Total Fat	8 g
Saturated Fat	2 g

Cholesterol	125 mg
Sodium	279 mg
Carbohydrate	61 g
Dietary Fiber	6 g
Sugars	13 g

Protein	44 g

2 Tbsp low-calorie margarine
2 Tbsp unbleached white flour
1 1/2 cups evaporated skim milk
1 cup water
1/4 cup low-fat, low-sodium chicken broth
Fresh ground pepper to taste
1/8 tsp cayenne pepper
1 10-oz package frozen peas
1/2 cup nonfat plain yogurt
2 Tbsp Parmesan cheese
2 cups sliced mushrooms
6 cups cooked egg noodles
1 1/2 lb cooked chicken breasts, cut into 2-inch cubes

1. Preheat the oven to 425 degrees. Melt the margarine in a medium saucepan. Blend in the flour until smooth. Stir in the milk, water, broth, pepper, and cayenne pepper. Cook over medium heat, stirring constantly, until mixture thickens and comes to a boil, about 10 minutes.

2. Stir in the peas, yogurt, and cheese. Mix the sauce with the mushrooms, cooked noodles, and chicken. Pour the mixture into a baking dish and bake for 15 minutes.

Ground Chicken Stroganoff

Crunchy water chestnuts add wonderful texture to this old-fashioned favorite.

Preparation Time:
20 minutes

6 Servings/Serving Size:
1/2 cup noodles with 4 oz chicken

Exchanges:

2	Starch
4	Very Lean Meat
1/2	Fat

Calories	322
Calories from Fat	70
Total Fat	8 g
Saturated Fat	3 g

Cholesterol	108 mg
Sodium	183 mg
Carbohydrate	30 g
Dietary Fiber	2 g
Sugars	6 g

Protein	31 g

1 1/2 lb ground chicken breast (have your butcher grind this for you)
1 medium onion, chopped
1 cup thinly sliced mushrooms
1 4-oz can sliced water chestnuts
Fresh ground pepper and salt to taste
2 Tbsp unbleached white flour
1 cup low-fat, low-sodium chicken broth
1 Tbsp white wine
1 Tbsp Worcestershire sauce
1 Tbsp Dijon mustard
1 cup low-fat sour cream
3 cups cooked wide noodles

1. In a medium skillet over medium-high heat, brown the chicken for about 3–4 minutes. Add the onion and saute for 3 minutes. Add the mushrooms and saute for 4 more minutes. Add the water chestnuts, pepper, and salt.

2. Sprinkle the flour over the mixture. Add the chicken broth. Mix together the wine, Worcestershire sauce, and mustard. Add to the skillet. Reduce heat to low and simmer for 10 minutes. Add the sour cream and heat on low for 1–2 minutes. Serve over cooked noodles.

Three Mushroom Stroganoff

Preparation Time:
20 minutes

12 Servings/Serving Size:
1/2 cup pasta with 1/2
cup stroganoff

Exchanges:
2 1/2	Starch
2	Very Lean Meat

Calories	258
Calories from Fat	18
Total Fat	2 g
Saturated Fat	0 g

Cholesterol	73 mg
Sodium	102 mg
Carbohydrate	34 g
Dietary Fiber	2 g
Sugars	5 g

Protein	23 g

10 dried shiitake mushrooms
15 dried porcini mushrooms
10 fresh white mushrooms or cremini
   mushrooms
1 medium onion, diced
2 garlic cloves, minced
1 tsp paprika
1 cup dry white wine
1 1/2 lb cooked ground turkey
2 Tbsp cornstarch or arrowroot powder
4 Tbsp water
1 1/4 cup low-fat, low-sodium chicken broth
2 cups nonfat sour cream
1/4 cup chopped scallions
1 Tbsp minced fresh parsley
6 cups cooked wide noodles

1. Rehydrate the shiitake and porcini
    mushrooms by pouring boiling water over
    them in a heatproof bowl. Let stand at room
    temperature for 20 minutes. Drain. Take
    stems off shiitake mushrooms and slice.
    Leave the porcini mushrooms whole. Stem
    and slice the fresh mushrooms. Heat the wine
    in a large nonstick skillet. Add the
    mushrooms, onion, garlic, and paprika and
    cook for 8 minutes.

2. Add the turkey and cook for 2 minutes. Add in
    the broth and bring to a boil. Lower the heat.
    Mix together the cornstarch or arrowroot
    powder and water and add to the skillet.
    Cook until thickened. Remove from the heat.
    Add in the sour cream, scallions, and parsley.
    Serve the stroganoff over cooked, hot
    noodles.

Turkey Tetrazzini

Use that leftover holiday turkey in this creamy dish.

| Preparation Time: |
| 20 minutes |

6 Servings/Serving Size:
1 cup

Exchanges:

2	Starch
1	Vegetable
1	Lean Meat

Calories	243
Calories from Fat	37
Total Fat	4 g
Saturated Fat	2 g
Cholesterol	19 mg
Sodium	154 mg
Carbohydrate	35 g
Dietary Fiber	2 g
Sugars	9 g
Protein	17 g

1 Tbsp low-calorie margarine
2 cups sliced mushrooms
2 Tbsp unbleached white flour
1 tsp paprika
2 cups evaporated skim milk
1/4 cup grated Swiss cheese
1/2 cup sliced scallions
1/4 cup diced red pepper
1/2 cup diced turkey
1 lb cooked thin spaghetti
1 Tbsp grated Parmesan cheese

1. Preheat the oven to 350 degrees. Melt the margarine in a heavy skillet over medium-high heat. Add the mushrooms and saute for 5 minutes. Sprinkle the flour and paprika over the mushrooms. Add the milk and stir until thickened.

2. Add the remaining ingredients except the Parmesan cheese. Pour the mixture into a 2-quart casserole dish. Sprinkle with the Parmesan cheese. Bake for 15 minutes until bubbly.

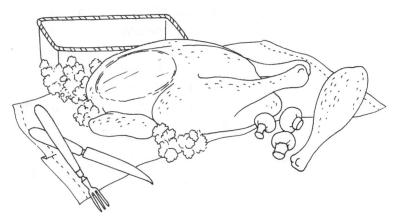

Asian Turkey Pasta

Warm, peanut-flavored turkey tops chewy soba noodles in this tasty dish. Look for soba noodles (Japanese buckwheat noodles) in the international food section of your grocery store.

1/4 cup reduced-fat peanut butter
2/3 cup low-fat, low-sodium beef broth
1/4 tsp ground red pepper
3 Tbsp lite soy sauce
1 Tbsp dry sherry
1 Tbsp cornstarch or arrowroot powder
2 Tbsp water
3 cups diced cooked turkey (preferably white meat)
1/2 cup thinly sliced carrots
1/4 cup diced red pepper
1/4 cup sliced scallions
3 cups cooked soba noodles (keep warm)
5 large romaine lettuce leaves
1 Tbsp toasted sesame seeds

1. In a large saucepan over medium heat, combine the peanut butter and the broth. Stir until smooth. Add the red peppers, soy sauce, and sherry. Bring to a boil. Lower the heat and simmer for 3 minutes. Combine the cornstarch or arrowroot powder with the water. Add to the sauce. Cook until thickened.

2. Add the cooked turkey, carrots, pepper, and scallions to the sauce. Toss to coat well. Place the romaine lettuce leaves on a platter. Place the warm soba noodles on top of the lettuce. Pile the turkey salad in the center of the noodles. Sprinkle on the sesame seeds and serve.

Low-Fat Macaroni and Cheese

Evaporated skim milk and low-fat cheeses make this a healthier version of an old favorite.

Preparation Time:
15 minutes

6 Servings/Serving Size:
1 cup

Exchanges:
2	Starch
1	Very Lean Meat

Calories	203
Calories from Fat	24
Total Fat	**3 g**
Saturated Fat	1 g

Cholesterol	**14 mg**
Sodium	**331 mg**
Carbohydrate	**28 g**
Dietary Fiber	1 g
Sugars	6 g

Protein	**16 g**

3/4 cup evaporated skim milk
1 cup low-fat cottage cheese
1/2 cup part-skim ricotta cheese
1/2 cup low-fat cheddar cheese
1/2 tsp nutmeg
Fresh ground pepper and salt to taste
1 lb cooked elbow macaroni
1 Tbsp Parmesan cheese
1 Tbsp dry bread crumbs

1. Preheat the oven to 350 degrees. Heat the milk in a saucepan over low heat. Add the cheeses until they melt, stirring constantly. Remove the cheese sauce from the heat. Add the cooked pasta to the cheese sauce and mix well.

2. Pour the mixture into a 2-quart casserole dish. Sprinkle with Parmesan cheese and bread crumbs. Bake the casserole for 15–20 minutes until bubbly and the top is browned.

Creamy Noodle Kugel

This pudding, traditionally served on Jewish holidays, marvelously warms your insides.

Preparation Time:
20 minutes

6 Servings/Serving Size:
1 cup

Exchanges:

1 1/2	Starch
1	Fruit
1	Very Lean Meat

Calories	214
Calories from Fat	16
Total Fat	2 g
Saturated Fat	1 g
Cholesterol	27 mg
Sodium	216 mg
Carbohydrate	38 g
Dietary Fiber	2 g
Sugars	18 g
Protein	12 g

1 lb cooked egg noodles
1 cup low-fat cottage cheese
3 egg substitutes
1/4 cup fresh orange juice
2 tsp vanilla
1 tart apple, unpeeled and diced
1 cup boiling water
1/2 cup raisins
1/2 cup canned crushed pineapple, canned in its own juice, drained
1 tsp cinnamon

Preheat the oven to 350 degrees. Combine all ingredients except the noodles and mix well. Add the noodles and pour the mixture into a 2-quart casserole dish. Bake the casserole for 50 minutes until set. Cut into squares and serve.

*The heart eats food
from every companion;
the head receives
nourishment from every
piece of knowledge.*

—Rumi

Pasta and White Bean Casserole

Here's everything you need for a healthy meal in one pot.

Preparation Time:
25 minutes

6 Servings/Serving Size:
1 cup pasta with 4 oz turkey

Exchanges:

4	Starch
1	Vegetable
4	Very Lean Meat

Calories	484
Calories from Fat	51
Total Fat	6 g
Saturated Fat	2 g

Cholesterol	82 mg
Sodium	371 mg
Carbohydrate	66 g
Dietary Fiber	7 g
Sugars	7 g

Protein	43 g

1 1/2 lb ground turkey (have your butcher grind this for you)
1 small onion, diced
2 cups chopped broccoli
1 tsp sage
1 tsp tarragon
1 15-oz can tomatoes, chopped fine, liquid reserved
1 1/2 cups low-fat, low-sodium chicken broth
2 cups canned white beans (navy or cannellini), drained and rinsed
6 cups cooked rotini pasta
2 Tbsp plain bread crumbs
2 Tbsp grated Parmesan cheese

1. Preheat the oven to 350 degrees. Crumble the turkey into a large skillet and place over medium heat. Cook, stirring occasionally, until turkey is cooked through, about 4 minutes. Pour off all but 1 Tbsp of the drippings in the pan. Add the onion, broccoli, sage, and tarragon to the pan. Cook until the vegetables are soft, about 4 minutes.

2. Add the tomatoes and heat to boiling, stirring occasionally. Boil 3 minutes. Remove skillet from heat and the add chicken broth and beans. Stir well. In a large bowl, combine the broccoli mixture and turkey with the cooked pasta. Toss well. Transfer the mixture to a baking dish. Combine the bread crumbs with the cheese and sprinkle over the casserole. Bake until heated through, about 20 minutes.

Baked Rotini with Chickpea Tomato Sauce

Try this tomato sauce over rice, too.

Preparation Time:
20 minutes

6 Servings/Serving Size:
1 cup

Exchanges:

5	Starch
2	Vegetable
1/2	Fat

Calories	493
Calories from Fat	63
Total Fat	7 g
Saturated Fat	1 g

Cholesterol	0 mg
Sodium	659 mg
Carbohydrate	88 g
Dietary Fiber	10 g
Sugars	14 g

Protein	20 g

2 15-oz cans chickpeas (garbanzo beans), drained and rinsed
1 18-oz can crushed tomatoes
1 1/4 cup spicy, low-sodium tomato juice
2 garlic cloves, minced
6 scallions, thinly sliced, green and white parts separated
1 tsp cumin
Fresh ground pepper and salt to taste
1/3 cup nonfat plain yogurt
6 cups cooked rotini pasta, undercooked by 3 minutes
1/2 cup plain, dry bread crumbs
1 Tbsp sesame seeds
1 Tbsp olive oil

1. Preheat the oven to 375 degrees. In a medium saucepan, combine the first seven ingredients (use only the white parts of the scallions). Heat to boiling, then reduce heat and simmer, covered, for 10 minutes. In a small bowl, slowly whisk about 1/4 cup of this mixture into the yogurt. Then add the yogurt to the saucepan and stir.

2. Stir in the cooked pasta and toss to coat. Transfer to a baking dish. Mix the bread crumbs, sesame seeds, oil, and green parts of the scallions in a small bowl until blended. Sprinkle the bread crumb mixture in an even layer over the top of the pasta. Bake until edges are bubbly and bread crumbs are golden brown, about 15 minutes.

Vegetable Lasagna

Preparation Time:
25 minutes

6 Servings/Serving Size:
1 cup

Exchanges:

3	Starch
1	Very Lean Meat

Calories	271
Calories from Fat	16
Total Fat	2 g
Saturated Fat	1 g

Cholesterol	10 mg
Sodium	520 mg
Carbohydrate	46 g
Dietary Fiber	4 g
Sugars	11 g

Protein	18 g

1 cup sliced carrot
1 cup sliced zucchini
1/2 cup diced red pepper
1 cup chopped spinach
1 cup low-fat cottage cheese
1/2 cup part-skim ricotta cheese
2 egg substitutes
1 tsp minced fresh basil
1 tsp minced fresh oregano
Fresh ground pepper to taste
2 cups low-fat, low-sodium marinara sauce
9 uncooked lasagna noodles

1. To prepare the vegetables, steam the carrots over boiling water for 2 minutes. Add the zucchini and steam 2 more minutes. Add the red pepper and steam for 2 more minutes. Add the spinach and steam 1 more minute. Remove the vegetables from the heat. Combine all remaining ingredients except the marinara sauce and lasagna noodles.

2. To assemble the lasagna, place a little sauce on the bottom of a casserole dish. Place 3 noodles on top of the sauce. Add a layer of vegetables and cover with a layer of the cheese mixture. Add some sauce. Repeat. Add the last layer of noodles and top with some sauce. Refrigerate overnight. The next day, preheat the oven to 350 degrees. Bake the lasagna for 40 minutes until bubbly. Let stand 10 minutes prior to serving. Cut into squares and serve. (If you prefer to bake the lasagna immediately, cook the pasta before layering it.)

Zippy Chicken Lasagna

| Preparation Time: |
| 25 minutes |

6 Servings/Serving Size:
1 cup

Exchanges:

| 3 | Starch |
| 4 | Very Lean Meat |

Calories	386
Calories from Fat	56
Total Fat	6 g
Saturated Fat	2 g

Cholesterol	56 mg
Sodium	542 mg
Carbohydrate	47 g
Dietary Fiber	5 g
Sugars	11 g

| Protein | 36 g |

1 Tbsp olive oil
1 medium onion, chopped
1 lb ground chicken breast (have your butcher grind this for you)
1/2 tsp crushed red pepper
1 tsp fennel seeds
Fresh ground pepper to taste
2 cups broccoli florets
1 cup sliced mushrooms
1 cup low-fat cottage cheese
1/2 cup part-skim ricotta cheese
2 egg substitutes
2 cups low-fat, low-sodium marinara sauce
9 uncooked lasagna noodles

1. Preheat the oven to 350 degrees. Heat the oil in a skillet over medium-high heat. Add the onion and saute for 5 minutes. Add the chicken and saute until the chicken is cooked through, about 5–8 minutes. Add the next 3 ingredients.

2. In a steamer over boiling water, steam the broccoli and mushrooms for 3 minutes. (Or microwave with 1 Tbsp water, covered, for 2 minutes.) Combine the cottage cheese, ricotta cheese and egg substitutes in a bowl. Mix well.

3. To assemble the lasagna, place a little sauce on the bottom of a casserole dish. Place 3 noodles on top of the sauce. Add the chicken, then the vegetables. Spread on a layer of the cheese mixture and some sauce. Repeat. Add the last layer of noodles and top with some marinara sauce. Refrigerate overnight. The next day, preheat the oven to 350 degrees. Bake the lasagna for 40 minutes until bubbly. Let stand for 10 minutes prior to serving. Cut into squares and serve.

Turkey Lasagna

Preparation Time:
35 minutes

6 Servings/Serving Size:
1 cup

Exchanges:

5	Starch
4	Very Lean Meat
1/2	Saturated Fat

Calories	574
Calories from Fat	83
Total Fat	9 g
Saturated Fat	4 g

Cholesterol	77 mg
Sodium	694 mg
Carbohydrate	77 g
Dietary Fiber	6 g
Sugars	12 g

Protein	45 g

2 tsp olive oil
1 lb ground turkey (have your butcher grind this for you)
1 cup chopped onion
2 garlic cloves, minced
2 tsp minced fresh oregano
1 Tbsp cumin
1 tsp minced fresh basil
2 tsp Worcestershire sauce
1 14-oz can crushed tomatoes
1 6-oz can tomato paste
3/4 cup low-fat cottage cheese
3/4 cup part-skim ricotta cheese
1 cup part-skim mozzarella cheese
1/4 cup Parmesan cheese
1 14-oz can artichoke hearts, packed in water, diced
1 package uncooked lasagna noodles

1. Preheat the oven to 375 degrees. Heat the oil in a large skillet over medium-high heat. Add the turkey and onion and saute until turkey is cooked through, about 10 minutes. Add the next 4 ingredients and saute for 1 minute. Add the next 3 ingredients and cook over medium heat for 15 minutes. Meanwhile, in a large bowl, combine all the cheeses. Add the artichokes.

2. To assemble the lasagna, place a little sauce on the bottom of a casserole dish. Place 3 noodles on top of the sauce. Place some of the cheese mixture on top of the noodles and layer on more sauce. Continue to layer the lasagna until you have three layers, ending with sauce. Cover and bake for about 35 minutes. Remove cover during last 5 minutes of baking. Let stand for 15–20 minutes before slicing.

White Lasagna

Preparation Time:
20 minutes

6 Servings/Serving Size:
1 cup

Exchanges:

3	Starch
3	Very Lean Meat
1/2	Monounsaturated Fat

Calories	364
Calories from Fat	61
Total Fat	7 g
Saturated Fat	2 g

Cholesterol	37 mg
Sodium	319 mg
Carbohydrate	45 g
Dietary Fiber	1 g
Sugars	12 g

Protein	30 g

2 Tbsp olive oil
10 garlic cloves, minced
1 medium onion, minced
1 1/2 cups evaporated skim milk
2 Tbsp minced fresh basil
2 tsp minced fresh oregano
Fresh ground pepper to taste
1/2 lb ground turkey (have your butcher grind this for you)
1 cup low-fat cottage cheese
1/2 cup part-skim ricotta cheese
2 egg substitutes
9 uncooked lasagna noodles

1. To make garlic sauce, heat the oil in a skillet over medium-high heat. Add the garlic and onion and saute for 5–6 minutes. Add the milk and lower the heat. Cook over low heat until thickened, stirring constantly. Add the basil, oregano, and pepper. Set aside. In a small nonstick skillet, brown the turkey until no longer pink, about 8 minutes. Combine the cottage cheese, ricotta cheese, and egg substitutes.

2. To assemble the lasagna, place a little sauce on the bottom of a casserole dish. Place 3 noodles on top of the sauce. Add a little of the sauce. Then add turkey. Spread the cheese mixture over the turkey. Repeat. Add the last layer of noodles and top with some garlic sauce. Refrigerate overnight. The next day, preheat the oven to 350 degrees. Bake the lasagna for 40 minutes until bubbly. Let stand 10 minutes before serving. Cut into squares and serve. (If you prefer to bake the lasagna immediately, cook the pasta before layering it.)

Saucy Stir-Frys

Stir-frys are a great way to get a meal on the table in a flash. You can wash, slice, and chop all of the ingredients a day in advance, and then it only takes minutes from the wok to your table.

Stir-frying is a wonderful method to use while teaching children how to cook. They'll enjoy adding different ingredients to the wok and stirring the mixture. A nonstick surface will assist in easy clean-up.

Be creative in your stir-frys—try many different vegetables paired with seafood, poultry, pork, and beef. You can think of stir-frys as consisting of four parts: seasoning such as garlic, scallions, and ginger; protein, either animal or soy; vegetables; and a sauce. Keep mixing and matching to find your favorite stir-fry combinations.

Southwestern Stir-Fry

If you're tired of Asian spices, try this differently flavored stir-fry.

Preparation Time:
20 minutes

6 Servings/Serving Size:
3 oz pork

Exchanges:
2	Vegetable
3	Lean Meat

Calories	212
Calories from Fat	74
Total Fat	8 g
Saturated Fat	2 g
Cholesterol	71 mg
Sodium	103 mg
Carbohydrate	7 g
Dietary Fiber	1 g
Sugars	4 g
Protein	26 g

2 Tbsp dry sherry
2 tsp cornstarch or arrowroot powder
1 tsp cumin
2 garlic cloves, minced
Fresh ground pepper and salt to taste
1 1/2 lb pork tenderloin, cut into 3-inch strips
1 Tbsp canola oil
1 green pepper, seeded and cut into strips
1 medium onion, thinly sliced
12 cherry tomatoes, halved

Combine the sherry, cornstarch or arrowroot powder, cumin, garlic, pepper, and salt in a plastic bag. Add the pork slices and shake to coat. Heat the oil in a medium skillet over medium-high heat. Add the pork mixture and stir-fry for 3–4 minutes. Add the remaining ingredients and steam, covered, for 3–5 minutes.

This adapted recipe is courtesy of the National Pork Producers.

Southern-Style Pork Stir-Fry

This is a decidedly different stir-fry from way down South.

Preparation Time:
20 minutes

6 Servings/Serving Size:
3–4 oz pork

Exchanges:

1	Starch
1/2	Fruit
3	Lean Meat

Calories	272
Calories from Fat	67
Total Fat	7 g
Saturated Fat	2 g

Cholesterol	71 mg
Sodium	81 mg
Carbohydrate	24 g
Dietary Fiber	3 g
Sugars	14 g

Protein	26 g

2 tsp canola oil
1 1/2 lb pork tenderloin, cut into strips
2 medium sweet potatoes, peeled and cut into 4-inch strips
1/2 cup water
1 medium onion, halved and sliced
2 Tbsp raisins
1 Tbsp cornstarch or arrowroot powder
1/4 cup dry white wine
2 cups thinly sliced apple wedges, unpeeled

1. Heat the oil in a heavy wok over medium-high heat. Add the pork and saute until the pork loses it pinkness, about 6–8 minutes. Remove the pork from the skillet. Add the sweet potatoes and water to the wok and cook, covered, for 5 minutes.

2. Return the pork to the wok, and add the onions and raisins. Continue to saute for 5 minutes. Mix the cornstarch or arrowroot powder and wine together and add to the pork. Cook, stirring, until sauce is thickened. Add the apple wedges and cook for 2–3 more minutes.

This adapted recipe is courtesy of the National Pork Producers.

Chicken Honey-Nut Stir-Fry

Just a few nuts add a crunch and taste to this stir-fry that can't be beat!

Preparation Time:
20 minutes

6 Servings/Serving Size:
3–4 oz chicken

Exchanges:
1	Starch
3	Very Lean Meat
1	Monounsaturated Fat

Calories	237
Calories from Fat	72
Total Fat	8 g
Saturated Fat	2 g

Cholesterol	69 mg
Sodium	396 mg
Carbohydrate	14 g
Dietary Fiber	2 g
Sugars	9 g

Protein	27 g

1 Tbsp peanut oil
2 medium carrots, peeled and diagonally sliced
2 stalks celery, diagonally sliced
1 1/2 lb boneless, skinless chicken breasts, cut into 3-inch strips
1 Tbsp cornstarch or arrowroot powder
3/4 cup fresh orange juice
3 Tbsp lite soy sauce
1 Tbsp honey
1 tsp minced ginger
1/4 cup chopped toasted cashews or peanuts, unsalted
1/4 cup minced scallions

1. Heat half of the oil in a wok over high heat. Add the carrots and celery and stir-fry for 3 minutes. Add the remaining oil and chicken breasts and stir-fry for 5 more minutes.

2. Dissolve the cornstarch or arrowroot powder in the orange juice. Mix in the soy sauce, honey, and ginger. Add the sauce to the wok and cook over medium heat until thickened. Top with nuts and scallions to serve.

This adapted recipe is courtesy of the National Honey Board.

Lemon Chicken Stir-Fry

Bean sprouts serve as the "noodles" in this stir-fry.

Preparation Time:
20 minutes

6 Servings/Serving Size:
3–4 oz chicken

Exchanges:
| 2 | Vegetable |
| 3 | Lean Meat |

Calories	215
Calories from Fat	68
Total Fat	8 g
Saturated Fat	2 g

Cholesterol	69 mg
Sodium	171 mg
Carbohydrate	9 g
Dietary Fiber	2 g
Sugars	4 g

Protein	27 g

2 Tbsp sesame oil
3 cups bean sprouts
2 garlic cloves, minced
2 tsp minced ginger
1 1/2 lb boneless, skinless chicken breasts, cut
   into 3-inch strips
1 cup fresh snow peas, trimmed
1/2 cup sliced red pepper
1 Tbsp lite soy sauce
1 Tbsp dry sherry
1 Tbsp fresh lemon juice
1 6-oz can bamboo shoots
1 6-oz can water chestnuts, slivered

1. Heat 1 Tbsp of the oil in a wok over high
    heat. Add the bean sprouts and stir-fry for
    1–2 minutes until crisp. Remove from wok
    and place on a platter. In the remaining oil,
    stir-fry the garlic and ginger for 30 seconds.
    Add the chicken and stir-fry for 4 minutes.
    Push the chicken up on the sides of the wok.

2. Add the snow peas and red pepper and stir-
    fry for 2 minutes. Combine the soy sauce,
    sherry, and lemon juice. Add to the wok along
    with the bamboo shoots. Add the chicken
    back to the center of the wok. Cook 2
    minutes. Place the chicken over the bean
    sprouts and top with water chestnuts to
    serve.

Korean Chicken Stir-Fry

Toast the sesame seeds for this recipe in a dry skillet over medium-high heat for 2–3 minutes, then place in a blender or coffee grinder until crushed.

Preparation Time:
15 minutes

6 Servings/Serving Size:
3 oz chicken with 1/2 cup rice

Exchanges:

2	Starch
3	Lean Meat

Calories	321
Calories from Fat	89
Total Fat	10 g
Saturated Fat	2 g

Cholesterol	69 mg
Sodium	370 mg
Carbohydrate	27 g
Dietary Fiber	2 g
Sugars	3 g

Protein	29 g

1 1/2 lb boneless, skinless chicken breasts, cut into strips
1 tsp grated fresh ginger
1 Tbsp lite soy sauce
2 Tbsp peanut oil
3 Tbsp crushed toasted sesame seeds
2 scallions, minced
2 garlic cloves, minced
3 cups fresh bean sprouts
3 cups cooked rice
2 Tbsp lite soy sauce

In a large bowl, combine the chicken, ginger, and soy sauce. Heat the oil in a wok over high heat. Add the chicken and stir-fry until the chicken is opaque, about 5 minutes. Add sesame seeds, scallions, and garlic and stir-fry for 2 minutes. Add the bean sprouts and cook for 2 minutes. Add the rice and soy sauce, toss well, and serve.

This adapted recipe is courtesy of the National Broiler Council.

Orange Chicken Stir-Fry

This stir-fry is served over aromatic jasmine rice.

Preparation Time:
20 minutes

6 Servings/Serving Size:
3–4 oz chicken with 1/2 cup rice

Exchanges:

2	Starch
1	Vegetable
3	Very Lean Meat

Calories	296
Calories from Fat	51
Total Fat	6 g
Saturated Fat	1 g

Cholesterol	69 mg
Sodium	269 mg
Carbohydrate	31 g
Dietary Fiber	1 g
Sugars	5 g

Protein	28 g

1 Tbsp canola oil
1 1/2 lb boneless, skinless chicken breasts, cut into strips
2 tsp minced ginger
1 cup sliced red pepper
1 cup sliced yellow pepper
1 cup sliced mushrooms
1/4 cup fresh orange juice
1/2 tsp orange extract
2 Tbsp lite soy sauce
2 tsp brown sugar
1/4 cup low-fat, low-sodium chicken broth
1 Tbsp cornstarch or arrowroot powder
3 cups cooked jasmine rice
1/2 cup sliced scallions

Heat the oil in a wok over high heat. Add the chicken and stir-fry for 5–6 minutes. Push the chicken up on the sides of the wok. Add the ginger and vegetables to the wok and stir-fry for 6 minutes. Combine remaining ingredients except the rice and scallions, add to the wok, and cook until sauce thickens. Add the chicken back to the center of the wok and cook for 1 minute. Serve over hot rice and garnish with scallions.

Apple-Turkey Stir-Fry

Apple juice adds a sweet touch to this stir-fry.

Preparation Time:
20 minutes

6 Servings/Serving Size:
3–4 oz turkey with 1/2 cup rice

Exchanges:

2 1/2	Starch
1	Vegetable
3	Very Lean Meat

Calories	320
Calories from Fat	30
Total Fat	3 g
Saturated Fat	0 g

Cholesterol	75 mg
Sodium	285 mg
Carbohydrate	39 g
Dietary Fiber	3 g
Sugars	11 g

Protein	31 g

2 Tbsp brown sugar
1/2 tsp red pepper flakes
2 garlic cloves, minced
2 Tbsp dry sherry
2 Tbsp lite soy sauce
1 Tbsp cornstarch or arrowroot powder
1/2 cup unsweetened apple juice
1 1/2 lb turkey breast, cut into thin strips
1 Tbsp canola oil
1 cup fresh snow peas, trimmed
2 cups thinly sliced carrot
2 Tbsp sliced scallions
3 cups cooked rice

Combine the first seven ingredients. Add the turkey and mix to coat well. Let stand for 30 minutes. Heat the oil in a wok over high heat. Add the turkey mixture and stir-fry for 5–7 minutes. Push the turkey up on the sides of the wok. Add the vegetables and stir-fry for 3 minutes. Push the turkey back to the center of the wok and stir-fry for 2–3 more minutes. Serve over hot rice.

Spicy Shrimp and Scallop Stir-Fry

Hot chili oil, made with sesame oil and chilies, is available in Asian grocery stores.

Preparation Time:
20 minutes

6 Servings/Serving Size:
3–4 oz seafood

Exchanges:

2	Vegetable
3	Very Lean Meat

Calories	161
Calories from Fat	37
Total Fat	4 g
Saturated Fat	1 g

Cholesterol	126 mg
Sodium	409 mg
Carbohydrate	8 g
Dietary Fiber	2 g
Sugars	4 g

Protein	23 g

1 Tbsp hot chili oil
2 garlic cloves, minced
1/4 cup minced scallions
1 small red chili, minced
2 medium carrots, thinly sliced
2 medium stalks celery, thinly sliced
1 lb medium shelled and deveined shrimp
1/2 lb sea scallops
1/4 cup low-fat, low-sodium chicken broth
1/2 cup chopped bok choy cabbage
1/2 cup fresh snow peas, trimmed
2 Tbsp lite soy sauce

Heat the oil in a wok over high heat. Add the garlic, scallions, and red chili and stir-fry for 30 seconds. Add the carrots and celery and stir-fry for 3 minutes. Add the shrimp and scallops and stir-fry for 1 minute. Add the broth, cover, and steam for 1 minute. Add the bok choy, snow peas, and soy sauce. Steam for 2 minutes until the snow peas are tender, but still crisp.

The easiest exercise is also the best: walk!

Holiday Shrimp Stir-Fry

Jumbo shrimp are spiced up with this Chinese ginger sauce.

Preparation Time:
20 minutes

6 Servings/Serving Size:
3–4 oz with 1/2 cup rice

Exchanges:

2	Starch
2	Very Lean Meat

Calories	214
Calories from Fat	26
Total Fat	3 g
Saturated Fat	1 g

Cholesterol	161 mg
Sodium	508 mg
Carbohydrate	26 g
Dietary Fiber	2 g
Sugars	2 g

Protein	21 g

1 1/2 lb fresh jumbo shrimp, peeled, deveined, and butterflied (you can have the seafood department do this for you)
1 tsp corn oil
2 scallions, minced
2 tsp minced ginger
2 garlic cloves, minced
3/4 cup low-fat, low-sodium chicken broth
3 Tbsp lite soy sauce
2 Tbsp cider vinegar
2 tsp rice vinegar
1/4 tsp chili powder
1 Tbsp cornstarch or arrowroot powder
2 Tbsp water
3 cups cooked brown rice

Heat the oil in a large skillet or wok over medium-high heat. Add the scallions, ginger, and garlic. Stir-fry for 30 seconds. Add the broth, soy sauce, cider vinegar, rice vinegar, and chili powder. Bring to a boil, then lower the heat. Add the shrimp and saute for 3–4 minutes, just until the shrimp turns pink. Mix together the cornstarch or arrowroot powder with the water. Add to the skillet and cook until thickened. Serve the shrimp over the rice.

Seafood and Asparagus Stir-Fry

You can use shrimp, crab, salmon, swordfish, or tuna in this recipe if you wish.

Preparation Time:
20 minutes

6 Servings/Serving Size:
3–4 oz seafood with 1/2 cup rice

Exchanges:

2	Starch
1	Vegetable
2	Very Lean Meat

Calories	270
Calories from Fat	36
Total Fat	**4 g**
Saturated Fat	1 g
Cholesterol	41 mg
Sodium	559 mg
Carbohydrate	34 g
Dietary Fiber	2 g
Sugars	8 g
Protein	24 g

1 Tbsp peanut oil
1 cup thinly sliced red pepper
1/2 cup thinly sliced yellow pepper
1/2 cup diced onion
2 cups sliced fresh asparagus
2 garlic cloves, minced
1 Tbsp minced ginger
1 lb sea scallops
1/2 lb sea bass, cut into 2-inch cubes
1/4 cup lite soy sauce
2 Tbsp rice vinegar
2 tsp sugar
3 cups cooked rice

Heat the oil in a wok over high heat. Add the peppers and onion and stir-fry for 3 minutes. Add the asparagus and stir-fry for 3 more minutes. Add the garlic and ginger and stir-fry for 3 minutes. Add the seafood, cover, and steam for 2 minutes. Mix together the soy sauce, rice vinegar, and sugar and add to the wok. Cook for 2–3 minutes and serve over hot rice.

Gingered Tuna Stir-Fry

Shredded cabbage, instead of rice or noodles, adds bulk to this stir-fry.

Preparation Time:
20 minutes

6 Servings/Serving Size:
3–4 oz tuna

Exchanges:
1	Vegetable
4	Very Lean Meat
1	Fat

Calories	218
Calories from Fat	71
Total Fat	8 g
Saturated Fat	2 g
Cholesterol	42 mg
Sodium	279 mg
Carbohydrate	7 g
Dietary Fiber	2 g
Sugars	4 g
Protein	27 g

1/2 cup dry sherry
3/4 cup orange juice
1/2 cup low-fat, low-sodium chicken broth
1/4 cup lite soy sauce
2 Tbsp minced ginger
1 1/2 lb tuna steaks, cut into 2-inch cubes
1 Tbsp sesame oil
1/2 cup chopped shallots
1 cup thinly sliced carrots
1/2 cup thinly sliced celery
1 cup shredded cabbage

Combine the first five ingredients. Add tuna and marinate for 30 minutes. Heat the oil in a wok over high heat. Add the shallots and stir-fry for 2 minutes. Add the carrots and celery and stir-fry for 3 minutes. Add the cabbage and stir-fry for 3 minutes. Push the vegetables up on the sides of the wok. Remove the tuna from the marinade and add it to the wok. Stir-fry for 3–4 minutes. Add the vegetables back to the center of the wok and stir-fry for 2 more minutes.

Orange Roughy Stir-Fry

Stir-fry orange roughy gently so it doesn't flake into tiny pieces.

Preparation Time:	
20 minutes	

6 Servings/Serving Size:	
3 oz fish with 1/2 cup rice	

Exchanges:	
2	Starch
1	Vegetable
2	Very Lean Meat

Calories	261
Calories from Fat	32
Total Fat	4 g
Saturated Fat	1 g

Cholesterol	23 mg
Sodium	408 mg
Carbohydrate	34 g
Dietary Fiber	3 g
Sugars	5 g

Protein	21 g

3 tsp peanut oil
2 scallions, minced
3 garlic cloves, minced
2 tsp minced ginger
1 1/2 lb orange roughy, cut into 2-inch cubes
1 cup diagonally sliced carrots
1 cup broccoli florets
1/2 cup sliced red pepper
1/2 cup fresh snow peas, trimmed
3 Tbsp lite soy sauce
2 Tbsp sherry
2 tsp sugar
1/2 cup low-fat, low-sodium chicken broth
2 Tbsp cornstarch or arrowroot powder
3 cups cooked rice

1. Heat 2 tsp of the oil in a wok over medium-high heat. Add the scallions, garlic, and ginger and stir-fry for 1 minute. Add the fish and stir-fry for 3–4 minutes, until it is almost cooked through. Remove the fish from the wok. Add the remaining oil to the wok and stir-fry the carrots for 2 minutes.

2. Add the broccoli and pepper and stir-fry for 4 more minutes. Add the snow peas and stir-fry for 1 minute. Mix together the soy sauce, sherry, sugar, broth, and cornstarch or arrowroot powder. Add the mixture to the wok and stir until sauce has thickened. Add the fish back to the wok and cook for 1 minute. Serve over hot rice.

Penne Pasta Stir-Fry

Penne pasta is a welcome surprise in this meatless Asian stir-fry.

Preparation Time:
20 minutes

6 Servings/Serving Size:
1 cup pasta with 1/2 cup vegetables

Exchanges:

3	Starch
1	Vegetable

Calories	262
Calories from Fat	28
Total Fat	3 g
Saturated Fat	0 g

Cholesterol	0 mg
Sodium	374 mg
Carbohydrate	50 g
Dietary Fiber	4 g
Sugars	6 g

Protein	9 g

2 tsp cornstarch or arrowroot powder
3 Tbsp lite soy sauce
3 Tbsp rice vinegar
1 cup low-fat, low-sodium chicken broth
2 tsp canola oil
2 large carrots, thinly sliced
3 garlic cloves, minced
1 cup fresh snow peas, trimmed
1/4 tsp red pepper flakes
6 cups cooked penne pasta
Fresh ground pepper and salt to taste

Combine the first four ingredients and set aside. Heat the oil in a large skillet or wok over high heat. Add the carrots and garlic and stir-fry for 5 minutes. Add the snow peas, lower heat to medium-low, and add the red pepper flakes and sauce. Add the pasta to the wok, bring to a boil, and cook for 2 minutes. Season with pepper and salt to serve.

Teriyaki Stir-Fry Salad

Stir-fry is great over mixed greens.

Preparation Time:	
20 minutes	

6 Servings/Serving Size:
3 oz pork

Exchanges:

2	Vegetable
3	Very Lean Meat
1	Fat

Calories	208
Calories from Fat	60
Total Fat	7 g
Saturated Fat	2 g

Cholesterol	66 mg
Sodium	350 mg
Carbohydrate	10 g
Dietary Fiber	3 g
Sugars	6 g

Protein	27 g

1/3 cup commercial teriyaki sauce
1/3 cup pineapple juice
1 Tbsp minced ginger
2 garlic cloves, minced
1 1/2 lb pork tenderloin, diagonally sliced across the grain into 1/4-inch strips
1 Tbsp peanut oil
1 cup diagonally sliced carrots
1 cup sliced shiitake mushrooms
1 cup fresh snow peas, trimmed
2 Tbsp minced scallions
6 cups mixed greens (try spinach, romaine, and watercress)

1. Combine the first four ingredients. Add the pork and marinate in the refrigerator for 2–24 hours. Then drain the marinade from the pork. Heat the oil in a wok over high heat. Add the pork and stir-fry for 5 minutes until the pork is cooked through. Push the pork up on the sides of the wok.

2. Add the carrots and stir-fry for 3 minutes. Add the mushrooms and stir-fry for 3 more minutes. Add the snow peas and stir-fry for 2 minutes. Add the scallions and stir-fry for 30 seconds. Line a platter with greens and place the pork and vegetable mixture on top to serve.

This adapted recipe is courtesy of the Association for Dressings and Sauces.

Speedy Stir-Fry

Rummage through your refrigerator for these easy stir-fry ingredients!

Preparation Time:
20 minutes

6 Servings/Serving Size:
3–4 meat with 1/2 cup rice

Exchanges:

2	Starch
1	Vegetable
3	Very Lean Meat

Calories	303
Calories from Fat	50
Total Fat	6 g
Saturated Fat	1 g
Cholesterol	69 mg
Sodium	282 mg
Carbohydrate	33 g
Dietary Fiber	2 g
Sugars	7 g
Protein	28 g

1 Tbsp canola oil
3 cups sliced raw vegetables (try carrots, broccoli, zucchini, and peppers)
2 garlic cloves, minced
1 1/2 lb boneless, skinless chicken breasts or lean sirloin steak, cooked and sliced into strips
2 Tbsp lite soy sauce
2 Tbsp brown sugar
1 Tbsp dry sherry
3 cups cooked rice
2 Tbsp toasted sesame seeds

Heat the oil in a wok over high heat. Add the vegetables and stir-fry for 4 minutes. Add the garlic and stir-fry for 2 more minutes. Add the chicken or beef and stir-fry 1 minute. Combine the soy sauce, sugar, and sherry and add to the wok. Cover and steam for 1 minute. Serve over hot rice and garnish with sesame seeds.

True silence is the rest of the mind; it is to the spirit what sleep is to the body— nourishment and refreshment.

—William Penn

Serving Squash

Colorful, plentiful squash is a classic fall favorite. Squash is an excellent source of vitamin A, vitamin C, riboflavin, and iron. A 3 1/2-oz serving of squash contains only 34 to 69 calories, depending on the type of squash and the cooking method used.

When selecting squash in the supermarket, always look for solid squash that feels heavy for its size. Uncooked squash should be kept on a cool, dry shelf. If you put uncooked squash in the refrigerator, it will become watery and lose its flavor quickly. Once cooked, squash should be refrigerated in a tightly covered container and used in 5 days. Cooked, mashed squash can be frozen for up to 6 months.

Squash can be cooked in the following ways:

* All types of squash can be baked. Just cut the squash in half, remove the seeds, and place cut side down on a cookie sheet. Bake the squash at 350 degrees for about 45 minutes (or more, depending on the size of the squash). When a fork slides through the skin easily, it's done.

* To boil squash, cut it in half and remove the seeds and fibers. Cut the squash into large chunks and peel each chunk. Add the squash to a pot of unsalted boiling water and boil gently for 20–40 minutes, depending on the quantity of squash. Drain and serve as chunks or mash.

* Squash can be microwaved. Follow the instructions for boiling squash and microwave on high until done. Then serve as chunks or mash.

Some favorite varieties of squash

* Acorn squash is probably the best-known of all the squashes. It is small, with a deep cavity ideal for stuffing.

* Buttercup squash is shaped like a turban, with a light green cap on a dark green base. The pulp is a creamy shade of yellow.

* Butternut squash has a smooth skin and looks like a tan, elongated pear. It has a sweet, orange pulp.

* Cushaw squash is globe-shaped at one end, and tapers to a narrow, curved neck. The pulp is white-gold.

* Hubbard squash resembles a football. It is lumpy-skinned, with colors ranging from dark green and light blue-gray to pumpkin and creamy white.

* Spaghetti squash is quite fun to prepare. The pulp cooks up into golden strands that are pulled from the shell. This squash is great with spaghetti sauce.

* Turkish Turban squash has a bright orange rind with deep green, white, and yellow splashes. It looks like a flattened pumpkin.

Squash is great used around the house as fall decoration, too. Pile colorful and differently-shaped squash in the center of your holiday table. Use a large turban squash as an edible serving tureen for soups and main courses. Acorn squash have attractive outer shells and look best served in scalloped halves.

Italian-Style Spaghetti Squash

Robust herbs and tomatoes are the perfect complement to chewy strands of squash.

Preparation Time:
25 minutes

6 Servings/Serving Size:
1 cup

Exchanges:

1	Starch
2	Vegetable
1	Lean Meat
1/2	Fat

Calories	209
Calories from Fat	56
Total Fat	6 g
Saturated Fat	2 g

Cholesterol	8 mg
Sodium	404 mg
Carbohydrate	27 g
Dietary Fiber	4 g
Sugars	8 g

Protein	12 g

1 small spaghetti squash, halved, seeds removed
1 Tbsp olive oil
1 cup chopped onion
2 garlic cloves, minced
2 cups thinly sliced mushrooms
2 medium tomatoes, seeded and chopped
1 tsp minced fresh oregano
2 tsp minced fresh basil
1/4 cup chopped fresh parsley
1 tsp minced fresh thyme
1 cup low-fat cottage cheese
1/2 cup grated part-skim mozzarella cheese
1 cup dry bread crumbs
2 Tbsp grated Parmesan cheese

1. Preheat the oven to 350 degrees. Place each squash half, cut side down, on a cookie sheet and bake, uncovered, for about 45–60 minutes until a fork goes easily into the shell. Meanwhile, heat the oil in a skillet over medium-high heat. Add the onion and garlic and saute for 5 minutes. Add the mushrooms and saute for 3 more minutes. Add the tomatoes and cook until the tomato liquid is evaporated. Add the herbs and cook for 5 minutes.

2. When the squash is done, scoop out the strands with a large fork or spoon. Combine the squash with the cheeses and place it in a casserole dish. Pour the sauce on top. Mix together the bread crumbs and Parmesan cheese and sprinkle over the sauce. Bake the casserole for 20 minutes and serve.

Spicy Spaghetti Squash

Spicy turkey tastes better than ground beef with this spaghetti squash.

Preparation Time:
25 minutes

6 Servings/Serving Size:
1 cup squash with 1/2 cup sauce

Exchanges:

1	Starch
1	Vegetable
2	Very Lean Meat

Calories	188
Calories from Fat	29
Total Fat	3 g
Saturated Fat	1 g

Cholesterol	47 mg
Sodium	286 mg
Carbohydrate	19 g
Dietary Fiber	5 g
Sugars	9 g

Protein	20 g

1 small spaghetti squash, halved, seeds removed
1 Tbsp olive oil
1/2 cup minced onion
3 garlic cloves, minced
2 scallions, minced
12 oz ground turkey (have your butcher grind this for you)
2 cups crushed tomatoes
2 Tbsp red wine
2 tsp capers
2 tsp minced fresh oregano
2 tsp crushed red pepper flakes
2 Tbsp minced fresh parsley

1. Preheat the oven to 350 degrees. Place each squash half, cut side down, on a cookie sheet and bake, uncovered, for about 45–60 minutes until a fork goes easily into the shell. Let cool slightly, scoop out the strands of squash with a large fork or spoon, and set aside. Discard shell.

2. Heat the oil in a skillet over medium-high heat. Add the onion, garlic, and scallions and saute for 2 minutes. Add the turkey and cook until it loses its pinkness, about 5–6 minutes. Add the tomatoes and wine. Bring to a boil, lower the heat, and simmer for 20 minutes.

3. Add the capers, oregano, and crushed red pepper flakes. Simmer for 5 minutes. Reheat the squash by microwaving it, covered, on high for 3 minutes. Top the squash with the sauce and garnish with parsley to serve.

Wild Rice- and Cranberry-Stuffed Acorn Squash

This squash is good served with Cornish game hens.

Preparation Time:
20 minutes

6 Servings/Serving Size:
1/2 small acorn squash
with 1/2 cup rice

Exchanges:

2 1/2	Starch

Calories	201
Calories from Fat	25
Total Fat	3 g
Saturated Fat	0 g
Cholesterol	0 mg
Sodium	17 mg
Carbohydrate	42 g
Dietary Fiber	8 g
Sugars	10 g
Protein	6 g

3 small acorn squash, halved, seeds removed
4 cups water
1 cup uncooked wild rice, rinsed
1 Tbsp olive oil
1 cup chopped onion
1/2 cup chopped celery
1/4 cup minced fresh parsley
1 cup dried cranberries, soaked in warm water
for 10 minutes, drained

1. Preheat the oven to 350 degrees. Place the halved squash, cut side down, on a cookie sheet and bake, uncovered, for about 45 minutes until a fork goes easily into the shell. Meanwhile, prepare the filling. In a large saucepan, combine water and rinsed rice. Bring to a boil, lower heat, and simmer for about 45 minutes.

2. Heat the oil in a skillet over medium-high heat. Add the onion and celery and cook for about 5 minutes. Add the parsley and drained dried cranberries. Add the cooked rice. Fill each acorn squash cavity with some of the rice mixture. Bake uncovered, filling side up, for 15 minutes.

Acorn Squash with Pineapple

Crushed pineapple enhances the sweet taste of acorn squash.

Preparation Time:
15 minutes

6 Servings/Serving Size:
1/2 cup

Exchanges:
1/2	Starch

Calories	47
Calories from Fat	1
Total Fat	0 g
Saturated Fat	0 g
Cholesterol	0 mg
Sodium	3 mg
Carbohydrate	12 g
Dietary Fiber	3 g
Sugars	6 g
Protein	1 g

1 large acorn squash
2 tsp cinnamon
1 tsp nutmeg
1/2 tsp allspice
1/2 tsp ginger
1/2 cup crushed pineapple, canned in its own
   juice, drained

1. Preheat the oven to 350 degrees. To prepare the squash, cut it in half and remove the seeds. Place each half, cut side down, on a baking sheet. Bake the squash for 45–60 minutes until soft and tender.

2. Turn the acorn squash over and scoop out all the squash. In a bowl, mix the squash with all the remaining ingredients. Place in a casserole dish and bake for 5 more minutes, until pineapple bubbles.

Butternut Squash Chicken Casserole

This is a tasty and satisfying one-dish meal.

Preparation Time:
20 minutes

6 Servings/Serving Size:
1 1/2 cups

Exchanges:
2 1/2	Starch
3	Very Lean Meat

Calories......................302
  Calories from Fat........56
Total Fat ....6 g
  Saturated Fat..............2 g

Cholesterol ....126 mg
Sodium...................206 mg
Carbohydrate............34 g
  Dietary Fiber ....8 g
  Sugars.....................19 g

Protein........................28 g

3 cups frozen peas, thawed
12 oz skinless, boneless cooked chicken breasts,
  cubed into 1-inch pieces
1 cup sliced cremini mushrooms
3 cups cooked, mashed butternut squash
2 Tbsp sugar
1 tsp lemon extract
1 Tbsp butter
2 eggs, beaten
1 cup evaporated skim milk

1. Preheat the oven to 350 degrees. Place the peas on the bottom of a casserole dish. Layer the chicken on top, then layer the mushrooms over the chicken.

2. Combine all remaining ingredients in a blender and mix well. Pour the mixture on top of the mushrooms. Bake for 30 minutes, covered. Uncover and bake for an additional 15 to 20 minutes.

Bourbon Acorn Squash

Try serving this squash with roasted pork.

Preparation Time:
10 minutes

6 Servings/Serving Size:
1/2 cup

Exchanges:
1   Starch

Calories.........................79
 Calories from Fat........19
Total Fat.......................2 g
 Saturated Fat.............1 g

Cholesterol...............5 mg
Sodium....................26 mg
Carbohydrate............14 g
 Dietary Fiber ....3 g
 Sugars.......................8 g

Protein..........................1 g

1 large acorn squash, halved, seeds removed
2 Tbsp brown sugar
1 Tbsp butter
1/4 cup bourbon

1. Preheat the oven to 350 degrees. Place the halved squash, cut side down, on a cookie sheet and bake for 45–60 minutes until a fork goes easily into the shell. Remove the squash from the oven and let cool for 20 minutes.

2. Scoop out the squash from the shell and place it in a mixing bowl. Add the remaining ingredients and beat well with electric beaters. Place the squash in a casserole dish and bake, uncovered, for 20 minutes.

Savor each bite of food

as though it were the

only one you had.

Portobello Mushroom-
Stuffed Zucchini

Serve this dish with rice and beans for a great vegetarian meal.

Preparation Time:
20 minutes

6 Servings/Serving Size:
1/2 medium zucchini with
2 Tbsp cheese

Exchanges:

2	Vegetable
1	Lean Meat
1/2	Fat

Calories......................116
  Calories from Fat........54
Total Fat ....6 g
  Saturated Fat.............3 g

Cholesterol ....11 mg
Sodium...................299 mg
Carbohydrate.............10 g
  Dietary Fiber ....2 g
  Sugars.......................5 g

Protein ....7 g

3 medium zucchini (halve lengthwise, scoop out
    and cube insides, reserve shells)
1/4 cup red wine
1 Tbsp olive oil
1 cup diced portobello mushrooms or white
    mushrooms
1/2 cup finely diced carrot
1/4 cup minced onion
2 garlic cloves, minced
1 10-oz can stewed tomatoes
1 tsp minced fresh basil
1 tsp minced fresh thyme
1/2 tsp minced fresh oregano
1/2 cup Parmesan cheese
1/2 cup shredded, part-skim mozzarella cheese

1. Preheat the oven to 350 degrees. Heat the
    wine and oil in a large skillet over medium-
    high heat. Add the cubed zucchini,
    mushrooms, carrot, and onion and saute for 5
    minutes. Add the garlic and saute for 3 more
    minutes. Add the tomatoes and herbs, lower
    the heat, and simmer for 5 minutes.

2. Stuff each zucchini shell with some of the
    mixture. Combine the cheeses and sprinkle
    on top of each shell. Place shells in a
    casserole dish. Pour in 1 inch of water. Cover
    and bake for 30 minutes.

Zucchini Mexican Style

Chili powder and cumin spice up fresh zucchini.

Preparation Time:
15 minutes

6 Servings/Serving Size:
1/2 cup

Exchanges:
1   Vegetable
1/2 Monounsaturated Fat

Calories........................51
 Calories from Fat........22
Total Fat ....2 g
 Saturated Fat.............0 g

Cholesterol ....0 mg
Sodium.....................13 mg
Carbohydrate..............8 g
 Dietary Fiber ....2 g
 Sugars.......................4 g

Protein ....1 g

1 Tbsp olive oil
1 Tbsp cumin seeds
1 medium onion, minced
3 garlic cloves, minced
1 1/2 cups sliced zucchini (1/4-inch-thick slices)
1/2 cup diced tomatoes
1/4 cup corn
3 Tbsp lime juice
2 tsp chili powder
Fresh ground pepper to taste

1. Heat the oil in a large skillet over medium-high heat. Add the cumin seeds and roast for 30 seconds. Add the onion and saute for 5 minutes. Add the garlic and saute for 3 more minutes.

2. Add the zucchini and saute for 2 minutes. Add the tomatoes and corn and saute for 2 more minutes. Add the lime juice and chili powder; cover and cook for 2 minutes. Grind in pepper and serve.

Summer Squash with Golden Raisins

This all-golden side dish is slightly sweet.

Preparation Time:	
10 minutes	

6 Servings/Serving Size:
1/2 cup

Exchanges:

1/2	Fruit
1	Vegetable

Calories	59
Calories from Fat	2
Total Fat	0 g
Saturated Fat	0 g
Cholesterol	0 mg
Sodium	2 mg
Carbohydrate	15 g
Dietary Fiber	1 g
Sugars	12 g
Protein	1 g

2 cups sliced summer squash (1/4-inch-thick slices)
1/2 cup golden raisins
1/2 cup sliced golden delicious apples (leave skin on)
1/2 cup water
2 tsp cinnamon
2 tsp honey

Combine all ingredients in a saucepan. Cook over medium-low heat for about 8 minutes until the squash and apples are tender.

Pumpkin Won Tons

This is an unusual, but very tasty, way to use pumpkin.

Preparation Time:
35 minutes

6 Servings/Serving Size:
3 won tons

Exchanges:
1 1/2	Starch
1/2	Fat

Calories	125
Calories from Fat	39
Total Fat	4 g
Saturated Fat	1 g

Cholesterol	2 mg
Sodium	108 mg
Carbohydrate	20 g
Dietary Fiber	3 g
Sugars	5 g

Protein	3 g

2 tsp peanut oil
2 tsp minced fresh parsley
2 garlic cloves, minced
1/2 cup minced onion
2 tsp lemon juice
1 tsp minced fresh rosemary
1 Tbsp minced golden raisins
2 cups canned pumpkin
1 tsp cinnamon
18 won ton wrappers
1 Tbsp peanut oil

1. Heat the oil in a skillet over medium-high heat. Add the parsley, garlic, and onion. Cook for about 5 minutes. Add the lemon juice, rosemary, raisins, pumpkin, and cinnamon.

2. Take out one won ton wrapper at a time and place some of the filling in the center of the square. Fold in half evenly and pinch the ends closed. Or pull the bottom corners toward each other, overlap the tips, and pinch together.

3. Cover finished won tons with a damp paper towel to keep them moist. Heat the oil in a nonstick skillet over medium-high heat. Add the won tons and saute until golden brown, about 2–3 minutes on each side.

Cranberry Festival

Cranberries are a welcome sight in the fall. Brightly colored and full of nutrients, cranberries are versatile enough to be part of a main dish, hearty breakfast, or sweet dessert. Buy cranberries in season, then freeze them to have through the winter. When cranberries are completely out of season, use the dried variety. Toss a handful of dried cranberries into sauces, cereals, and salads to give them a nice, tart lift.

Game Hens with Cranberry Barbecue Sauce

Try using this sauce with pork roast, too.

Preparation Time:
20 minutes

6 Servings/Serving Size:
1/2 hen, no skin

Exchanges:

1/2	Carbohydrate
3	Medium-Fat Meat
1/2	Fat

Calories	288
Calories from Fat	158
Total Fat	18 g
Saturated Fat	5 g

Cholesterol	124 mg
Sodium	169 mg
Carbohydrate	10 g
Dietary Fiber	1 g
Sugars	8 g

Protein	21 g

1 1/2 cup fresh cranberries
1/4 cup orange juice
1/4 cup commercial barbecue sauce
2 Tbsp sugar
3 Cornish game hens, split
Fresh ground pepper and salt to taste

1. Preheat the oven to 350 degrees. Combine the cranberries, juice, barbecue sauce, and sugar and bring to a boil over high heat. Lower heat and simmer for 10 minutes. Place the hens in a roasting pan. Sprinkle with pepper and salt.

2. Roast the hens, uncovered, for 30 minutes. Baste hens with some of the sauce and continue to roast for an additional 20 minutes, until juices run clear. Serve with additional warm sauce on the side.

Allan's Cranberry Chicken

This dish is great served with rice.

<table>
<tr><td>

Preparation Time:
15 minutes

---

6 Servings/Serving Size:
3–4 oz

Exchanges:

1/2	Carbohydrate
1	Vegetable
3	Very Lean Meat
1/2	Fat

Calories 196
 Calories from Fat 41
Total Fat .... 5 g
 Saturated Fat .... 1 g

Cholesterol .... 69 mg
Sodium .... 76 mg
Carbohydrate .... 12 g
 Dietary Fiber .... 2 g
 Sugars .... 9 g

Protein .... 26 g

</td></tr>
</table>

1 cup boiling water
1/2 cup dried cranberries
2 tsp canola oil
1 1/2 lb skinless, boneless chicken breasts,
    halved and pounded to 1/2-inch thickness
1 large carrot, peeled and diagonally sliced
1 red pepper, julienned
1 yellow pepper, julienned
2 scallions, sliced
2 Tbsp honey
1 Tbsp lemon juice

1. Heat the oil in a large skillet over medium-high heat. Add the chicken breasts and saute on each side for a total of 10 minutes. Remove from the skillet. Add the carrot and peppers and saute for 5 minutes. Add the scallions and saute for 3 more minutes.

2. Mix together the honey and lemon juice. Add the cranberries and the juice mixture to the skillet and cook 1 minute. Add the chicken breasts, cover, and simmer on low for 5 minutes.

Stuffed Cranberry and Rice Chicken

Juicy, tart cranberries surprise you in every bite!

Preparation Time:
30 minutes

6 Servings/Serving Size:
3–4 oz chicken and vegetables with 1/2 cup rice

Exchanges:

2	Starch
3	Very Lean Meat
1/2	Monounsaturated Fat

Calories	296
Calories from Fat	57
Total Fat	6 g
Saturated Fat	1 g

Cholesterol	73 mg
Sodium	80 mg
Carbohydrate	27 g
Dietary Fiber	3 g
Sugars	3 g

Protein	30 g

3 whole chicken breasts, halved, boned, skinned, and pounded to 1/2-inch thickness
3 cups cooked brown rice
1/2 cup rehydrated cranberries, drained (to rehydrate dried cranberries, pour boiling water over 1/2 cup cranberries, let sit for 10 minutes, and drain)
1 Tbsp olive oil
1/2 cup diced celery
1/2 cup diced onion
2 tsp minced fresh thyme
1 cup dry white wine

1. Prepare the chicken breasts and set aside. Combine the rice and rehydrated cranberries and mix well. Set aside. Heat the oil in a small saucepan over medium-high heat. Add the celery and onion and saute for 5 minutes. Add the vegetables and thyme to the rice.

2. On a flat surface, take about 1/2 cup of the rice mixture and place on the lower third of each chicken breast. Fold over the sides of the chicken breast and roll up. Secure each breast with a toothpick. Continue with all chicken breasts. Place all the chicken rolls in a casserole dish. Pour wine in the bottom of the dish. Cover and bake in a preheated 350-degree oven for 20 minutes. Uncover and bake for 10 more minutes.

Turkey and Wild Rice Salad

Use leftover roasted turkey and extra rice from stuffing for this hearty salad.

Preparation Time:
17 minutes

---

6 Servings/Serving Size:
1 cup

Exchanges:
1	Starch
3	Very Lean Meat
1/2	Monounsaturated Fat

Calories	222
Calories from Fat	63
Total Fat	7 g
Saturated Fat	1 g

Cholesterol	49 mg
Sodium	49 mg
Carbohydrate	16 g
Dietary Fiber	2 g
Sugars	4 g

Protein	24 g

Salad
3 cups diced cooked turkey (preferably white meat)
2 cups leftover cooked wild rice
1/2 cup rehydrated cranberries, drained (to rehydrate dried cranberries, pour boiling water over 1/2 cup cranberries, let sit for 10 minutes, and drain)
1/4 cup diced red onion
1/4 cup diced yellow pepper

Dressing
1/2 cup raspberry vinegar
2 Tbsp olive oil
2 Tbsp minced fresh parsley
1 Tbsp minced scallions
Fresh ground pepper to taste

Combine all salad ingredients. In a blender, combine all dressing ingredients. Pour the dressing over the salad and toss well. Serve at room temperature.

Cranberry Rice Salad

This salad will look festive on your fall table.

Preparation Time:
25 minutes

6 Servings/Serving Size:
1 cup

Exchanges:
2 1/2   Starch
1/2 Monounsaturated Fat

Calories	213
Calories from Fat	45
Total Fat	5 g
Saturated Fat	0 g
Cholesterol	0 mg
Sodium	14 mg
Carbohydrate	38 g
Dietary Fiber	2 g
Sugars	6 g
Protein	3 g

3 Tbsp Cranberry Orange Cinnamon Sauce (see recipe, p. 377)
1/2 cup orange juice
2 Tbsp canola oil
2 tsp sugar
4 cups cooked rice (white or brown)
1/4 cup sliced scallions
1/2 cup sliced celery
1/2 cup diced yellow or red pepper
1/2 cup thinly sliced carrots
1/2 cup fresh or dried cranberries (to rehydrate dried cranberries, pour boiling water over 1/2 cup cranberries, let sit for 10 minutes, and drain)

Whisk together the first four ingredients to make the dressing. Combine all remaining ingredients and pour the dressing over the salad. Toss well and chill before serving.

Cranberry Couscous Salad

Here's another great salad using fiber-rich grain and dried cranberries.

Preparation Time:
20 minutes

6 Servings/Serving Size:
1 cup

Exchanges:
1 1/2	Starch
1	Vegetable
1	Monounsaturated Fat

Calories	191
Calories from Fat	58
Total Fat	6 g
Saturated Fat	1 g

Cholesterol	0 mg
Sodium	57 mg
Carbohydrate	30 g
Dietary Fiber	3 g
Sugars	10 g

Protein	4 g

3/4 cup dry couscous
2 1/2 cups boiling water
1 cup dried cranberries
2 cups diced carrot
1 cup diced celery
2 Tbsp chopped toasted walnuts
1/2 cup unsweetened apple juice
2 Tbsp canola oil
1 Tbsp honey
1 Tbsp fresh lemon juice
Pinch salt

1. Rehydrate the dry couscous in 1 1/2 cups of the boiling water. Let couscous stand for 5–10 minutes until water is absorbed. Rehydrate the dried cranberries in the remaining boiling water. Let stand for 10 minutes and drain.

2. Combine the rehydrated couscous and drained cranberries with the carrot, celery, and walnuts in a large salad bowl. Whisk together the remaining ingredients and pour over the salad. Chill for several hours before serving.

Cranberry Pear Crumble

Two of fall's finest fruits combine for a sweet treat.

Preparation Time:
20 minutes

6 Servings/Serving Size:
1/2 cup fruit with 1/4 cup topping

Exchanges:

1	Starch
1	Fruit
1/2	Fat

Calories	147
Calories from Fat	34
Total Fat	4 g
Saturated Fat	1 g
Cholesterol	0 mg
Sodium	49 mg
Carbohydrate	27 g
Dietary Fiber	4 g
Sugars	15 g
Protein	3 g

1 cup fresh cranberries
2 cups diced Red d'Anjou pears
2 Tbsp fresh lemon juice
2 tsp almond extract
1 tsp cinnamon
1/4 tsp nutmeg
1 1/2 cups rolled oats
1/4 cup whole wheat flour
3 Tbsp low-calorie margarine
2 Tbsp brown sugar
1 tsp cinnamon
1/2 cup orange juice

1. Preheat the oven to 350 degrees. Combine the first six ingredients and place in a casserole dish. Mix together the oats and flour. Add the margarine and brown sugar and mix well until the margarine is incorporated into the oats. Add the cinnamon.

2. Add the orange juice a little at a time until mixture is moist but still a little crumbly (you may not need all of the juice). Bake, covered, for 30 minutes. Uncover and bake for an additional 15 minutes until pears are soft and topping is browned.

Cranberry-Orange Cinnamon Sauce

This recipe makes cranberry sauce a little more special.

Preparation Time:	
5 minutes	

6 Servings/Serving Size:	
1/2 cup	

Exchanges:	
1	Fruit

Calories	63
Calories from Fat	2
Total Fat	0 g
Saturated Fat	0 g

Cholesterol	0 mg
Sodium	2 mg
Carbohydrate	19 g
Dietary Fiber	3 g
Sugars	13 g

Protein	1 g

3 cups cranberries
2 small oranges, unpeeled and sliced into rings
   (remove seeds)
1 cup water
1/4 cup orange juice
3 cinnamon sticks
2 Tbsp honey

Combine all ingredients in a saucepan and bring to a boil. Lower the heat and simmer for 15 minutes until cranberries pop. Chill and serve.

Diet is a four-letter word.
Forget about it.
Diets are punishing; good eating
habits are rewarding.
A well thought-out eating plan
makes room for treats.
It encourages variety. It's about
saying "yes" to good food
and good habits.

Cranberry Apple Swirl

This dessert looks beautiful served on your holiday table, with its sparkling red layers alternating with snowy white ones.

Preparation Time:
10 minutes

---

6 Servings/Serving Size:
1 cup

Exchanges:

1 1/2	Carbohydrate
1	Saturated Fat

Calories	160
Calories from Fat	58
Total Fat	6 g
Saturated Fat	4 g

Cholesterol	28 mg
Sodium	68 mg
Carbohydrate	23 g
Dietary Fiber	2 g
Sugars	19 g

Protein	5 g

1 1/2 cups Cranberry Orange Cinnamon Sauce (see recipe, p. 377)
1 1/2 cups diced apple (any variety)
1 cup nonfat plain yogurt
2 cups low-fat sour cream
2 Tbsp orange juice
2 tsp honey
1 tsp cinnamon
2 Tbsp grated orange peel

Combine the cranberry sauce and apples. Mix together the yogurt, sour cream, juice, honey, and cinnamon. In six wine, parfait, or champagne glasses, place a layer of the cranberry-apple mixture. Add a layer of the yogurt mixture. Keep layering, ending with the yogurt mixture. Sprinkle orange peel on top and serve.

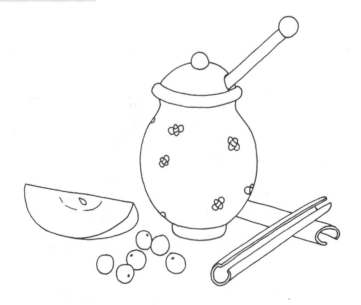

Cranberry Banana Bread

This moist tea bread gives traditional banana bread more color and tartness.

Preparation Time:
15 minutes

9 Servings/Serving Size:
1 1-inch slice

Exchanges:
2	Starch
1/2	Monounsaturated Fat

Calories	186
Calories from Fat	50
Total Fat	6 g
Saturated Fat	1 g

Cholesterol	47 mg
Sodium	166 mg
Carbohydrate	30 g
Dietary Fiber	3 g
Sugars	6 g

Protein	5 g

1 1/2 cups unbleached white flour
1/2 cup whole-wheat flour
2 tsp baking powder
1/2 tsp baking soda
2 eggs, beaten
1/2 cup unsweetened applesauce
2 Tbsp canola oil
1 cup mashed bananas (about 2 bananas)
1 cup coarsely chopped fresh cranberries (or leave whole if you wish)
2 Tbsp minced toasted pecans

1. Preheat the oven to 350 degrees. Combine the flours, baking powder, and baking soda in a medium bowl. Combine the eggs, applesauce, oil, and bananas in a large bowl. Mix well.

2. Slowly add the dry ingredients to the large bowl and mix until blended. Fold in the cranberries. Pour the batter into a nonstick 9-inch loaf pan. Top with pecans. Bake for about 45 minutes until a toothpick comes out clean.

Cranberry Muffins

This muffin will perk you up on a brisk autumn morning.

Preparation Time:
20 minutes

12 Servings/Serving Size:
1 muffin

Exchanges:
2   Starch

Calories 152
  Calories from Fat 32
Total Fat .... 4 g
  Saturated Fat .... 0 g

Cholesterol .... 35 mg
Sodium .... 72 mg
Carbohydrate .... 27 g
  Dietary Fiber .... 2 g
  Sugars .... 7 g

Protein .... 4 g

1 1/2 cups unbleached white flour
1 cup whole-wheat flour
2 tsp baking powder
2 tsp cinnamon
2 eggs, beaten
1/4 cup sugar
1/2 cup unsweetened applesauce
2 Tbsp canola oil
1/4 cup orange juice
1 tsp orange extract
1 cup fresh cranberries

1. Preheat the oven to 350 degrees. Combine
   the flours, baking powder, and cinnamon in a
   medium bowl. Set aside. In a large bowl,
   combine the remaining ingredients. Add the
   dry ingredients slowly to the large bowl and
   mix until blended. Do not overbeat.

2. Pour the batter into 12 nonstick muffin cups
   and bake for 20–25 minutes. Remove muffins
   from oven and let cool slightly. Remove
   muffins from pan and let cool completely.

Creamy Turkey and Apple Soup

This hearty soup has a subtle Indian flavor.

Preparation Time:
20 minutes

6 Servings/Serving Size:
1 cup

Exchanges:

1	Starch
1/2	Skim Milk
2	Very Lean Meat

Calories......................190
 Calories from Fat........30
Total Fat ....3 g
 Saturated Fat.............1 g

Cholesterol ....40 mg
Sodium..................168 mg
Carbohydrate.............19 g
 Dietary Fiber ....1 g
 Sugars.....................10 g

Protein........................21 g

2 tsp canola oil
12 oz uncooked turkey breast, cut into 2-inch
 cubes
1 cup diced onion
1 cup minced celery
1/2 cup diced zucchini
1/2 cup diced tomatoes
1/2 cup white wine
2 tsp curry powder
3 cups low-fat, low-sodium chicken broth
1/2 cup cooked basmati rice (white or brown)
1 1/2 cups evaporated skim milk
1/2 cup diced Granny Smith apples
1 Tbsp cornstarch or arrowroot powder
2 Tbsp water

1. Heat the oil in a stockpot over medium-high
 heat. Add the turkey and saute for 5 minutes.
 Add the onion, celery, and zucchini and saute
 for 5 more minutes. Add the tomatoes and
 saute for 3 minutes. Add the wine and
 simmer for 7–8 minutes.

2. Add the curry powder, broth, and rice and
 simmer for 20 minutes. Add the milk and
 simmer for 5 minutes. Add the apples and
 simmer for 3 more minutes. Mix together the
 cornstarch or arrowroot powder and water.
 Add to the soup and cook over medium-low
 heat until thickened.

Asian Apple Pork

Asian spices and apples go well together.

<table>
<tr><td>

Preparation Time:
10 minutes

---

6 Servings/Serving Size:
3 oz pork with 1/2 cup rice

Exchanges:
2	Starch
3	Very Lean Meat
1/2	Fat

Calories	285
Calories from Fat	55
Total Fat	6 g
Saturated Fat	2 g

Cholesterol	65 mg
Sodium	268 mg
Carbohydrate	30 g
Dietary Fiber	1 g
Sugars	5 g

Protein	26 g

</td></tr>
</table>

2 tsp peanut oil
2 tsp minced ginger
2 Tbsp minced scallions
1 1/2 lb pork tenderloin, cut into 3-inch strips
1 cup diced Gala apples
2 Tbsp lite soy sauce
1 Tbsp rice vinegar
1 cup low-fat, low-sodium chicken broth
1 Tbsp brown sugar
2 tsp dry sherry
1 Tbsp cornstarch or arrowroot powder
2 Tbsp water
3 cups cooked jasmine, white, or brown rice

1. Heat the oil in a wok over high heat. Add the ginger and scallions and stir-fry for 30 seconds. Add the pork and stir-fry for 7–9 minutes until pork loses its pinkness. Add the apple and stir-fry for 3 more minutes.

2. Combine the soy sauce, vinegar, broth, brown sugar, and sherry. Add to the wok, lower heat, cover, and simmer for 5 minutes. Combine the cornstarch or arrowroot powder and water. Add to the wok and cook until thickened, about 3 minutes. Serve over cooked rice.

Granny Smith Pork

This apple-spiced dish is great served over rice.

Preparation Time:
15 minutes

6 Servings/Serving Size:
3 oz

Exchanges:

1 1/2	Fruit
3	Very Lean Meat
1	Fat

Calories......................244
  Calories from Fat.......50
Total Fat......................6 g
  Saturated Fat............2 g

Cholesterol.............56 mg
Sodium.................135 mg
Carbohydrate.............26 g
  Dietary Fiber.............3 g
  Sugars.....................18 g

Protein.......................20 g

1 tsp canola oil
1 1/2 lb boneless pork, cut into 1/2-inch cubes
4 medium Granny Smith apples, cored and sliced
    into 1/2-inch wedges
1 cup dry white wine
2 Tbsp brown sugar
1/4 cup cider vinegar
3 Tbsp cornstarch or arrowroot powder
2 Tbsp Worcestershire sauce
Fresh ground pepper and salt to taste

1. Heat the oil in a skillet over medium-high heat. Add the pork and brown on all sides. Add the apple slices and saute for 3 minutes. Add 1/2 cup of the wine, reduce the heat, cover, and simmer for 10 minutes.

2. Mix the other 1/2 cup of wine together with the remaining ingredients and add to the skillet. Cook over medium heat, stirring constantly, until sauce thickens.

This adapted recipe is courtesy of the National Pork Producers.

Apple-Stuffed Pork Chops

Preparation Time:
20 minutes

6 Servings/Serving Size:
3 oz

Exchanges:

1 1/2	Starch
1	Fruit
3	Lean Meat
1/2	Fat

Calories.......................370
 Calories from Fat......115
Total Fat.....................13 g
 Saturated Fat.............4 g

Cholesterol.............67 mg
Sodium..................222 mg
Carbohydrate............38 g
 Dietary Fiber ....2 g
 Sugars.....................20 g

Protein.......................25 g

6 pork loin rib chops, cut 1 1/4 inches
  thick
2 oranges
1 Tbsp canola oil
1/2 cup finely minced onion
1 cup bread crumbs
1 cup coarsely chopped tart apple, unpeeled
1/2 tsp sage
1 Tbsp butter
2 Tbsp cornstarch or arrowroot powder
1/2 tsp cinnamon
1 1/4 cup apple juice or cider
1/2 cup raisins

1. Preheat the oven to 325 degrees. Cut an
   opening in each pork chop to form a pocket.
   Set aside. Shred 2 tsp orange peel and set
   aside. Squeeze the oranges, reserving the
   juice. Heat the oil in a skillet over medium-
   high heat. Add the onion and saute until
   tender, about 5 minutes. Add the bread
   crumbs, apple, and sage, along with 1 Tbsp of
   the reserved orange juice.

2. Fill each pork chop pocket with an equal
   amount of stuffing. Brush both sides of the
   chops with some of the remaining orange
   juice. Place the chops in an 8-inch square
   baking dish and bake for 25–30 minutes or
   until tender, basting with orange juice. Melt
   the butter in a saucepan. Add in the
   cornstarch or arrowroot powder and
   cinnamon, mixing well. Gradually stir in the
   apple juice. Add the raisins and reserved
   orange peel. Cook over medium heat until
   thickened and bubbly. Serve the sauce with
   the chops.

This adapted recipe is courtesy of the National Pork Producers.

Apple Orchard Pork Chops

Try serving these hearty pork chops with wide noodles.

Preparation Time:
15 minutes

6 Servings/Serving Size:
3–4 oz

Exchanges:

2 1/2	Fruit
4	Very Lean Meat
1/2	Fat

Calories	313
Calories from Fat	62
Total Fat	7 g
Saturated Fat	2 g
Cholesterol	71 mg
Sodium	226 mg
Carbohydrate	36 g
Dietary Fiber	3 g
Sugars	30 g
Protein	26 g

2 tsp canola oil
1 1/2 lb boneless pork chops
2 cups apple cider
1/3 cup German-style mustard
3 medium apples, unpeeled, sliced 1/2 inch thick
1/2 cup currants or raisins
1/2 cup sliced scallions
2 Tbsp cornstarch or arrowroot powder
1/4 cup water

1. Heat the oil in a large skillet over medium-high heat. Add the pork chops and brown for about 4 minutes on each side. Combine the cider and mustard and pour over the pork chops. Cover and cook over medium-low heat for 25–30 minutes.

2. Add the apples, currants, and scallions. Cover and cook 5–10 minutes longer. Place the pork chops and apples on serving platter and keep warm. Combine the cornstarch or arrowroot powder and water. Add to the cider liquid; cook and stir until thickened. Serve the sauce over the pork chops and apples.

This adapted recipe is courtesy of the National Pork Producers.

Recommended Uses for Apples

Flavor, Variety	Fresh Texture	Salads	Pie	Baking	Season
Red Delicious	Sweet, Crisp	Excellent	Fair	No	Year-round
Golden Delicious	Sweet, Tender	Very Good	Excellent	Very Good	Year-round
Granny Smith	Tart, Crisp	Very Good	Very Good	Very Good	Year-round
Gala	Sweet, Crisp	Very Good	Good	Good	Aug.–Mar.
Fuji	Sweet-Spicy, Crisp	Excellent	Good	Good	Year-round
Rome Beauty (Red Rome)	Slightly Tart, Firm	Good	Very Good	Excellent	Sept.–July
Jonagold	Sweet-Tart, Crisp	Very Good	Very Good	Very Good	Sept.–April
Braeburn	Very Firm	Good	Good	Good	Oct.–July
Criterion	Sweet/ Complex, Crisp	Very Good	Very Good	Good	Oct.–Mar.
Winesap	Slightly Tart, Spicy, Firm	Excellent	Good	Good	Oct.–Aug.
Newtown Pippin	Slightly Tart, Firm	Very Good	Excellent	Very Good	Sept.–June
Elstar	Tart-Sweet, Firm	Very Good	Good	Very Good	Sept.–Mar.

This adapted chart is courtesy of the Washington Apple Commission.

Bean and Apple Bake

This is a heartier and healthier version of baked beans.
(However, it is relatively high in sodium.)

Preparation Time:
20 minutes

6 Servings/Serving Size:
1 cup (3 oz turkey, about
1/2 cup beans)

Exchanges:

2	Starch
1	Vegetable
3	Very Lean Meat

Calories	291
Calories from Fat	28
Total Fat	3 g
Saturated Fat	1 g

Cholesterol	75 mg
Sodium	578 mg
Carbohydrate	35 g
Dietary Fiber	7 g
Sugars	14 g

Protein	34 g

2 tsp olive oil
1 1/2 lb ground turkey (have your butcher grind this for you)
1/2 cup minced onion
1 24-oz can vegetarian baked beans
2 cups canned, no-sodium tomato sauce
1 Tbsp brown sugar
2 Tbsp Dijon mustard
1/2 cup diced Gala apples
1/4 cup red wine vinegar

Preheat the oven to 325 degrees. Heat the oil in a skillet over medium-high heat. Add the turkey and saute until the turkey is almost cooked through, about 7 minutes. Add the onion and saute for 5 more minutes. Combine the turkey with the remaining ingredients and place into a casserole dish. Bake, covered, for 45 minutes until bubbly.

Honey-Yogurt Dumplings with Apples

These low-fat dumplings are still chewy and comforting.

Preparation Time:
15 minutes

6 Servings/Serving Size:
1/2 cup apples with 1 2-inch dumpling

Exchanges:

1	Starch
2	Fruit

Calories	190
Calories from Fat	13
Total Fat	1 g
Saturated Fat	0 g

Cholesterol	37 mg
Sodium	266 mg
Carbohydrate	42 g
Dietary Fiber	2 g
Sugars	23 g

Protein	4 g

3 cups apple slices, peeled
1 1/2 cups cranberry juice
1 Tbsp honey
1 cinnamon stick
1/4 tsp nutmeg
1 cup unbleached white flour
4 tsp baking powder
1 tsp cinnamon
1 egg
6 Tbsp low-fat plain yogurt
1 Tbsp honey
1 Tbsp skim milk
1 tsp grated orange peel

1. Combine the apple, juice, honey, cinnamon stick, and nutmeg in a heavy skillet. Bring to a boil, then reduce the heat to simmer. Combine the flour, baking powder, and cinnamon in a mixing bowl.

2. Mix together the remaining ingredients in a separate bowl; stir into flour mixture to form a moist batter. Drop the dough by tablespoonful onto the hot fruit. Cover and simmer for 15 to 20 minutes until a toothpick inserted in the dumpling centers comes out clean.

This adapted recipe is courtesy of the National Honey Board.

Fried Apples

These apples are great served with any pork or ham dish.

Preparation Time:	
15 minutes	

6 Servings/Serving Size:
1/2 cup

Exchanges:
1	Fruit
1/2	Monounsaturated Fat

Calories	83
Calories from Fat	23
Total Fat	3 g
Saturated Fat	0 g

Cholesterol	0 mg
Sodium	2 mg
Carbohydrate	16 g
Dietary Fiber	1 g
Sugars	14 g

Protein	0 g

1 Tbsp canola oil
3 cups diced, peeled baking apples
2 Tbsp fresh lemon juice
3/4 cup unsweetened apple juice
1 Tbsp honey
2 tsp cinnamon
1 tsp nutmeg
2 Tbsp water
1 Tbsp cornstarch or arrowroot powder

Heat the oil in a skillet over medium heat. Add the apples and lemon juice and saute for 10 minutes, being careful not to let them burn. Mix together the remaining ingredients until cornstarch or arrowroot powder is dissolved. Add the mixture to the apples and cook over medium heat until sauce is thickened. Serve warm.

Eating properly will not, by itself,

keep well a person who does not exercise,

for food and exercise, being opposite in effect,

work together to produce health.

—*Hippocrates*

Sweet and Sour Chicken Salad

Sweet apples add a twist to basic chicken salad.

Preparation Time:
15 minutes

6 Servings/Serving Size:
3 oz chicken

Exchanges:

1	Carbohydrate
3	Lean Meat
1/2	Monounsaturated Fat

Calories	268
Calories from Fat	114
Total Fat	13 g
Saturated Fat	2 g

Cholesterol	72 mg
Sodium	114 mg
Carbohydrate	11 g
Dietary Fiber	2 g
Sugars	8 g

Protein	27 g

Salad

18 oz boneless, skinless cooked chicken breast, cut into 2-inch cubes
1 1/2 cups diagonally sliced celery
1 cup fresh snow peas, trimmed
1/2 cup diced red pepper
1 cup diced, unpeeled Gala apples

Dressing

1/4 cup vinegar
1/4 cup canola oil
2 Tbsp sugar
1 tsp paprika
1 tsp celery seeds
Fresh ground pepper and salt to taste

Combine all salad ingredients. Whisk together the dressing ingredients. Pour the dressing over the salad and serve.

Apple Crunch Salad

Adding three different apples triples the crunch value of this fruit salad!

Preparation Time:
20 minutes

---

6 Servings/Serving Size:
1 cup

Exchanges:
1 1/2	Fruit
1	Saturated Fat

Calories 125
  Calories from Fat........43
Total Fat ....5 g
  Saturated Fat.............2 g

Cholesterol ....10 mg
Sodium...................20 mg
Carbohydrate.............22 g
  Dietary Fiber ....3 g
  Sugars......................16 g

Protein...........................2 g

1 cup diced Granny Smith apples, unpeeled
1 cup diced Golden Delicious apples, unpeeled
1/2 cup diced Red Delicious apples, unpeeled
1 cup sectioned oranges
1 medium banana, sliced
2 Tbsp toasted walnuts
2 Tbsp lemon juice
3/4 cup low-fat sour cream
2 Tbsp fresh orange juice
2 tsp sugar
2 Tbsp toasted, shredded coconut

Combine the fruit and walnuts with the lemon juice. Whisk together the sour cream, orange juice, and sugar. Add to the fruit and mix well. Top with toasted coconut and serve.

Apple Cinnamon Cobbler

This slim version of the traditional cobbler will warm your holidays.

Preparation Time:
20 minutes

6 Servings/Serving Size:
1 2-inch biscuit with 1/2 cup fruit filling

Exchanges:
2 1/2   Carbohydrate
1 1/2 Monounsaturated Fat

Calories......................258
 Calories from Fat........92
Total Fat ....10 g
 Saturated Fat.............1 g

Cholesterol ....1 mg
Sodium....................83 mg
Carbohydrate.............41 g
 Dietary Fiber ....4 g
 Sugars.....................23 g

Protein ....4 g

4 medium baking apples, peeled and sliced thin
1 cup water
2 tsp cinnamon
2 Tbsp cornstarch or arrowroot powder
1/4 cup sugar
1 cup whole-wheat pastry flour
1 tsp baking powder
1/4 cup canola oil
1 Tbsp honey
1/2 cup low-fat buttermilk

1. Preheat the oven to 375 degrees. In a large saucepan over medium heat, combine the apples, water, cinnamon, cornstarch or arrowroot powder, and sugar. Cook until the apples are soft and the mixture is thickened, about 10 minutes.

2. Meanwhile, combine the whole-wheat pastry flour and baking powder. Add in the oil, honey, and buttermilk. Stir until biscuits are moist. Add additional milk if necessary. Pour the apple mixture into a casserole dish. Drop the biscuit dough by tablespoonsful on top of the apples. Place in the oven and bake for 20 minutes until biscuits are golden brown. Serve warm.

Fresh Apple Crisp

This is a healthy version of an old-fashioned favorite.

Preparation Time:
15 minutes

---

6 Servings/Serving Size:
1 medium apple with 1/4 cup topping

Exchanges:

1	Starch
2	Fruit
1	Monounsaturated Fat

Calories 248
 Calories from Fat 58
Total Fat ....6 g
 Saturated Fat ....1 g

Cholesterol ....0 mg
Sodium ....4 mg
Carbohydrate ....47 g
 Dietary Fiber ....7 g
 Sugars ....28 g

Protein ....4 g

6 medium Granny Smith apples, unpeeled and
  sliced
2 Tbsp fresh lemon juice
2 tsp cinnamon
1 tsp nutmeg
1 1/4 cups rolled oats
1/4 cup whole-wheat flour
2 Tbsp honey
2 Tbsp apple juice concentrate, thawed
2 Tbsp canola oil
2 Tbsp water

Preheat the oven to 350 degrees. Sprinkle the apples with lemon juice and add the spices. Place the apples in a casserole dish. In a separate bowl, combine the oats and flour. Add the honey, apple juice concentrate, oil, and water. Work the mixture until it resembles crumbs and is moist. Sprinkle the topping over the apples. Bake for 30 minutes until topping is browned and apples are soft.

Currant and Wine Apples

This baked apple dessert is the perfect ending to any meal.

Preparation Time:
15 minutes

6 Servings/Serving Size:
1 apple

Exchanges:

2 1/2	Fruit
1	Fat

Calories	184
Calories from Fat	42
Total Fat	5 g
Saturated Fat	1 g

Cholesterol	0 mg
Sodium	49 mg
Carbohydrate	35 g
Dietary Fiber	5 g
Sugars	29 g

Protein	1 g

6 medium Rome apples
3 Tbsp low-calorie margarine
1/2 cup currants
2 Tbsp toasted walnuts
2 tsp cinnamon
1 1/2 cups dry red wine

1. Preheat the oven to 350 degrees. Core each apple, but do not go through the bottom. Peel each apple about one fourth of the way down. Combine the margarine, currants, walnuts, and cinnamon.

2. Stuff each apple with some of the currant mixture and place in a casserole dish. Pour wine over the apples. Bake the apples, uncovered, for about 40–50 minutes until soft and tender. Serve hot or cold.

Apples and Pears with Whole Spices

This spicy, seasonal fruit dessert looks festive served with the whole spices.

Preparation Time:
10 minutes

6 Servings/Serving Size:
1/2 cup

Exchanges:
1	Fruit

Calories	67
Calories from Fat	3
Total Fat	0 g
Saturated Fat	0 g

Cholesterol	0 mg
Sodium	4 mg
Carbohydrate	17 g
Dietary Fiber	2 g
Sugars	15 g

Protein	0 g

2 medium baking apples, unpeeled, cubed into
   1-inch pieces
1 medium Red d'Anjou or Bartlett pear, unpeeled,
   cubed into 1-inch pieces
2 Tbsp lemon juice
3/4 cup water
1/4 cup apple juice concentrate
3 whole cloves
2 cinnamon sticks
2 cardamom pods
2 allspice berries

Combine all ingredients in a large saucepan. Bring to a boil, lower the heat, and simmer for 20 minutes until apples and pears are soft. Add more water if necessary to prevent burning (water should be just about absorbed by the end of the cooking time). Serve with the whole spices.

Apple Muffins

Sauteed apples in sweet spices make this muffin special.

Preparation Time:
20 minutes

12 Servings/Serving Size:
1 muffin

Exchanges:
1 1/2   Starch
1/2 Monounsaturated Fat

Calories 160
  Calories from Fat 40
Total Fat .... 4 g
  Saturated Fat .... 1 g

Cholesterol .... 36 mg
Sodium .... 94 mg
Carbohydrate .... 26 g
  Dietary Fiber .... 2 g
  Sugars .... 6 g

Protein .... 5 g

2 Tbsp low-calorie margarine
1 cup diced apple, unpeeled
2 Tbsp brown sugar
2 tsp cinnamon
1/2 tsp nutmeg
1 1/2 cups unbleached white flour
1 cup whole-wheat flour
2 tsp baking powder
2 eggs, beaten
1/2 cup unsweetened applesauce
2 Tbsp canola oil
1 Tbsp sugar
1/4 cup evaporated skim milk

1. Preheat the oven to 350 degrees. In a saucepan over medium heat, melt the margarine. Add the apple and saute for 5 minutes. Add the sugar, cinnamon, and nutmeg and saute for 2–3 minutes. Remove from heat. Combine the flours and baking powder in a medium bowl. Combine the eggs, applesauce, oil, sugar, and milk in a large bowl.

2. Slowly add the dry ingredients to the large bowl and mix until blended. Add the apple mixture and stir lightly to mix. Pour the batter into 12 nonstick muffin cups and bake for 25–30 minutes. Remove muffins from oven and let cool slightly. Remove muffins from pan and let cool completely.

Warm Up and Go!

On chilly fall mornings, it's more important than ever to start your day with a warm and nutritious meal. You'll be rewarded with higher spirits, more energy, and a more productive morning. There are many ways to make breakfast more interesting and fun. Here are some creative ways to liven up hot cereals:

* When cooking oats, use half apple juice and half water. The apple juice will give the oats an extra sweetness.

* Instead of the same old hot cereals, try cooking different grains like millet, quinoa, or barley. They are easily digestible and delicious.

* A little topping can go a long way! By using just one tablespoon, you can even include a few nuts. Try these tasty toppings: raisins, wheat germ, walnuts, almonds, peanuts, nut butters (use 1 tsp), bananas, pears, apples, or fresh berries.

Try some of these tasty alternatives to toast:

* Brush tortillas with a little canola oil (1/4 tsp per tortilla), sprinkle with cinnamon, and bake for 3 minutes at 350 degrees, until the tortillas are lightly toasted.

* Use toasted whole wheat pita bread and fill with scrambled eggs or fruit and cottage cheese.

* Cook chapatis, the bread of India. Chapatis can be found at Indian grocery stores and some natural food stores. Just cook them on each side in a nonstick skillet until they puff up, and drizzle with 1/2 tsp honey to serve.

Or make pancakes, muffins, and smoothies more nutritious:

* In a standard 12-muffin recipe, add to the dry mixture 2 Tbsp toasted wheat germ, 1/4 cup nonfat dry milk, and 2 Tbsp bran.

* Try substituting different flours for wheat flour when making pancakes. Consider rice flour, buckwheat, ground oats, or adding blue cornmeal to the batter.

* Drink your breakfast with this California-style smoothie: simply blend together 1 cup nonfat milk, 1 cup any diced fruit, 2 tsp honey, and 6 large ice cubes (makes 2 servings). Add 2 tsp wheat germ for an extra healthy punch.

Stuffed French Toast

There's a creamy surprise stuffed inside this French toast.

Preparation Time:
20 minutes

6 Servings/Serving Size:
1 slice

Exchanges:
2 1/2	Starch
2	Very Lean Meat

Calories	286
Calories from Fat	38
Total Fat	4 g
Saturated Fat	2 g

Cholesterol	8 mg
Sodium	645 mg
Carbohydrate	38 g
Dietary Fiber	2 g
Sugars	7 g

Protein	21 g

6 slices challah or French bread, cut 2 inches
   thick (12 oz total)
1/4 cup part-skim ricotta cheese
1/4 cup low-fat cottage cheese
2 Tbsp low-fat cream cheese
2 tsp sugar
2 tsp any extract (try orange, vanilla, strawberry,
   or almond)
12 egg substitutes
1/4 cup evaporated milk
Nonstick cooking spray

1. Cut a pocket in each slice of bread. Open
    carefully. With an electric beater, whip
    together the cheeses, sugar, and extract.
    Divide the mixture evenly into 6 portions and
    insert a portion into each bread pocket.

2. Beat together the egg substitutes and milk.
    Dip the bread slices in the mixture. Turn to
    coat both sides. Spray a nonstick pan lightly
    with nonstick cooking spray and heat over
    medium-high heat. Cook the French toast for
    about 3–4 minutes on each side until golden
    brown.

Pumpkin Pear Waffles

These spicy waffles make a great fall breakfast.

Preparation Time:	
15 minutes	
6 Servings/Serving Size:	
1/2 waffle	
Exchanges:	
1 1/2	Starch
Calories......................122	
Calories from Fat........19	
Total Fat ....2 g	
Saturated Fat.............1 g	
Cholesterol ....71 mg	
Sodium...................116 mg	
Carbohydrate.............22 g	
Dietary Fiber ....3 g	
Sugars.......................7 g	
Protein..........................5 g	

1 cup whole-wheat pastry flour
1 1/2 tsp baking powder
1 tsp cinnamon
1/2 tsp nutmeg
2 eggs, beaten
2 Tbsp brown sugar
1/2 cup pumpkin puree
1/4 cup finely diced pear
Nonstick cooking spray

Mix together the flour, baking powder, cinnamon, and nutmeg. Beat together the eggs and sugar. Add in the flour mixture. Fold in the pumpkin and pear. Pour batter into a hot waffle iron coated with nonstick cooking spray and cook until waffles are crisp and browned. The batter will make 3 waffles.

You are what you eat!

Whole-Wheat Pancakes

You can modify this basic recipe by adding fruit, nuts, or flavored extracts.

Preparation Time:
15 minutes

6 Servings/Serving Size:
2 pancakes

Exchanges:
2   Starch
1/2   Monounsaturated Fat

Calories	194
Calories from Fat	42
Total Fat	5 g
Saturated Fat	1 g
Cholesterol	72 mg
Sodium	516 mg
Carbohydrate	31 g
Dietary Fiber	4 g
Sugars	6 g
Protein	9 g

1 1/2 cups whole-wheat flour
1/2 cup crushed low-sugar bran cereal
2 tsp baking soda
3/4 cup evaporated skim milk
2 eggs, beaten
1 Tbsp brown sugar
1 Tbsp canola oil
2 tsp vanilla
Nonstick cooking spray

Combine all ingredients and mix until blended. Drop batter, 1/4 cup at a time, onto a hot griddle sprayed with nonstick cooking spray. Cook until brown on both sides, turning once, about 5–6 minutes. Serve with jam or fruit if desired.

Pancakes with Cottage Cheese and Fruit

These delicious pancakes are loaded with calcium.

Preparation Time:	
15 minutes	

6 Servings/Serving Size:
2 pancakes

Exchanges:

1 1/2	Starch
1	Fruit
2	Lean Meat

Calories	280
Calories from Fat	58
Total Fat	6 g
Saturated Fat	1 g
Cholesterol	74 mg
Sodium	348 mg
Carbohydrate	40 g
Dietary Fiber	2 g
Sugars	15 g
Protein	15 g

2 cups low-fat cottage cheese
2 eggs, beaten
1/2 cup whole-wheat flour
1 cup unbleached white flour
1 1/2 Tbsp canola oil
2 Tbsp brown sugar
1/2 cup low-sugar jam
1/2 cup fresh or frozen berries, thawed (any kind)

1. Mix the cottage cheese in a blender until smooth. Combine all ingredients except the jam and fruit in a bowl, add the cottage cheese, and mix until blended.

2. Cook on a nonstick griddle over medium heat until browned on both sides, about 5–7 minutes.

3. Meanwhile, heat the jam in a saucepan until melted. Add the fruit and heat for 2 minutes. Pour over hot pancakes to serve.

Apple Raisin Pancakes

Leftover pancakes from this breakfast make a great snack, too.

Preparation Time:
10 minutes

6 Servings/Serving Size:
2 pancakes

Exchanges:

1 1/2	Starch
1	Fruit

Calories	196
Calories from Fat	19
Total Fat	2 g
Saturated Fat	1 g

Cholesterol	71 mg
Sodium	145 mg
Carbohydrate	40 g
Dietary Fiber	3 g
Sugars	14 g

Protein	6 g

2 eggs, beaten
1 cup unsweetened applesauce
1 tsp cinnamon
2 tsp sugar
1 cup unbleached white flour
1/2 cup whole-wheat flour
2 tsp baking powder
2 tsp vanilla
1/2 cup golden raisins

Combine all ingredients until blended. Cook on a nonstick griddle over medium heat until both sides are browned, about 5–7 minutes.

Butterscotch Pancakes

A weekend morning is the perfect time to savor these butterscotch-rich pancakes.

Preparation Time:
10 minutes

6 Servings/Serving Size:
2 pancakes

Exchanges:
2 1/2   Starch

Calories	190
Calories from Fat	22
Total Fat	2 g
Saturated Fat	1 g
Cholesterol	73 mg
Sodium	183 mg
Carbohydrate	34 g
Dietary Fiber	2 g
Sugars	10 g
Protein	8 g

2 eggs, beaten
1/4 cup butterscotch liqueur or schnapps
2 tsp vanilla
1 cup unbleached white flour
1/2 cup whole-wheat flour
1/2 cup evaporated skim milk
2 tsp baking powder
1/2 cup low-fat vanilla yogurt
1 tsp sugar

Combine all ingredients until blended. Cook on a nonstick griddle over medium heat until browned on both sides, about 5–7 minutes.

New England Mini Corn Cakes

Make silver dollar pancakes the easy way with a muffin tin.

Preparation Time:
10 minutes

12 Servings/Serving Size:
2 cakes

Exchanges:
2   Starch

Calories.......................163
  Calories from Fat........23
Total Fat.......................3 g
  Saturated Fat............1 g

Cholesterol ....54 mg
Sodium..................177 mg
Carbohydrate............29 g
  Dietary Fiber ....1 g
  Sugars.......................5 g

Protein..........................6 g

Nonstick cooking spray
1 1/3 cup yellow corn meal
1 1/3 cup unbleached white flour
4 tsp baking powder
3 eggs, beaten
1 cup evaporated skim milk
2 Tbsp honey
2 Tbsp low-calorie margarine
3 tsp maple extract

Preheat the oven to 400 degrees. Spray 24 muffin cups with nonstick cooking spray. Combine all ingredients and mix until blended. Fill each muffin cup one-third full with batter. Bake for 13 minutes until browned. Each pancake should be 1/2 inch high.

Sweet Cornmeal Cakes

These hearty cakes are good served at dinnertime, too.

Preparation Time:	
10 minutes	
6 Servings/Serving Size:	
2 pancakes	
Exchanges:	
2	Starch
1/2	Fat
Calories	202
Calories from Fat	42
Total Fat	5 g
Saturated Fat	1 g
Cholesterol	74 mg
Sodium	203 mg
Carbohydrate	33 g
Dietary Fiber	3 g
Sugars	5 g
Protein	7 g

1 1/2 cups yellow cornmeal
2 tsp baking powder
2 Tbsp low-calorie margarine
1 cup low-fat vanilla yogurt
2 eggs, beaten
1 Tbsp brown sugar
1 tsp cinnamon

Combine all ingredients and mix until blended. Cook on a nonstick griddle over medium heat until browned on both sides, about 5–7 minutes.

*You don't have to be
a great chef to cook;
all you need is
interest
and a little time.*

Great Grains Granola

It's fun to make your own granola, because you can choose all your favorite ingredients!

Preparation Time:
15 minutes

6 Servings/Serving Size:
1/2 cup

Exchanges:

2	Starch
2	Fruit
1/2	Fat

Calories	294
Calories from Fat	41
Total Fat	5 g
Saturated Fat	1 g
Cholesterol	0 mg
Sodium	31 mg
Carbohydrate	61 g
Dietary Fiber	6 g
Sugars	35 g
Protein	7 g

2 cups quick-cooking oats
2 Tbsp toasted wheat germ
1/4 cup bran flakes
2 Tbsp brown sugar
1/2 cup apple juice concentrate, thawed
1 Tbsp canola oil
1 Tbsp cinnamon
2 tsp nutmeg
1 cup raisins
1/2 cup chopped dried apricots

Preheat the oven to 350 degrees. Combine all ingredients except the raisins and apricots and mix well. Spread the granola out on a nonstick cookie sheet. Bake the granola for about 45–55 minutes, turning often, until toasted and dry. Add the raisins and apricots and store in an airtight container.

Fruited Couscous Breakfast

Couscous is a welcome change from other hot cereals. It's easy to digest and quick to prepare.

Preparation Time: 15 minutes	
6 Servings/Serving Size: 1/2 cup	
Exchanges:	
2 1/2	Starch
2	Fruit
Calories 303	
Calories from Fat 4	
Total Fat ....0 g	
Saturated Fat.............0 g	
Cholesterol ....0 mg	
Sodium....................10 mg	
Carbohydrate............69 g	
Dietary Fiber ....5 g	
Sugars.....................28 g	
Protein........................7 g	

1 1/2 cups water
1 1/2 cups unsweetened apple juice
1 1/2 cups dry couscous
3/4 cup golden raisins
3/4 cup diced dried apricots
2 tsp cinnamon
1/2 tsp nutmeg
1/4 tsp allspice
2 tsp honey

In a medium saucepan, bring the water and apple juice to a boil. Add the couscous, raisins, and apricots. Remove from the stove and let rehydrate, uncovered, for about 5–6 minutes. Drain any excess liquid. (Couscous should be soft.) Add the spices and honey and serve.

Potato Pancakes

A delicious classic without all the fat.

Preparation Time:
20 minutes

6 Servings/Serving Size:
1/2 cup

Exchanges:
1 1/2   Starch

Calories.......................123
  Calories from Fat........31
Total Fat......................3 g
  Saturated Fat.............1 g

Cholesterol.............71 mg
Sodium....................24 mg
Carbohydrate.............19 g
  Dietary Fiber.............2 g
  Sugars.......................2 g

Protein........................4 g

2 medium potatoes, peeled
1 medium zucchini, unpeeled
1 small onion
2 eggs, beaten
1/2 cup matzo meal or dry bread crumbs
Nonstick cooking spray
2 tsp canola oil

1. Grate the potato and zucchini. Drain any accumulated liquid, or the potatoes will turn green. Grate the onion. Combine the potatoes, zucchini and onion in a bowl. Add the eggs and matzo meal or bread crumbs. Mix well.

2. Preheat the oven to 300 degrees. Spray a skillet with nonstick cooking spray. Heat the oil in the skillet over medium-high heat. Add 1/2 cup portions of the potato mixture. Cook for about 5 minutes on one side, turn, and cook on the other side for 3 minutes until golden brown. Transfer cooked cakes to the oven to keep warm. Repeat until all the mixture is used.

Fresh Herb Omelet

This one-dish meal is loaded with fresh herb flavor.

Preparation Time:
25 minutes

6 Servings/Serving Size:
1/6 of recipe

Exchanges:

1	Starch
1	Vegetable
2	Lean Meat

Calories	222
Calories from Fat	62
Total Fat	7 g
Saturated Fat	2 g

Cholesterol	144 mg
Sodium	483 mg
Carbohydrate	18 g
Dietary Fiber	2 g
Sugars	8 g

Protein	22 g

1 Tbsp olive oil
1 cup diced red pepper
1 cup sliced mushrooms
1 cup sliced scallions
2 garlic cloves, minced
4 slices whole-wheat bread, crusts removed (3 oz total)
1 cup low-fat cottage cheese
4 eggs
8 egg whites
3/4 cup evaporated skim milk
1 Tbsp minced fresh basil
1 Tbsp minced fresh rosemary
2 tsp minced fresh chives
1 Tbsp minced fresh parsley
Fresh ground pepper and salt to taste

1. Preheat the oven to 350 degrees. Heat the oil in a skillet over medium-high heat. Saute the pepper, mushrooms, and scallions for 6 minutes. Add the garlic and saute for 3 more minutes.

2. Place the bread slices in a large casserole dish. Combine the remaining ingredients and pour the egg mixture on top of the bread. Add the cooked vegetables. Bake for about 25–30 minutes until the omelet is slightly puffed and set.

Asian Frittata

You can serve this nutritious meal for a light lunch, too.

Preparation Time:
15 minutes

6 Servings/Serving Size:
1 wedge

Exchanges:
| 2 | Vegetable |
| 2 | Very Lean Meat |

Calories	125
Calories from Fat	28
Total Fat	3 g
Saturated Fat	1 g

Cholesterol	0 mg
Sodium	426 mg
Carbohydrate	9 g
Dietary Fiber	1 g
Sugars	5 g

Protein	15 g

1 Tbsp peanut oil
3 scallions, minced
2 tsp grated fresh ginger
2 garlic cloves, minced
1 cup diced red pepper
12 egg substitutes
2 Tbsp lite soy sauce
1 cup fresh bean sprouts
1 cup fresh snow peas, trimmed and halved
1 Tbsp toasted sesame seeds

1. Preheat the oven to 350 degrees. Heat the oil in a large, nonstick, ovenproof skillet over medium-high heat. Add the scallions, ginger, and garlic and saute for 1–2 minutes. Add the red pepper and saute for 3 more minutes. Mix together the egg substitutes and soy sauce and add to the skillet. Cook over medium heat for 8–10 minutes until the egg substitutes are set on the bottom.

2. Place the bean sprouts and snow peas over the eggs. Sprinkle with sesame seeds. Place in the oven and bake just until the top is set, about 8–10 minutes. (Watch carefully that eggs do not overcook, or they will become tough.) Turn the oven up to broil for about 30 seconds, just until the frittata is browned. Serve in six wedges.

Fall Menus

Home from School

Spicy Apple Cider

Popcorn Crunch

Homemade Pizza

Fruit and Cereal Balls

414–417

After the Hayride

Ginger and Lemon Cider

Hearty Fall Stew

Drop Biscuits

Shredded Carrot and Raisin Salad

418–421

Octoberfest

German Sauerkraut Balls

Applesauce-Stuffed Pork Tenderloin

Celery Root Salad

Poached Pear Halves with Red Wine Sauce

422–425

The Big Game

Creamy Herb Yogurt Dip

Pork and Bean Chili

Onion Beer Bread

Crunchy Bananas

426–429

Spooky Halloween

Sparkling Garnet Punch

Corn Tortilla Pizzas

Spinach and Red Swiss Chard Salad

Carob-Dipped Dried Apricots

430–433

Thanksgiving Feast

Cream of Carrot Soup

Roasted Thanksgiving Turkey

Fall Vegetable Medley

Pumpkin Pie

434–437

Spicy Apple Cider

This is a great drink to warm the kids up on a chilly fall day.

Preparation Time:
5 minutes

6 Servings/Serving Size:
1 cup

Exchanges:

2	Fruit

Calories	116
Calories from Fat	2
Total Fat	0 g
Saturated Fat	0 g

Cholesterol	0 mg
Sodium	7 mg
Carbohydrate	29 g
Dietary Fiber	0 g
Sugars	27 g

Protein	0 g

6 whole cloves
2 cinnamon sticks
6 allspice berries
2 cardamom pods
6 cups apple cider
Cinnamon sticks for stirring

In a spice bag or a piece of cheesecloth tied tightly at the top, combine the cloves, cinnamon sticks, berries, and cardamom. Place the cider and spice bag in a large saucepan and bring to a boil. Lower the heat and simmer for 20 minutes. Remove the spice bag. Pour into mugs and serve with cinnamon sticks.

Popcorn Crunch

Popcorn makes a great snack, but some people find air-popped corn to be a bit dry. Try misting the popcorn with olive oil from a spray bottle and seasoning it with chili powder, dried basil and oregano, cinnamon and nutmeg, curry powder, or onion and garlic powder. Or try the recipe below for a crunchy treat.

Preparation Time:
5 minutes

6 Servings/Serving Size:
1 cup

Exchanges:
1	Starch
1/2	Fat

Calories	93
Calories from Fat	24
Total Fat	3 g
Saturated Fat	0 g

Cholesterol	0 mg
Sodium	463 mg
Carbohydrate	15 g
Dietary Fiber	1 g
Sugars	1 g

Protein	2 g

3 cups air-popped corn
2 cups whole-grain pretzel sticks
1 cup Cherrios® cereal
2 Tbsp lite soy sauce
2 tsp garlic powder
1 tsp onion powder
1 Tbsp Worcestershire sauce
2 Tbsp melted low-calorie margarine

Preheat the oven to 300 degrees. Combine all ingredients and bake for 20–30 minutes. Let cool before serving.

Homemade Pizza

When it gets chilly outside, gather everyone into the kitchen to make this easy pizza.

<table>
<tr><td colspan="2">Preparation Time:
20 minutes</td></tr>
<tr><td colspan="2">6 Servings/Serving Size:
1 4-inch square</td></tr>
</table>

Exchanges:

3	Starch
1	Vegetable
2	Monounsaturated Fat

Calories	356
Calories from Fat	111
Total Fat	12 g
Saturated Fat	1 g

Cholesterol	1 mg
Sodium	560 mg
Carbohydrate	54 g
Dietary Fiber	4 g
Sugars	5 g

Protein	9 g

2 1/2 cups unbleached white flour
1 Tbsp baking powder
1/4 cup canola oil
1/2 tsp salt
Water
2 tsp olive oil
2 cups steamed vegetables (try broccoli, onions, or spinach)
1 1/2 cups low-sugar, low-sodium tomato sauce
1 cup rehydrated, whole sun-dried tomatoes
2 tsp minced fresh oregano
2 Tbsp grated Parmesan cheese

1. Preheat the oven to 375 degrees. In a large bowl, combine the flour and the baking powder. Add the oil and mix with a fork until the oil is incorporated. Add water a little at a time until the crust is still soft, but is able to be formed into a ball. Press dough on the bottom and up the sides of a nonstick baking sheet. Brush with olive oil. Bake for 8 minutes and remove from the oven.

2. Spread the tomato sauce on the cooked dough. Add the vegetables and sun-dried tomatoes. Sprinkle with oregano and Parmesan cheese. Bake for another 5–8 minutes until the cheese melts. Cut into squares.

Fruit and Cereal Balls

These crunchy balls make great snacks.

Preparation Time:
15 minutes

10 Servings/Serving Size:
3 balls

Exchanges:

1/2	Starch
2	Fruit

Calories	144
Calories from Fat	5
Total Fat	1 g
Saturated Fat	0 g

Cholesterol	0 mg
Sodium	44 mg
Carbohydrate	35 g
Dietary Fiber	3 g
Sugars	24 g

Protein	2 g

1 cup chopped raisins
1 cup chopped dates
1/2 cup Grape-Nuts® cereal
3/4 cup oats
1/4 cup apple juice concentrate

Combine the dried fruit and Grape-Nuts®
cereal in a bowl. Add the oats and mix well.
Slowly add the juice until the mixture is firm
enough to handle in your hands. Roll into small
balls and refrigerator for 2 hours.

*You can slash your
grocery bill with scissors.
Companies put out more than
300 billion coupons each year.*

*Spend a little time organizing
the coupons you cut out,
and you'll save quite a bit
of money at the store.*

Ginger and Lemon Cider

Pack this cider in a thermal bottle and take it with you on the ride!

Preparation Time:	
10 minutes	

6 Servings/Serving Size:
1 cup

Exchanges:	
2	Fruit

Calories	121
Calories from Fat	2
Total Fat	0 g
Saturated Fat	0 g
Cholesterol	0 mg
Sodium	6 mg
Carbohydrate	30 g
Dietary Fiber	0 g
Sugars	29 g
Protein	0 g

1 cup minced fresh ginger
3 Tbsp sugar
3 1/2 cups water
3 strips lemon rind
5 cups unsweetened apple juice
4 cinnamon sticks

Bring the ginger, sugar, water, and lemon rind to a boil in a medium saucepan. Continue to cook until the syrup is reduced to 1 cup. Strain, remove the ginger, and let cool. In another saucepan, warm the apple juice with the cinnamon sticks until it comes to a simmer. Add in the ginger syrup. Serve hot or warm.

Hearty Fall Stew

Try dipping Drop Biscuits (see recipe, p. 420) into this
tasty stew.

Preparation Time:
20 minutes

---

6 Servings/Serving Size:
1 cup

Exchanges:

1	Starch
4	Very Lean Meat
1	Monounsaturated Fat

Calories	286
Calories from Fat	87
Total Fat	10 g
Saturated Fat	3 g

Cholesterol	88 mg
Sodium	224 mg
Carbohydrate	16 g
Dietary Fiber	4 g
Sugars	7 g

Protein	32 g

1 Tbsp olive oil
1 1/2 lb boneless beef chuck, cut into 1 1/2-inch
  cubes
1 cup minced onion
2 garlic cloves, minced
1 cup burgundy wine
2 cups low-sodium tomato sauce
1 cup low-fat, low-sodium beef broth
2 tsp minced fresh rosemary
1 bay leaf
Fresh ground pepper to taste
2 large carrots, cut into chunks
1/2 cup sliced celery
1/2 cup frozen peas, thawed

1. Heat the oil in a large stockpot over medium-
    high heat. Add the beef and saute for 5
    minutes, browning all sides. Remove the meat
    from the pan. Add the onion and garlic to the
    pan and saute for 5 minutes.

2. Add the wine, tomato sauce, broth, rosemary,
    bay leaf, and pepper and bring to a boil. Add
    the beef and simmer for 1 hour. Add more
    liquid if necessary. Add the vegetables to the
    pot and simmer for 30 minutes. Remove the
    bay leaf and serve.

Drop Biscuits

Low-fat sour cream makes these biscuits chewy and rich.

Preparation Time:
10 minutes

12 Servings/Serving Size:
1 biscuit

Exchanges:

1/2	Starch

Calories	52
Calories from Fat	11
Total Fat	1 g
Saturated Fat	1 g
Cholesterol	5 mg
Sodium	165 mg
Carbohydrate	8 g
Dietary Fiber	0 g
Sugars	1 g
Protein	1 g

1 cup self-rising flour
1/4 tsp baking soda
3/4 cup low-fat sour cream
1/2 tsp minced fresh rosemary
2 tsp grated onion
Nonstick cooking spray

Preheat the oven to 425 degrees. Mix all ingredients together just until blended, being careful not to overbeat. The biscuit dough will be sticky. Drop dough onto a cookie sheet lightly sprayed with nonstick cooking spray. Bake for 10–12 minutes until biscuits are golden brown. Do not overbake; biscuits should be flaky inside.

Don't worry if some recipes are more than 30% fat. You want your fat intake for the whole day to be less than 30% of your calories. Each item on your plate doesn't need to be. For example, your favorite salad dressing may be 90% fat. But if you eat wisely all day, you can have dressing on your salad and still meet the 30%-or-less guideline.

*S*hredded Carrot and Raisin Salad

This colorful classic is good for you, too.

Preparation Time:
15 minutes

6 Servings/Serving Size:
1/2 cup

Exchanges:
1/2	Fruit
1	Vegetable
1/2	Saturated Fat

Calories.........................79
  Calories from Fat........16
Total Fat ....2 g
  Saturated Fat.............1 g

Cholesterol ....7 mg
Sodium.....................27 mg
Carbohydrate.............15 g
  Dietary Fiber ....2 g
  Sugars.......................13 g

Protein...........................1 g

1 1/2 cups shredded, peeled carrot
1 1/2 cups thinly sliced, peeled apples (any
    variety)
1/4 cup golden raisins
1/2 cup low-fat sour cream
1/3 cup skim milk
1 Tbsp fresh lemon juice
1 Tbsp sugar
1/4 tsp cinnamon
1/4 tsp nutmeg
1/8 tsp allspice

Combine the carrots, apples, and raisins.
Whisk together the dressing ingredients. Toss
the dressing with salad and chill before
serving.

German Sauerkraut Balls

Sauerkraut adds the Octoberfest flavor to these meatballs.

Preparation Time:
35 minutes

6 Servings/Serving Size:
4 balls

Exchanges:
1	Starch
1	Medium-Fat Meat

Calories.......................148
 Calories from Fat........54
Total Fat ....6 g
 Saturated Fat.............1 g

Cholesterol ....77 mg
Sodium...................341 mg
Carbohydrate............16 g
 Dietary Fiber ....2 g
 Sugars.......................4 g

Protein.........................8 g

1 16-oz can sauerkraut
1/4 cup white wine
1 Tbsp canola oil
2 Tbsp finely minced scallions
3 Tbsp flour
2/3 cup evaporated skim milk
1/2 Tbsp caraway seeds
1/2 cup crumbled cooked turkey bacon
Fresh ground pepper and salt to taste
1/2 cup dry bread crumbs
Nonstick cooking spray
2 eggs, beaten
1 1/2 tsp flour

1. Boil the sauerkraut for 15 minutes. Remove from heat and squeeze out any excess moisture. Chop very fine. Preheat the oven to 350 degrees. Heat the wine and oil in a skillet over medium-high heat. Add the scallions and saute for 1 minute. Add the flour slowly and cook for 1 minute. Lower the heat and add the milk, stirring constantly.

2. Add the sauerkraut, caraway seeds, and bacon and cook for 2 minutes. Add in the pepper and salt. Remove from heat and add in the bread crumbs. Form the mixture into balls and place on a cookie sheet sprayed with nonstick cooking spray. Brush each ball with some egg and dust with flour. Bake for 30–35 minutes until golden brown.

Applesauce-Stuffed Pork Tenderloin

Peanuts are a welcome surprise in this stuffed pork roast.

Preparation Time:
15 minutes

6 Servings/Serving Size:
3 oz

Exchanges:
4	Very Lean Meat
1	Fat

Calories	197
Calories from Fat	67
Total Fat	7 g
Saturated Fat	2 g
Cholesterol	71 mg
Sodium	124 mg
Carbohydrate	5 g
Dietary Fiber	1 g
Sugars	3 g
Protein	27 g

1 1/2 lb boneless pork tenderloin
1/4 cup dry vermouth
Nonstick cooking spray
2/3 cup unsweetened chunky applesauce
1/4 cup finely chopped toasted peanuts, unsalted
1/4 tsp finely crushed fennel seeds
Fresh ground pepper and salt to taste

1. Using a sharp knife, form a pocket in the pork tenderloin by cutting a lengthwise slit down the center almost to, but not through, the bottom of the tenderloin. Place the pork in a dish and pour the vermouth in the pocket. Cover the dish and marinate in the refrigerator about 1 hour.

2. Preheat the oven to 375 degrees. Spray a shallow roasting pan with nonstick cooking spray. In a small bowl, combine the applesauce, peanuts, fennel seeds, pepper, and salt. Place the roast in the dish, spoon the mixture into the pocket and secure with toothpicks. Roast for 30–40 minutes until juices run clear. Let stand 5 to 10 minutes before slicing.

This adapted recipe is courtesy of the National Pork Producers.

Celery Root Salad

Celery root, also known as celeriac, is wonderful when julienned and eaten cold. Celeriac can also be cooked and pureed. It is delicious in soups.

Preparation Time:	
15 minutes	

6 Servings/Serving Size:
1/2 cup

Exchanges:	
1/2	Starch
1 1/2	Fat

Calories	108
Calories from Fat	66
Total Fat	7 g
Saturated Fat	1 g
Cholesterol	5 mg
Sodium	406 mg
Carbohydrate	9 g
Dietary Fiber	1 g
Sugars	4 g
Protein	2 g

2 cups julienned celery root, peeled
1/2 cup julienned red pepper
1/2 cup julienned carrot
2 tsp lemon juice
1/2 cup Dijon mustard
1 Tbsp olive oil
2 tsp lemon juice
2 garlic cloves, minced
2 Tbsp red wine vinegar
1/3 cup low-fat mayonnaise
1 Tbsp minced fresh basil
2 tsp minced fresh oregano

Combine celery root, red pepper, carrot, and lemon juice in a bowl. Whisk together the remaining ingredients. Pour the dressing over the salad and toss well. Refrigerate for 1 hour before serving.

Poached Pear Halves with Wine Sauce

Whole nutmeg and cinnamon sticks add punch to these pears.

Preparation Time:	
10 minutes	

6 Servings/Serving Size:
1 pear

Exchanges:

3	Fruit

Calories	200
Calories from Fat	8
Total Fat	1 g
Saturated Fat	0 g

Cholesterol	0 mg
Sodium	3 mg
Carbohydrate	46 g
Dietary Fiber	5 g
Sugars	39 g

Protein	1 g

2 cups blush wine
1 cup apple juice
2 cinnamon sticks
1 whole nutmeg
3 cloves
6 d'Anjou pears, peeled, cored, and cut in half
2 Tbsp cornstarch or arrowroot powder
1/4 cup cold water
1/4 cup sugar
Mint sprigs

1. Combine the wine, apple juice, cinnamon sticks, nutmeg, and cloves in a large skillet and heat to simmering. Add the pears, cut sides down. Simmer, covered, for 10–15 minutes until the pears are tender. Carefully remove the pears and place them on serving dishes. Discard the spices.

2. Heat the wine mixture to boiling. Mix the cornstarch or arrowroot powder with water and add to the wine. Boil, stirring constantly, until thickened. Remove the sauce from the heat and let stand for 2–3 minutes. Stir in the sugar. Spoon the sauce over the pears. Garnish with mint to serve.

Creamy Herb Yogurt Dip

Choose your favorite herb to flavor this yogurt dip.

Preparation Time:
5 minutes

---

12 Servings/Serving Size:
2 Tbsp

Exchanges:
Free Food

Calories......................25
 Calories from Fat..........7
Total Fat ....1 g
 Saturated Fat.............0 g

Cholesterol ....5 mg
Sodium....................75 mg
Carbohydrate..............3 g
 Dietary Fiber ....0 g
 Sugars........................2 g

Protein..........................2 g

1/2 cup part-skim ricotta cheese
1/2 cup low-fat plain yogurt
2 Tbsp low-fat mayonnaise
3 minced rehydrated sun-dried tomatoes
1 Tbsp minced fresh herbs (try dill, basil, or
   chives)
1 tsp fresh lemon juice

Place all ingredients in a blender and blend until smooth. Serve with crackers or raw vegetables.

Pork and Bean Chili

Using lean pork tenderloin helps keep this chili low in fat.

Preparation Time:
15 minutes

6 Servings/Serving Size:
1 cup

Exchanges:

1	Starch
2	Vegetable
4	Very Lean Meat

Calories	280
Calories from Fat	57
Total Fat	6 g
Saturated Fat	2 g

Cholesterol	73 mg
Sodium	512 mg
Carbohydrate	24 g
Dietary Fiber	7 g
Sugars	8 g

Protein	32 g

1 1/2 lb lean pork tenderloin, cut into 2-inch cubes
1 medium onion, chopped
3 garlic cloves, minced
1/2 cup green pepper, diced
1 28-oz can tomatoes, chopped, undrained
1 cup low-fat, low-sodium beef broth
1 Tbsp chili powder
1 tsp ground cumin
1 tsp minced fresh oregano
1 tsp cayenne pepper
2 cups canned black beans, drained and rinsed
Fresh ground pepper and salt to taste
Sprigs of fresh cilantro
6 Tbsp low-fat sour cream

In a stockpot over medium-high heat, saute the pork for about 10 minutes until it is no longer pink. Add the onion, garlic, and pepper and saute for 5 more minutes. Add the remaining ingredients. Bring to a boil, lower the heat, and simmer for 35 minutes. Serve with sprigs of cilantro and garnish with sour cream.

Onion Beer Bread

Onion lovers will love this bread!

Preparation Time: 5 minutes	

9 Servings/Serving Size:
1 1-inch slice

Exchanges:

2	Starch

Calories	178
Calories from Fat	14
Total Fat	2 g
Saturated Fat	0 g

Cholesterol	47 mg
Sodium	674 mg
Carbohydrate	34 g
Dietary Fiber	2 g
Sugars	3 g

Protein	6 g

3 cups self-rising flour
1 tsp sugar
1/2 tsp salt
10 oz room-temperature beer
2 eggs, beaten
3/4 cup minced onion
Nonstick cooking spray

Preheat the oven to 350 degrees. Combine all ingredients. Pour into a lightly sprayed 9-inch loaf pan and bake for 50 minutes until a toothpick comes out clean.

Results!

Why, man, I have gotten a lot of

results. I know several thousand

things that won't work.

—*Thomas A. Edison*

Crunchy Bananas

Eat these slowly to savor their crunchy goodness.

Preparation Time:	
10 minutes	

6 Servings/Serving Size:
1/2 banana

Exchanges:
2 1/2	Carbohydrate
1	Saturated Fat

Calories	247
Calories from Fat	81
Total Fat	9 g
Saturated Fat	7 g

Cholesterol	2 mg
Sodium	30 mg
Carbohydrate	43 g
Dietary Fiber	4 g
Sugars	33 g

Protein	4 g

1 cup low-fat vanilla yogurt
2 Tbsp honey
3 medium bananas
Wooden sticks
3/4 cup unsweetened coconut
1/4 cup carob chips

1. Combine yogurt and honey in a bowl and mix well. Cut each banana in half and insert a wooden stick into the cut end. Roll the bananas in some of the honey-yogurt mixture and then place on a cookie sheet lined with waxed paper. Place the bananas in the freezer until the yogurt is hard, about 1 hour.

2. Combine the coconut and carob chips. Remove the bananas from the freezer and re-dip in the remaining yogurt. Roll the bananas in the coconut mixture. Return the bananas to the freezer and freeze until firm. Let bananas sit at room temperature 5 minutes before serving.

Sparkling Garnet Punch

Ward off mischievous spirits with this potent brew.

Preparation Time:
5 minutes

---

6 Servings/Serving Size:
1/2 cup

Exchanges:
1/2   Fruit

Calories 36
 Calories from Fat 1
Total Fat ....0 g
 Saturated Fat ....0 g

Cholesterol ....0 mg
Sodium ....1 mg
Carbohydrate ....9 g
 Dietary Fiber ....0 g
 Sugars ....9 g

Protein ....0 g

1 1/2 cups cranberry juice
4 whole cloves
3 cinnamon sticks
1 whole nutmeg
1 1/2 cups no-calorie sparkling water
1 tsp almond extract

Combine the cranberry juice, cloves, cinnamon, and nutmeg in a saucepan. Bring to a boil, then lower heat and simmer for 10 minutes. Add the extract. Strain and remove the spices. Refrigerate for several hours. Just before serving, combine the cranberry juice with the water and almond extract. Serve from a small punch bowl or pitcher.

Corn Tortilla Pizzas

This is a great low-fat Mexican food and pizza combination!

Preparation Time:
15 minutes

6 Servings/Serving Size:
1 tortilla pizza

Exchanges:

1	Starch
1	Vegetable
2	Lean Meat

Calories	220
Calories from Fat	62
Total Fat	7 g
Saturated Fat	2 g
Cholesterol	44 mg
Sodium	399 mg
Carbohydrate	19 g
Dietary Fiber	4 g
Sugars	4 g
Protein	19 g

1 Tbsp olive oil
12 oz ground turkey (have your butcher grind this for you)
1 cup finely diced zucchini
1 cup finely diced red pepper
2 tsp minced fresh oregano
1 tsp minced fresh basil
6 6-inch corn tortillas (yellow or blue)
1 1/2 cups marinara sauce
1/4 cup sliced black olives
1/2 cup part-skim mozzarella cheese

1. Preheat the oven to 350 degrees. Heat the oil in a skillet over medium-high heat. Add the ground turkey and saute for 3 minutes. Add the zucchini and red pepper and continue to cook until the turkey is cooked through, about 3–4 minutes. Add the oregano and basil.

2. To assemble the pizzas, spoon some of the sauce over each tortilla. Add the turkey mixture. Dot with olives and sprinkle with cheese. Place the pizzas on a baking sheet and bake until the cheese melts and the tortilla is crisp, about 5–6 minutes.

Spinach and Red Swiss Chard Salad

Red Swiss chard is not only delicious, but an appealing color change from greens. If you can't find it, use spinach.

Preparation Time:
15 minutes

---

6 Servings/Serving Size:
1 cup

Exchanges:
1/2   Carbohydrate
2 1/2   Monounsaturated Fat

Calories 154
 Calories from Fat 115
Total Fat ....13 g
 Saturated Fat ....1 g

Cholesterol ....0 mg
Sodium ....65 mg
Carbohydrate ....10 g
 Dietary Fiber ....2 g
 Sugars ....7 g

Protein ....2 g

3 cups washed and torn spinach leaves
2 1/2 cups washed and torn red Swiss chard
1/2 cup sectioned oranges
1/4 cup toasted walnuts
3 Tbsp canola oil
1/4 cup white wine vinegar
2 Tbsp fresh orange juice
2 Tbsp sugar
1 tsp paprika
1 tsp celery seeds
1 tsp dry mustard
Fresh ground pepper and salt to taste

Combine the spinach, chard, oranges, and walnuts in a large salad bowl. Whisk all remaining ingredients together. Pour the dressing over the salad and serve.

Carob-Dipped Dried Apricots

This dessert's orange and black colors are perfect for Halloween.

Preparation Time:
5 minutes

6 Servings/Serving Size:
4 apricots

Exchanges:
| 1 1/2 | Carbohydrate |
| 1/2 | Saturated Fat |

Calories	134
Calories from Fat	39
Total Fat	4 g
Saturated Fat	2 g

Cholesterol	0 mg
Sodium	4 mg
Carbohydrate	26 g
Dietary Fiber	3 g
Sugars	19 g

Protein	2 g

1/2 cup carob chips
24 whole dried apricots

In a double boiler over hot, not boiling, water, melt the carob chips. Dip each apricot in the melted carob so that the carob covers half of the apricot. Work quickly. Chill the apricots in the refrigerator to harden the carob before serving.

Soften dried fruits in your

microwave in less than a minute.

Put in a covered dish with a bit of

water and heat on

high for about

30 seconds.

Cream of Carrot Soup

This bright, delicious soup is the perfect beginning to any meal.

Preparation Time:
15 minutes

6 Servings/Serving Size:
1 cup

Exchanges:
1	Starch
1/2	Low-Fat Milk

Calories......................141
  Calories from Fat........27
Total Fat ....3 g
  Saturated Fat.............1 g

Cholesterol ....3 mg
Sodium..................218 mg
Carbohydrate.............22 g
  Dietary Fiber ....3 g
  Sugars.....................11 g

Protein........................9 g

2 Tbsp low-calorie margarine
1/4 cup minced shallots
2 Tbsp unbleached white flour
2 cups evaporated skim milk, hot
2 cups pureed cooked carrots
2 cups low-fat, low-sodium chicken broth
2 tsp cinnamon
1 Tbsp chopped fresh parsley

Melt the margarine in a stockpot over medium-high heat. Add the shallots and saute for 3 minutes. Sprinkle with flour and cook for 2 minutes. Add the remaining ingredients and simmer on low for 20 minutes. Garnish with chopped parsley to serve.

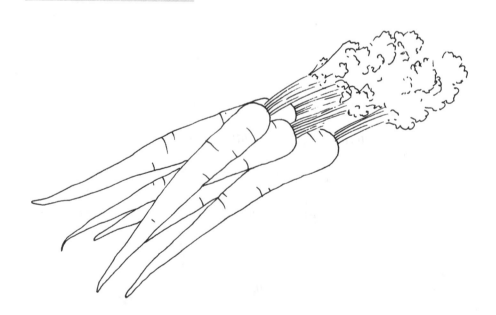

Roasted Thanksgiving Turkey

This turkey is moist and flavorful due to whole herbs placed underneath the skin and oranges and onions roasting in the cavity.

Preparation Time:
10 minutes

**Makes 1 12-lb turkey/
Serving Size:**
3–4 oz

Exchanges:

1/2	Starch
4	Lean Meat

Calories	265
Calories from Fat	121
Total Fat	13 g
Saturated Fat	3 g
Cholesterol	81 mg
Sodium	69 mg
Carbohydrate	9 g
Dietary Fiber	2 g
Sugars	4 g
Protein	29 g

1 12-lb turkey, giblets removed, washed inside and out
3 sprigs thyme
2 sprigs oregano
2 sprigs sage
3 sprigs fresh parsley
3 Tbsp olive oil
2 Tbsp dry white wine
2 Tbsp paprika
Fresh ground pepper to taste
3 small oranges, unpeeled and cut into wedges
2 onions, cut into wedges
1 cup low-fat, low-sodium chicken broth

1. Preheat the oven to 325 degrees. With your fingers, lift up the skin covering the turkey breast. Slip the thyme, oregano, sage, and parsley underneath the skin. Combine the oil, wine, paprika, and pepper. Rub this mixture over the surface of the turkey. Place the oranges and onions inside the turkey.

2. Place the turkey, breast side down, in a roasting pan. Pour the chicken broth into the bottom of the pan. Cover loosely with aluminum foil. Roast for 20–25 minutes per pound, basting periodically. Halfway through, place breast side up. During last 45 minutes of roasting, remove cover. Continue to roast until the leg moves easily and juices run clear. Let stand for 20 minutes to help let juices settle for easier carving.

Fall Vegetable Medley

You can surround your turkey with these vegetables during the last 45 minutes of cooking to soak up some natural juices.

<table>
<tr><td>

Preparation Time:
20 minutes

---

6 Servings/Serving Size:
1/2 cup

Exchanges:
1	Vegetable
1	Monounsaturated Fat

Calories 76
  Calories from Fat 42
Total Fat ....5 g
  Saturated Fat ....1 g

Cholesterol ....0 mg
Sodium ....35 mg
Carbohydrate ....9 g
  Dietary Fiber ....1 g
  Sugars ....5 g

Protein ....1 g

</td></tr>
</table>

1 large red pepper, cut into 2-inch squares
1 large yellow pepper, cut into 2-inch squares
1 medium carrot, cut into 2-inch chunks
1 small red onion, cut into wedges
6 garlic cloves, skin on, left whole
2 Tbsp olive oil
1/4 cup balsamic vinegar
Fresh ground pepper and salt to taste

Preheat the oven to 325 degrees. Combine all ingredients in a roasting pan. Roast uncovered, basting with turkey juices, for about 45 minutes, until vegetables are soft.

Pumpkin Pie

This is the perfect finale to any fall feast.

Preparation Time:	
10 minutes	

9 Servings/Serving Size:
1 1-inch slice

Exchanges:

2	Carbohydrate
1/2	Monounsaturated Fat

Calories	181
Calories from Fat	47
Total Fat	5 g
Saturated Fat	1 g
Cholesterol	49 mg
Sodium	218 mg
Carbohydrate	28 g
Dietary Fiber	2 g
Sugars	13 g
Protein	7 g

2 cups crushed graham crackers
3 Tbsp low-calorie margarine
2 Tbsp brown sugar
2 tsp cinnamon
2 cups pumpkin puree
1 12-oz can evaporated skim milk
2 eggs, beaten
1 tsp cinnamon
1/2 tsp nutmeg
1/2 tsp allspice

1. Preheat the oven to 425 degrees. Combine the graham crackers, margarine, sugar, and cinnamon and press into the bottom and sides of a 9-inch pie plate. Place in the oven and bake for 5 minutes. Remove and set aside.

2. Beat together all remaining ingredients in the order given. Pour into the crust and bake for 15 minutes. Lower temperature to 350 degrees and bake for about 35 minutes until set. Cool slightly or chill before serving.

Index

Alphabetical List of Recipes

Subject Index

About the Author

Robyn Webb has made her mark in the field of nutrition. In addition to her well-known nutritional practice consisting of counseling services, low-fat catering, a low-fat cooking school, and lecture services, she is also the successful author of *Diabetic Meals In 30 Minutes—Or Less!* (American Diabetes Association, 1996) and *A Pinch of Thyme: Easy Lessons for a Leaner Life* (Kendall/Hunt Publishing, 1994).

Webb specializes in providing fast and easy ways for people to maintain their health. Recipes developed by Webb are designed with the busy person in mind. Most take less than an hour to prepare and are simple to follow. The results are delicious.

Her expertise and eye-opening ideas have been noted by the media. Webb has been featured in articles in *Woman's Day, Cosmopolitan, USA Today,* The Associated Press, *Virginia Business Magazine, Washingtonian, The Washington Business Journal,* and the *Washington Post.* Webb has appeared nationally on CBS News with Dan Rather, on ESPN with fitness expert Denise Austin, The TV Food Network, and Working Woman. Her local Washington, D.C., credits include Broadcast House Live, WJLA Channel 7, News Channel 8, and WRC-TV's "Fighting Fat" series. Webb has also been the guest on several radio talk shows, including WTOP AM and WPGC AM.

Webb's career spans twelve years. She received her Master of Science degree in nutrition from Florida State University. Her work with the American Diabetes Association includes the taste analysis for five cookbooks in the *Healthy Selects* series and taste analysis for *Forecast* magazine recipes. Webb grew up in a family challenged by diabetes and is well versed in the need for careful meal planning and food preparation.

New Books from the American Diabetes Association Library of Cooking and Self-Care

Diabetic Meals In 30 Minutes—Or Less!

Put an end to bland, time-consuming meals with more than 140 fast, flavorful recipes. Complete nutrition information accompanies every recipe, and a number of "quick tips" will have you out of the kitchen and into the dining room even faster! Here's a quick sample: Salsa Salad, Oven-baked Parmesan Zucchini, Roasted Red Pepper Soup, and Layered Vanilla Parfait. #CCBDM
Nonmember: $11.95; ADA Member: $9.55

Diabetes Meal Planning Made Easy

The new Diabetes Food Pyramid helps make nutritious meal planning easier than ever. This new guide simplifies the concept by translating diabetes food guidelines into today's food choices. Simple, easy-to-follow chapters will help you understand the new food pyramid; learn all about the six food groups and how to incorporate them into a healthy diet; make smart choices when it comes to sweets, fats, and dairy products; shop smart at the grocery store; make all your meals easier by planning ahead; more. #CCBMP
Nonmember: $14.95; ADA Member: $11.95

Magic Menus for People With Diabetes

Mealtime discipline can be a major struggle—calculating exchanges, counting calories, and figuring fats is complicated and time-consuming. But now you have more than 200 low-fat, calorie-controlled selections—for breakfast, lunch, dinner, and snacks—to automatically turn the struggle into a smorgasbord. Choose from Chicken Cacciatore, Veal Piccata, Chop Suey, Beef Stroganoff, Vegetable Lasagna, plus dozens more. But don't worry about calculating all your nutrients—it's done for you automatically. #CCBMM
Nonmember: $14.95; ADA Member: $11.95

World-Class Diabetic Cooking

Travel around the world at every meal with a collection of 200 exciting new low-fat, low-calorie recipes. Features Thai, Caribbean, Scandinavian, Italian, Greek, Spanish, Chinese, Japanese, African, Mexican, Portuguese, German, and Middle Eastern recipes. All major food categories—appetizers, soups, salads, pastas, meats, breads, and desserts—are highlighted. Includes a nutrient analysis and exchanges (conveniently converted to U.S. exchanges) for each recipe. #CCBWCC
Nonmember: $12.95; ADA Member: $10.35

Southern-Style Diabetic Cooking
Dig into a savory collection of Southern-style recipes without guilt. *Southern-Style Diabetic Cooking* takes traditional Southern dishes and turns them into great-tasting, but good-for-you, recipes. Features more than 100 selections, including appetizers, soups, salads, breads, main dishes, vegetables, side dishes, and desserts. Complete nutrient analysis with each recipe. Suggestions on appropriate frequency of serving and ways to fit special treats or holiday menus into a meal plan. (Available in November 1996.) #CCBSSDC
Nonmember: $11.95; ADA Member: $9.55

How to Cook for People with Diabetes
Finally, here's a collection of reader favorites from the delicious, nutritious recipes featured every month in *Diabetes Forecast*. But you don't only get ideas for pizza, chicken, unique holiday foods, vegetarian recipes and more, you also get nutrient analysis and exchanges for each recipe. (Available in November 1996.) #CCBCFPD
Nonmember: $11.95; ADA Member: $9.55

American Diabetes Association Complete Guide to Diabetes
Finally, all areas of diabetes self-care are covered in the pages of one book. Whether you have type I or type II diabetes, you'll learn all about symptoms and causes, diagnosis and treatment, handling emergencies, complications and prevention, achieving good blood sugar control, and more. You'll also discover advice on nutrition, exercise, sex, pregnancy, travel, family life, coping, and health insurance. 464 pages. Hardcover. Conveniently indexed for quick reference to any topic. #CSMCGD
Nonmember: $29.95; ADA Member: $23.95

How to Get Great Diabetes Care
This book explains the American Diabetes Association's Standards of Care and informs you—step-by-step—of the importance of seeking medical attention that meets these standards. You'll learn about special concerns and treatment options for diabetes-related diseases and conditions. #CSMHGGDC
Nonmember: $11.95; ADA Member: $9.55

Reflections on Diabetes
A collection of stories written by people who have learned from the experience of living with diabetes. Selected from the *Reflections* column of *Diabetes Forecast* magazine, these stories of success, struggle, and pain will inspire you. #CSMROD
Nonmember: $9.95; ADA Member: $7.95

Sweet Kids: How to Balance Diabetes Control and Good Nutrition with Family Peace

At last! A professionally developed collection of advice for parents and caregivers of children with diabetes. Learn all about nutrition and meal planning in diabetes: food, diabetes, and proper development; special areas of concern, such as low blood sugar; self-care techniques for caregivers of children with diabetes; much more. Take advantage of this practical way to educate yourself about how to properly care for a person with diabetes. #CSMSK

Nonmember: $14.95; ADA Member: $11.95

101 Tips for Staying Healthy With Diabetes (and Avoiding Complications)

Developing complications of diabetes is a constant threat without proper self-care. *101 Tips for Staying Healthy* offers the inside track on the latest tips, techniques, and strategies for preventing and treating complications. You'll find simple, practical suggestions for avoiding complications through close blood-sugar control, plus easy-to-follow treatment strategies for slowing and even halting the progression of existing complications. Helpful illustrations with each tip. #CSMFSH

Nonmember: $12.50; ADA Member: $9.95

BESTSELLERS

Diabetes A to Z

In clear, simple terms, you'll learn all about blood sugar, complications, diet, exercise, heart disease, insulin, kidney disease, meal planning, pregnancy, sex, weight loss, and much more. Alphabetized for quick reference. #CGFDAZ

Nonmember: $9.95; ADA Member: $7.95

Managing Diabetes on a Budget

For less than $10 you can begin saving hundreds and hundreds on your diabetes self-care. An inexpensive, sure-fire collection of "do-it-this-way" tips and hints to save you money on everything from medications and diet to exercise and health care. #CSMMDOAB

Nonmember: $7.95; ADA Member: $6.25

The Fitness Book: For People with Diabetes

You'll learn how to exercise to lose weight, exercise safely, increase your competitive edge, get your mind and body ready to exercise, much more. #CSMFB

Nonmember $18.95; ADA Member: $14.95

Raising a Child with Diabetes

Learn how to help your child adjust insulin to allow for foods kids like to eat, have a busy schedule and still feel healthy and strong, negotiate the twists and turns of being "different," accept the physical and emotional challenges life has to offer, and much more. #CSMRACWD
Nonmember: $14.95; ADA Member: $11.95

The Dinosaur Tamer

Enjoy 25 fictional stories that will entertain, enlighten, and ease your child's frustrations about having diabetes. Each tale warmly evaporates the fear of insulin shots, blood tests, going to diabetes camp, and more. Ages 8–12. #CSMDTAOS
Nonmember: $9.95; ADA Member: $7.95

101 Tips for Improving Your Blood Sugar

101 Tips offers a practical, easy-to-follow roadmap to tight blood sugar control. One question appears on each page, with the answers or "tips" below each question. Tips on diet,, exercise, travel, weight loss, insulin injection, illness, sex and much more. #CSMTBBGC
Nonmember: $12.50; ADA Member $9.95

Order Toll-Free! 1–800–ADA–ORDER (232–6733)
VISA • MasterCard • American Express

Or send your check or money order to:
American Diabetes Association
ATTN: Order Fulfillment Department
P.O. Box 930850
Atlanta, GA 31193–0850

Shipping & Handling:
up to $30 . . . . add $3.00
$30.01–$50 . . . . add $4.00
above $50 . . . . add 8% of order

Allow 2–3 weeks for shipment. Add $3 to shipping & handling for each extra shipping address. Add $15 for each overseas shipment. Prices subject to change without notice.

Also available in bookstores nationwide